Toronto Telegram

A policeman to the rescue in the raging Humber River during Hurricane Hazel.

Illustrated London News

Survivors of the Empress of Ireland drew this picture of the sinking liner.

Geological Survey of Canada

Dominion Avenue in Frank, Alberta,
before the avalanche struck.

The residential section in the heart of Regina after the "twister" had done its work.

Toronto Telegram

A hundred thousand volunteer rescue workers battled the Winnipeg Flood.

Miners trapped in the Springhill disaster stoically awaited rescue.

Ontario Department of Lands and Forests

Blazing forests like this one razed Porcupine and Haileybury in northern Ontario.

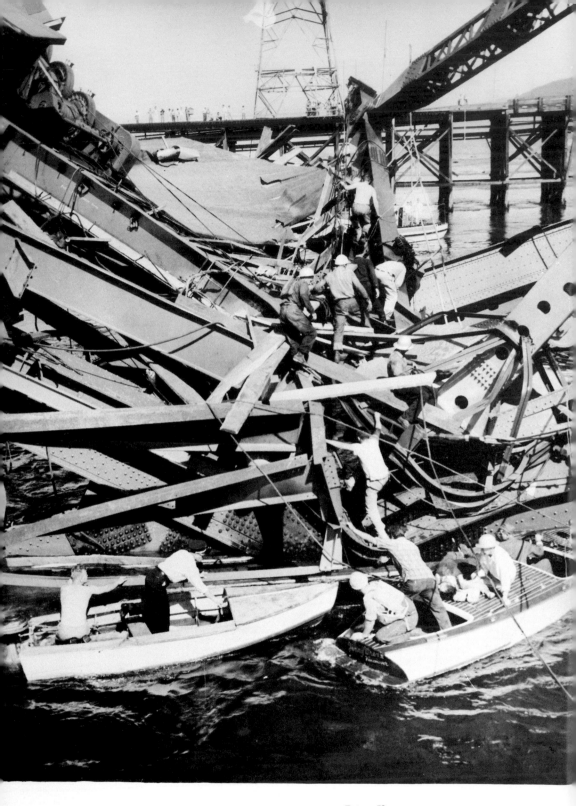

Brian Kent

Rescue workers climb over the mangled wreckage of Vancouver's Second
Narrows Bridge:

Great Canadian Disasters

GREAT
CANADIAN
DISASTERS

by Frank Rasky

with photographs

LONGMANS GREEN
& COMPANY – TORONTO

Longmans, Green & Company
137 Bond Street, Toronto 2

Printed and Bound in Canada
by Richardson, Bond & Wright Ltd.

•

by the same author

Gay Canadian Rogues

Roy Rogers, King of the Cowboys

DEDICATED

*to the thousands
who survived
and helped to tell
their story*

CONTENTS

PREFACE

Leo Tolstoy describes an interesting character in his story, *The Death of Ivan Ilyich*. The man is dying, and as he faces death, he suddenly remembers a school essay he had to study as a boy which began, "All men are mortal . . ." Only when death is imminent does the phrase really become meaningful. "It is not all other men who are mortal," Ivan Ilyich realizes with a swift and awful awareness. "It is I who am mortal."

How men face impending death has always fascinated me. It is the sovereign drama of life, and each of us is destined some day to play his role in that supreme and ultimate piece of theatre. Will we make of it a comedy or a tragedy? Will we behave as Falstaff or Hamlet?

In the stories of Canadian disasters that follow, I have tried wherever possible to discover what people immediately think and do when death threatens. The primary reaction seems to be one of feeling lonely and lost, and there is an overwhelming need to communicate with other doomed souls groping similarly for life. In the crow-black catacombs, two miles beneath the crust of the earth in the caved-in coal mine of Springhill, Nova Scotia, where the lethal gas smelled like burnt rubber, the survivors automatically reached out their fingers to touch the human warmth of their companions.

Women appear to respond differently from men. When the *Empress of Ireland* was being sucked under the St. Lawrence River, mothers on the sloping deck thought only of handing their babies to men who could swim. Fathers, however, seem more concerned with perpetuating the family name, leaving some mark to show that they themselves once lived on this earth. I find infinitely pathetic the comment of Lindsay Morton, the English mining agent, crouched on the lake shore with his wife and baby, while the forest fire devastated the South Porcupine gold camp: "The whole thing resolved itself into a question of dying decently. We lay in the mud, sometimes crawling into the water and then out again to gasp a breath of air. But it wasn't air we got to breathe. Just smoke, so bitter that it made the baby cry out, 'Mama, O Mama, give me air!' At last, I became so exhausted, I buried the family books and papers close beside me, so as to make sure I would leave a trace of identity behind me."

In the case of childless couples, I found that wives more often than husbands reach out amid catastrophe to say, "If we must die, let us die together." Yet resignation to the fact of death, of course, depends on individual temperament. During Hurricane Hazel, when the Humber River tossed their floating bed down Raymore Drive, the philosophic editor, Walter Harwood, folded his arms as he sat on the mattress, and said to his wife and mother-in-law: "I love you both. But this is the end, and we're going to die. Life, after all, is the only nightmare that is real." His wife, however, blazing with a more aggressive will to live, clenched her fists and cried out with magnificient defiance, "I'm not going to die! I'm not going to die!"

I have tried to make these more than adventure stories. Violence in itself does not interest me, although I realize that it has the power to create taut suspense. I have been more interested in presenting these disasters within a social framework, in pinpointing them on the board of Canadian history.

To be sure, I have been interested in learning what people ate and said and put on and sang and thought and feared during each disaster. But I have been equally interested in learning what things they did immediately before and after.

It has been difficult to ferret out these intimate things; and it has not been easy to get accurate accounts of the disasters themselves. Eyewitnesses contradict each other right and left, memories distort, and newspapers conflict strongly. For days after the avalanche in Frank, Alberta, the *Victoria Times* persisted in calling it an earthquake. Today, years after the event, the *Leader-Post* still refers to the Regina tornado as a cyclone, although the old Regina *Leader* vainly explained in an editorial the difference between the two, and correctly defined the Regina wind as a tornado.

Wherever possible, I have relied upon the transcript of eyewitness evidence given in coroners' inquiries or during investigations by special commissions. For example, in writing the chapter "Inferno in Newfoundland", I drew largely on the report of the inquiry conducted by the St. John's Supreme Court justice, Sir Brian Dunfield. It was a model investigation, and Sir Brian would make a model journalist.

Fantastic things turn up in these yellowing transcripts. Imbedded in the 612 pages of Lord Mersey's report on the sinking of the *Empress of Ireland* you will find the testimony of Captain Kendall, the skipper of the ill-fated ocean liner. He testifies how, after his ship had sunk, he stalked up to the bridge of the coal boat that had rammed her and, like an angry boy, confronted Captain Andersen with hot words of accusation. You would not believe a scene like this in a work of fiction. It is too melodramatically pat, and smacks of ham. And yet it is all there, written into the official records. "You have sunk my ship," Captain Kendall said. "You were going full speed, and in that dense fog." Captain Andersen glared and replied, "I was not going full speed. *You* were going full speed."

I have been surprised how keenly — nay, ferociously — these disasters live on in the memories of old-timers in local communities. Originally these chapters appeared in condensed form in either *Liberty* magazine or *Argosy*. My reconstruction of the Regina tornado, the Halifax explosion, and the St. John's fire provoked the fiercest conflict among survivors. Everybody nurtured a different version of the events, and some incensed correspondents wrote to me as though I myself were responsible for the local disaster. In a moment of foolishness, I originally described the water-front houses of St. John's as being "unpainted shanties". I touched a raw nerve, evidently, because among the spirited letters I received was one signed "The Butcher" which threatened, "If you ever come to St. John's, I will kill you with my bare hands."

Happily, I found most of the elderly survivors a serene and spry lot, brimming with health and delighted to share their memories with posterity. Having lived through a major disaster, it was as though they had learned to cope with the lesser dilemmas of life with grace and a smile.

Frank Rasky
Toronto, 1961

_ 1 _

St. Lawrence Shipwreck

HIGH IN THE CROW'S-NEST OF THE CANADIAN Pacific ocean liner, the *Empress of Ireland,* Look-out Jock Carroll gazed out at the dark green waters of the St. Lawrence River. It was a beautiful summery night, shortly after 1 A.M. on Friday, May 29, 1914. Overhead a young moon displayed its slender shoulder in a sky brightly pearled with stars. In his thirty years of sea-going, Carroll couldn't recall the Gulf of St. Lawrence ever looking so polished and unwrinkled by wind.

It seemed to him that the transatlantic liner — a 14,000-ton floating palace, complete with her own cricket pitch, five sumptuous decks, and Rudolph Valentino-style décor — was off to a splendid voyage, this time to Liverpool.

Just yesterday afternoon, the *Empress* had picked up at Quebec City her 1,057 passengers and million-dollar cargo of bars of silver from Cobalt, Ontario. At 1:20 A.M., after a stately two-hundred-mile cruise down the St. Lawrence, she had landed her French-Canadian river pilot at the Marconi wireless station of Father Point, near the tiny Quebec town of Rimouski. Now her twin screws were pushing her away from the south shore, and she was slitting through the unruffled waters at a speed of eighteen knots toward the open sea.

She was indeed an Edwardian dowager empress. Sedate in white and grey, steel-corseted with her ten watertight compartments, she imparted an air of truly impregnable safety. Her unsinkability was

1

serenely taken for granted by her passengers. They were a mixed *Grand Hotel* of personalities, and their thoughts were now on other things.

In his green-velvet stateroom in first class, Laurence Irving, the actor, with long locks of brown hair and a theatrical pince-nez, was having a late cup of tea with his beautiful wife, Mabel Hackney, who had been leading lady opposite his father, Sir Henry Irving. They were talking about the success they'd enjoyed while touring Canada in the melodrama *Typhoon*.

In his stateroom, Sir Henry Seton-Karr, walrus-moustached big-game hunter, explorer, and author of sporting books, was admiring the trophies he'd bagged in the wilds of British Columbia. As he sipped his usual nightcap of whisky and soda, he mused over the jolly tales of adventure he'd have to tell the gentlemen at the Athenaeum Club in London.

Mrs. Ethel Sabina Grundy Paton, the stout and merry society queen of Sherbrooke, Quebec, wife of its wealthiest woollen manufacturer, removed her diamonds. She fingered them impatiently. She could hardly wait to meet her two celebrated journalist brothers in London and Paris.

Just about to retire for the night was Major Henry Herbert Lyman, president of Montreal's oldest wholesale drug firm, a bearded and bald tycoon of sixty. He was passionately dedicated to British imperialism, insect-collecting, and his mother. After her recent death, he had had the door of her bedroom in their McTavish Street home in Montreal padlocked, and worshipped before the shrine of her furniture that was never to be touched. Now, he smiled at the young lady he had fallen in love with and married, and was about to take on a romantic tour of Europe.

In his second-class cabin, with his wife and three children, the grey, spade-beared commander of the Canadian Salvation Army, Commissioner David Rees, was on his knees praying thankfully. (He was known never to leave a street-car without saying a humble "Thank you" to the conductor.) He was praying for the two hundred Salvationists with him, voyaging to Albert Hall in London for their international congress.

They were the hand-picked "flower of the Canadian Salvation Army". There was the one-week-married Captain Eddy Dodd, *War Cry* editor, who had just posted at Rimouski the first installment of his

2

"Travel Jottings", with the modest copy instruction: "If you can conveniently do so, give this a two-column heading — not deep." There was Major George Attwell, baritone player in the forty-member brass band. Having admired the pretty sunset on deck with his wife, Captain Hattie, he had donned his white nightshirt and entered in his diary: "It looks as if we are going to have an excellent journey. Everything seems favourable!" And there was, among other gentle souls in the flock, Bandsman Teddy Gray, editorial cartoonist for the Toronto *Star* — who had prudently made his will and taken out a $2,000 insurance policy before embarking.

In his second-class cabin, nineteen-year-old Cedric ("Ritchie") Gallagher of Winnipeg, who had recently completed his second year of medicine at the University of Manitoba, was laughing. He was reading aloud to his mother Stephen Leacock's new best-seller, *Sunshine Sketches of a Little Town*. His mother, Louise, was laughing too, partly because of the humour, and partly because of her joy in her son. She had promised him this trip to Germany as a reward for success in his examinations.

In her cabin nearby, Mrs. Florrie Green, a short, brown-eyed Toronto Quaker of twenty-nine, her black tresses flowing over her pink nightgown, was reading with nostalgia back copies of the Birmingham *Daily Mail* and the Birmingham *Weekly Post*, which her father had sent her from England. Her husband Walter, an electrician with the Toronto Electric Light Company, had known she was homesick. He had been sensible enough to send Florrie on a vacation alone back to the Old Country.

In third class, Mrs. Pearl Cohen, a slight, thin-lipped Toronto immigrant of twenty-four, was moaning in pain. She was in what was then called "a delicate condition", and she desperately wanted her baby to be born "back home" in London where her mother was. Her husband Abe, a clothes peddler, caressed her damp forehead. He reminded her of the two thousand dollars they'd scrimped together these last four years in their Toronto flat on D'Arcy Street in the Jewish Kensington area, and how wonderful it would be when they invested their fortune in a nice little fish-and-chip shop on their arrival in London.

She cheered up, and didn't bother Abe to summon the ship's physician, Dr. James F. Grant, of Victoria, British Columbia. Like most

3

of the other 420 members of the *Empress* crew, the handsome young doctor — he'd graduated from McGill University only the year before — was fast asleep in his quarters.

Also sound asleep, far down in the ship's sixteen-berth glory-hole, was the assistant steward, William ("Billy Boy") Lawrence Hughes. A cocky, wisecracking lad of seventeen, with a heavy Lancashire accent, he'd run away from home in Liverpool to become a sea-going bellhop; now he was proud of earning eleven dollars a month, plus tips, aboard the *Empress*. But he was dog-tired from having sorted out baggage all day. In the glory-hole, he hung up his navy-blue "monkey jacket" on a steel peg, and kissed the signet ring on his finger that was a gift from his brunette sweetheart, Annie Veronica. And the last thing he saw before he snoozed off was the gleaming bald head in the opposite bunk of old John Cheetham, the silver-man in charge of the ship's cutlery.

Down in the deepest bowels of the ship, in the boiler-room, his naked chest sweaty and grease-blackened and lit up from the scarlet glow of the furnaces, Ted Fitchett, the well-known English boxer, was very much awake, as he heaved coal and cursed his luck. His star had been on the decline ever since Darky Allen had fought him to a draw at the Canadian Club in Montreal. He'd tried his hand as a trainer at the Hochelaga Club, and taken on some Royal Highlander kilties as pupils at Montreal's National Sporting Club. But everybody regarded him as a has-been in the ring. Now he was working his way as a stoker back to Bradford in England where his brother, William Fitchett, was making a big name in boxing circles. He swore he'd return to Montreal in the fall to show them all who was really champ. A lucky break was all Ted Fitchett needed; just a lucky break.

Standing on the bridge of the *Empress,* peering into the empty night, was her skipper, Captain Henry George Kendall. Six feet of punctilio, impeccably uniformed, he was a commanding figure. At thirty-nine he was earning what was then considered a handsome salary, $4,250 a year. As Father Point receded into the night, the Captain was thinking of how a notorious murderer, at that very place, had put a curse on his head.

It was just four years ago that Captain Kendall had quietly taken on board here Scotland Yard Inspector Walter Dew, who had then arrested the London wife-butcher, Dr. Hawley Crippen. After chopping

4

up his wife, Crippen had wrapped her up tidily in a plum-coloured curtain, and buried her in the cellar of his Highgate home in north London. Then he had fled with his mistress, Ethel Le Neve. Before boarding Captain Kendall's ship bound for Canada, Crippen had disguised his mistress as a boy, and they had masqueraded as "Mr. and Master Robinson". His suspicions aroused by the "boy's" girlish figure, Captain Kendall had radioed Scotland Yard.

It was the first time the relatively new invention of wireless had been used to capture fugitives on the high seas, and Captain Kendall's name was headlined around the world. Scotland Yard wirelessed back that they were sending a detective by fast steamer to net in the murderer on his arrival at Father Point on the St. Lawrence. When Crippen was arrested, the enraged killer fixed his bulging eye on Captain Kendall and uttered his malevolent curse, like something out of a bad melodrama. "You will suffer for this treachery, sir," he said.

Now, just six minutes after he'd landed his river pilot at Father Point, Captain Kendall was suddenly jolted out of his reverie into the present by the urgent clanging of a bell. It was the signal struck by Lookout Jock Carroll high in the crow's-nest: "A ship's masthead light spotted on the starboard bow." The Irish seaman had sighted, six miles away, the approaching Norwegian collier, Storstad — a six-thousand-ton "coal nigger" nosing up-river to Montreal with her load of ten thousand tons of coal from Sydney, Nova Scotia. Just as suddenly, a bank of low-lying fog rolled out from the Quebec shore. It shrouded both ships so completely that they were in a sightless world.

Jock Carroll heard the warning siren wail a mournful "whoo-whoo-whoo" from the Empress, and heard a long, ghostly blast of the whistle from the Storstad; but noise could not rip away the curtain of fog between them. At 1:55 A.M., the black Storstad loomed out of the even blacker mist, and her steel-sheathed bow sliced twenty feet clean through to the vitals of the Empress, fatally wounding her. Within fourteen minutes, the great luxury liner keeled over on her right side, like a whale pierced by a pygmy swordfish, and sank. A thousand and twelve people, with their mortal dreams and aspirations, died with her.

Jock Carroll was one of the 465 who survived. As soon as the Empress was rammed and began listing, he leaped for the ladder. By an acrobatic feat, he scrambled down through the lacework of rigging to

5

the forecastle head. He ran up the tilting deck, tore off all his clothing except his pants, and cannon-balled into the water in a belly-flopper dive.

"And how were you saved?" the Irishman was later asked at the official inquiry conducted by Lord Mersey, who also investigated the sinking of the *Titanic*.

"Begorra, I couldn't tell you, sir," Jock Carroll replied. "I was picked up by some boat."

The world wanted to know far more about it than that. The sinking of the *Empress* was the most dreadful marine disaster in Canadian history, and everywhere the agonized cry was raised: "Why?"

Rudyard Kipling was reminded that he'd been aboard the ocean liner on her maiden voyage to Quebec eight years ago; he'd almost been tempted then to write a poem extolling her absolute invulernability.

A few days after the tragedy, Sir Arthur Conan Doyle arrived in Montreal on a lecture tour, and was asked if he could solve the mystery. The creator of Sherlock Holmes shook his head and said he was baffled.

In England, the *Illustrated London News* devoted a whole issue to the catastrophe, and assigned the world's most renowned sea expert, Joseph Conrad, to write an article on "The Lesson of the Collision". The best explanation that the author of *Typhoon, Chance,* and *Twixt Land and Sea* could come up with was cryptic. "It seems to me that the resentful sea gods never do sleep," he wrote, "and as long as men will travel on the water, the sea gods will take their toll."

The mystery was all the more perplexing because the *Empress* was far safer than the *Titanic*. Just two years before, that allegedly unsinkable White Star giant had hit an iceberg off the Grand Banks of Newfoundland; she had gone to her grave with 1,513 people, drowning such millionaires as John Jacob Astor and Benjamin Guggenheim, while a ragtime band played "Nearer My God to Thee". The lesson learned from her foundering was that the *Titanic* had carried life-boats enough for 1,178 persons — only sixteen boats, or one-third of her capacity. The rules had since been tightened for all ocean liners; and consequently the *Empress of Ireland* had increased her life-boat capacity to 1,860 — a total of forty boats, or more than enough for all aboard.

Indeed, Captain Kendall had put his crew through a scrupulous life-boat drill and safety inspection while the *Empress* was still moored at her berth in Quebec City. It was a clear, sunshiny afternoon on Thursday, May 28, when the Canadian Pacific Railway liner prepared to cast off. The only untoward incident was that the ship's cat, Emmy, a veteran of a dozen voyages, insisted stubbornly on staying behind on the pier. It was odd, because she was deserting her litter of kittens on board.

Shrugging off this peculiar omen, the Salvation Army's staff band—dressed in red tunics and Mountie-style stetsons — assembled on the upper deck. They struck up "O Canada" and "Auld Lang Syne." At 4:20 p.m., as the ship slid away from the quay, Bandmaster Edward Hanagan, aware of the adoring eyes of his seven-year-old daughter Gracie on him, led the forty brass-players in the rousing favourite, "God Be with You Till We Meet Again." It was to become the theme song of that ill-fated voyage.

That evening, in the candelabra-lit dining saloon, the ship's five-piece orchestra played the lugubrious tune, "The Funeral March of a Marionette". Billy Boy Hughes, the jocular assistant steward, tried his hand at cheering up Sir Henry Seton-Karr, the explorer, and the society queen, Mrs. Ethel Sabina Grundy Paton. "Don't eat too heavy," he joked. "You'll be sea-sick in the morning. Then you'll miss our bee-ootiful breakfast." They laughed politely.

After dinner, the contingent of Salvationists indulged in their own form of entertainment. A group of them lingered in the lounge. There Bandsman Ernest Green and his sister Jessie encouraged their father, Adjutant Harry Green, to play on the piano a round of his own comical tunes. In the music-room there was a hymn sing-song. Bandsman Herbert Booth Greenaway, in honour of his honeymooning brother Tom Greenaway and Tom's bride Margaret, requested "There Is Sweet Rest in Heaven". On deck, Captain Rufus Spooner, a cockney cut-up from Moose Jaw, Saskatchewan, organized a rough-house game of "Dead Man" — in which a male Salvationist tried to fall down, while those in the circle around him tried to keep him on his feet.

Most of the Salvationists emulated the actions of Captain George Wilson, the pious but practical horn-player of Toronto. He wrote a sweet letter to his wife, Captain Annie, thanking her for the Bible she

7

had loaned him. He borrowed a stamp from Deputy Bandmaster Willy Wakefield of Vancouver. Then he posted the letter in time for it to be taken off by the mail tender, *Lady Evelyn*, when the *Empress* reached the Quebec town of Rimouski. At 1:20 A.M. the liner stopped again at Father Point, about three miles down-river from Rimouski. There she discharged her pilot, Adélard Bernier, onto the tug *Eureka*. But by then Captain George Wilson was fast asleep in the upper bunk of the second-class cabin he shared with three other male Salvationists. His wallet containing three hundred dollars was snug under his pillow, and he was blissfully secure, because he'd first knelt to say his nightly prayer, "Thank you, Lord, for the day's happenings."

Aboard the *Storstad* all was not so secure. The squat Norwegian collier with her crew of thirty-six, chartered by the Dominion Coal Company, was then speeding up-river to Father Point to pick up her St. Lawrence pilot, who would guide her to Montreal. Her captain was not at the helm. He was Captain Thomas Andersen, a portly and jovial Norwegian with a droopy handle-bar moustache, asleep in his cabin with his wife. He'd left strict orders that he was to be summoned the moment fog showed. These orders were disobeyed by the chief officer on the bridge, Alfred Toftenes, thirty-three years old and ambitious, who had been promoted to first mate only five weeks ago. (At the official inquiry later, he was asked if it was true that the collier was promised a bonus for making a speedy coal delivery. Toftenes denied it, but it was noted that he "smiled a crooked smile" while saying no.)

Nobody will ever know for sure what warning whistle blasts were sounded by Chief Officer Toftenes and Captain Kendall when their vessels were enveloped in fog. At the inquiry, their accusations were hotly conflicting. Each claimed the other was a liar who had changed course in midstream. "If the evidence of the two officers was correct," wrote the Montreal *Gazette* in deadpan prose, "then the two vessels must have been lying about two miles apart, neither of them moving, when they collided so violently."

What is certain is that Chief Officer Toftenes did not awaken his skipper until the *Empress* was little more than eight hundred feet away. On the *Storstad* bridge, he called through the speaking-tube connecting him with Captain Andersen: "It's getting hazy, sir. And the Father Point light is just closing off now."

8

The hapless officer didn't bother to mention the ocean liner on his port bow, that had vanished from his vision and that he'd been dodging in the river black-out.

Captain Andersen pulled on his pants and sweater and hastened on deck. He was aghast to see the hull of the *Empress*, a dim green-lit phantom, looming toward him at a forty-degree angle in the foggy night. He raced to the bridge and frantically rang his order to the engines: "Full speed astern!"

It was too late. The collier ploughed on intently, and her prow slashed through the steel plates amidships of the *Empress* like tearing Cellophane. Tendrils of yellow flame shot out, as steel ground shrieking against steel. The *Storstad* bow ripped on through twenty feet of the liner's steel decks, her anchor hooking cruelly into the very entrails of the *Empress*.

On the flying bridge of the *Empress*, Captain Kendall yelled through his megaphone toward the collier: "Go full speed astern!" He hoped the coal vessel, by staying inside the gash, might plug up the wound, like a cork in a bottle.

Captain Andersen cupped his hands and shouted back: "I *am* going astern full speed!"

But the speed and impact of the mighty liner were too much for him; her headway twisted the *Storstad* out of the hole. The collier limped off into the fog, halted a half-mile away, and hooted her hoarse-voiced whistle, but received no answer from the monster she had just stabbed.

Captain Andersen, peering futilely into the darkness, was joined on the bridge by his wife. She had tossed a fur coat over her shoulders.

"I suppose we're going down?" she asked her husband quietly.

"It might be," he replied. "But take it easy, and don't cry."

"My place is here on the bridge with you," she said. "Let us go down in the ship together."

But his officers reported that the *Storstad* was not badly crippled, after all, and Captain Andersen and his wife then heard the piteous cries of the drowning in the water. "At first I didn't know what it was," he later said. "It was like one long, moaning sound." Captain Andersen ordered the *Storstad's* four life-boats to be lowered and sent to the rescue.

Aboard the *Empress*, Captain Kendall was desperate. The collision had ruptured the liner's two boiler-rooms, and tons of water were spouting in by the second through her gashed stokeholes. He gave the order, "Close the doors of the ten watertight compartments." But only one of the bulkhead compartments could be slammed shut in time. He telephoned Chief Engineer William Sampson: "For heaven's sake, give her all you've got. We'll try to beach her." But Sampson replied, "The steam is all gone."

The Captain sounded the high, screaming crescendo of the distress siren to signify, "Prepare to abandon ship." Then he turned wearily to his Chief Officer, M. R. Steed. "Have Sparks send the SOS signal to Father Point," he said.

In the liner's lurching wireless cabin, senior Marconi operator Ronald Ferguson, in his pajamas, calmly tapped out the newly adopted international distress signal: Dot-dot-dot. Dash-dash-dash. Dot-dot-dot.

At the Father Point wireless shack, Operator Bill Whiteside, aroused from his bed and also in pajamas, replied: "Okay. Here we are."

The blue dots danced in the *Empress* cabin: "We have struck something. Sinking fast. Ship listing terribly. Stand by."

"Okay, old man," replied Father Point. "Where are you?"

"Twenty miles past Rimouski."

"Okay, old man. Am sending *Eureka* from Father Point and *Lady Evelyn* from Rimouski to render you assistance. Did you say twenty miles?"

Marconi Operator Ferguson was just about to send out the word "Yes", when the dynamos failed, and all the lights on the *Empress* sputtered out into blackness.

As the ship began to heel over violently, Chief Steward Augustus Gaade, clutching his dressing-gown, scrambled up the main saloon deck on starboard. He spoke crisply to the sailor on duty, "Call all passengers you can. Tell them to get life-belts on, and muster on the top deck." Then he made his way to the dangerously tilting bridge, where Captain Kendall was standing with his megaphone.

Gaade, who'd been with the *Empress* since her christening eight years ago, choked and spoke softly. "Well, this looks to be about the finish, sir," he said.

"Yes," said the Captain, "and a terrible finish it is, too."

The finish was described by one survivor, Salvationist Kenneth McIntyre, as "a picture from Dante's *Inferno*". Down below in third class, 584 of the 717 poorer passengers, lost in the bewildering warren of ship corridors, were almost instantly drowned "like rats trapped in a maze". When the boilers exploded, stokers like Ted Fitchett, the luckless boxer, were scalded to death, "amid the nasty smell that usually arises when you throw water on live coals".

Only forty-eight of the total 253 second-class passengers, only thirty-six of the eighty-seven first-class passengers, managed to live. Some died because they were too sleepy to budge from their bunks (Major Henry Herbert Lyman, the bald tycoon, and his young bride), or too dazed (Teddy Gray, the *Star* cartoonist, who'd made his will), or too slow-moving (Captain Eddy Dodd, the *War Cry* editor, who had posted the first and last instalment of his "Travel Jottings").

Some died trying to crawl up the stairs to the slanting deck, where a floor had suddenly become a wall and a wall a ceiling. Some died when the life-boats crashed down from their swaying davits and crushed women and children to death. Some died because they couldn't hold on along with the others, who sat clinging to the upturned, slimy bottom of the liner, like a grandstand of doomed spectators; who wailed in despair as she was finally sucked down, "My God! My God! My God!"

Some died while bobbing in the freezing water, like a village of floundering ants, unable to swim. Some died of heart attack after they were pulled aboard the four *Empress* life-boats that got away. And some died after they were yanked up to the deck of the *Storstad*, the cold and shock too much for them, though Captain Andersen's wife ministered to them with bottles of whisky and Benedictine, and tore up curtains and tablecloths and her own petticoats to cover their nakedness.

The calmness of the 248 crew members who survived out of the total 420 was apparently almost saint-like. It was so eulogized before the official inquiry by George Bogue Smart, a first-class passenger, employed as Ottawa's Chief Inspector of British Immigrant Children in Canada.

"The discipline on board after the collision was really marvellous," he testified. "I never heard people who spoke with such tenderness to each other in that time of great distress. There was no bad language. No panic to speak of. No violence at all. All good-natured.

"No, I wasn't shaken up seriously when the vessels came together," Smart said. "I can best define the jar by saying it reminded me of the rude impact of a couple of coaches on a railway. I crawled upstairs to the upper deck, and climbed out on the port railing. And I put my arm around the post, you know, and I just sat and waited until the ship went down. I will never know the man in charge of the life-raft who picked me up, but whoever he was, he spoke in the kindest way to me. It was really delightful to me then, under those trying circumstances."

In first class, as one survivor phrased it, "the gentlemen by and large behaved like gentlemen and the ladies like ladies."

Mrs. Ethel Sabina Grundy Paton, the society dowager of Sherbrooke, behaved as though she were going to the annual tea-dance of the Daughters of the Empire. A steward knocked on the door of her stateroom, No. 32 on the upper deck, and said politely, "If you want to be saved, ma'am, please put on your life-belt and go on deck."

"Will I have time to save any of my personal effects?" she asked.

"No, ma'am," he replied. "Not if you wish to save your life."

She snorted, and had him hand her the life-preserver — cork blocks sewn in canvas — from the top of her stateroom wardrobe. After he left, she put on her diamonds and dressed impeccably. She even took along her reticule sewing-bag, containing her nail scissors and extra pair of glasses.

On the sloping deck, she found the starboard rail almost immersed in water. Holding her skirts, she imperturbably stepped off the rail into a collapsible life-boat nearby, not wetting her button shoes at all, and thanking the officer who held her arm. Aboard the *Storstad*, Captain Andersen's wife found her "a self-possessed darling", and her nail scissors were quite handy. The society dowager used them to cut up a pillowcase and make a dress of sorts for naked little Florence Barbour. The eight-year-old girl lost her parents, but was saved by riding the back of a swimmer, Robert Crellin, a wealthy miner from Silverton, British

Columbia, who later adopted the orphan. At Rimouski, Mrs. Paton wired her brother, G. C. Grundy, general manager of the Temiscouata Railway, that she was "none the worse" for her escape. He rushed to the scene in his private train, the *Madawaska*, and Mrs. Paton returned to Sherbrooke in style, entertaining on the way lady survivors fortunate enough to accompany her.

Laurence Irving, the actor, behaved in the manner befitting a tragedian playing his last great scene. His death scene was played before only one spectator, F. E. Abbott, owner of a millinery store on Bay Street in Toronto.

"I met Irving first in the passage-way," Abbott later recalled, "and he said calmly, 'Is the boat going down?' I said that it looked like it.

" 'Dearie,' Irving then said to his wife, 'there is no time to lose.' Mrs. Irving began to cry, and the actor reached for his life-belt. The boat suddenly lurched forward, and he was thrown against the door of his cabin. His face was bloody, and Mrs. Irving became frantic. 'Keep cool,' he warned, but she persisted in holding her arms around him. He forced the life-belt over her, and practically carried her upstairs.

"I said: 'Can I help you?' And Irving said, 'Look after yourself first, old man. But God bless you all the same.' I dived overboard, and I clung like grim death to a deck-chair. I looked back and saw two figures on the sinking deck. Irving was kissing his wife as the ship went down, and they were clasped in each other's arms."

The Toronto milliner performed in his own touching scene. "I became unconscious in the water," Abbott remembered, "and then I heard someone say, 'Are you alive?' I opened my eyes, and saw two men close to me on a raft. One man stretched out a broken oar and he said, 'Grab it, and I will pull you on with us.' When I touched the oar, the man said to his companion, 'Come and give me a hand, or I shall have to let go.' I pleaded with him, 'For God's sake, don't let me go!' He answered simply, 'No, I won't let you go — even if you pull me off the raft.' I do not know the name of my rescuer. I only know he was an Englishman, and he was a brave man."

Later, Abbott wept when they found Laurence Irving floating in his life-jacket, dead, with a shred of his wife's night-dress still clutched in his hand.

Sir Henry Seton-Karr, the big-game hunter, behaved in a manner befitting a graduate of Harrow and Oxford, son of the resident commissioner at Baroda, India, during the Indian mutiny. He dressed himself meticulously in a starched white shirt and evening clothes, saved a man's life, and then returned for his hunting trophies.

"My cabin was opposite Sir Henry's," recalled M. D. A. Darling, a young Englishman returning home from Shanghai. "When I opened my door, he opened his, and we bumped into each other in the passage-way. He had a life-belt in his hand, and I was empty-handed. Sir Henry offered me the life-belt and I refused it.

"He said, 'Go on, man, take it! Or I will try to get another man.' I told him to rush out himself, and save his own life, while I looked after myself.

"Sir Henry got angry. He actually forced the life-belt over me. Then he pushed me along the corridor. I never saw him after that. He went back to his cabin, and he never came out again, because the ship disappeared a few minutes later."

Darling then saved a life on his own — the life of the young ship's surgeon, Dr. James F. Grant. Thrown out of his bunk, the physician tried to squeeze through a narrow porthole; but his shoulders got caught, and his feet danced helplessly in midair, like a wedged beetle. After Darling pulled him through, Dr. Grant was surprised to find himself on the plated side of the *Empress,* now lying almost flat in the water on her starboard flank. "Several hundred people were crouched together there," he later said, "and as the ship canted over further, they'd slide down into the water, as though walking down a sandy beach into the water to bathe."

Dr. Grant was stark naked and unconscious by the time a life-boat hoisted him aboard the *Storstad.* There he was put in Captain Andersen's bunk along with a couple of other men, who huddled together and slapped themselves for warmth. As soon as he recovered, the doctor exclaimed, "There's better work for me than remaining here. Lend me a pair of pants, so I can get busy and do some good."

He had to deal with several striking shock cases, of the kind he'd never been taught about at McGill. One traumatic man was pulled out of the river while he was swimming madly for his life. Even when he

14

was laid flat on the *Storstad* deck, he continued his swimming strokes for one hour, like a fish out of water seized with maniac motion. Another man, his broken leg swollen to the size of a log, fought desperately when Dr. Grant tried to put it in a splint. The surgeon finally found the reason: secreted under the man's night-shirt, next to his skin, was a foot-wide money belt holding five purses stuffed with dollar bills. And perhaps most poignant was the woman who died talking to a husband who wasn't there: "She used all the endearing little names — you know, the silly names — a wife calls out to her husband when she is happy. She babbled in rapture, and died smiling."

Helping Dr. Grant massage the numb victims with heavy towels was Cedric ("Ritchie") Gallagher, the young Winnipeg medical student, who'd been laughing with his mother at the Stephen Leacock stories. He wasn't laughing now. His mother had paused to slip her wedding ring on her finger. Then they had leaped together from the promenade deck of the floundering *Empress*, the mother's hands linked in her son's. But his mother got her neck noosed in the fallen rigging of the mainmast. She was torn from his grasp, and he last saw her bubbling below with the sinking ship. "Poor mother was swallowed up," was all Cedric would say, in a flat and expressionless voice.

Nor was there much life in the voice of Abe Cohen, the London immigrant, who had tried to cheer up his pregnant wife with dreams of their fish-and-chip shop. They were just about to jump together when the ship's boiler explosion ripped them apart, and now he was haunted by the memory of his wife's last anguished cry, "Oh, God! Save me for the sake of my unborn son!"

Mrs. Florrie Green, the Quaker homesick for Birmingham, had reason to bless the swimming lessons given her there by the Quakers' Severn Street Swimming Club. As the ship's keel made its final plunge, sucking her deep down into the water, she prayed silently to herself, "God help me." Just as she was choking for air, the boilers exploded, and the convulsion shot her up to the surface again. At the same time, she experienced the painfully odd sensation of being scalded all over her body in the icy-cold water.

Despite her blistering burns, she swam to an upturned life-boat and clutched it for what seemed hours. Four men held on beside her, too numb to talk, except when a life-boat from the *Lady Evelyn* came along-side, and then one man managed to croak, "There's a lady here!"

Later, aboard the *Storstad*, after she peeled of her soaked nightgown and borrowed a skirt from the captain's wife, she retained her sense of humour. Looking even more ridiculous was a bedraggled man, clad only in a woman's petticoat and fifty-cent straw hat. Today she still recalls the laughter at the quip, "Why, you look all dolled up for the bloomin' Easter Parade!"

The contingent of two hundred Salvationists behaved as you would expect them to behave under pressure: gently, gallantly, devoutly. One hundred and sixty-seven of them died, or, in the Salvation Army phrase, "were promoted to glory".

The spade-bearded Commissioner David Rees, surrounded by his wife and three children, was praying when promoted to his glory. As the deck finally turned turtle, the Commissioner was seen clasping his daughter Annie in his arms, and stroking her forehead; and the last thing he said was, "Thy will be done."

Bandmaster Edward Hanagan and his wife were promoted to glory while trying to save their flaxen-haired seven-year-old daughter Gracie. Until she could cling to a plank in the water, the little girl found herself perched on the floating back of her dead father, his hand still clutching the arm of her dead mother. "For long after," says Gracie, now a London, Ontario housewife, "a tap running in a bathtub would frighten me into terrible shivers."

Adjutant Harry Green, the composer of comical tunes, went down with his wife Nellie and daughter Jessie, while putting his trust in Providence. His twenty-three-year-old son, Bandsman Ernie Green, found his family group grasping the deck rail. "When I last saw my father," the son recalls, "he said: 'Well, whatever happens, my boy, we are in God's hands.' And I said, 'Yes, Father.' A second later, the *Empress* rolled like a tar-barrel, and my father and my mother and my sister were washed away before my eyes."

The horrified son dived into the salt water, kicked off his red-striped pajamas, and saved himself by clutching the cold and waxy corpse of a drowned man whose life-belt had slipped around his loins. "For long nights after," says the son, now a retired Salvationist lieutenant-

16

colonel, employed as a floorwalker at Simpson's in Toronto, "I would wake up in a clammy sweat from that nightmare vision of my family."

Major George Attwell, the diary keeper, who'd admired the lovely sunset with his wife Captain Hattie, almost went to his glory by agreeing to rescue a baby. On the heaving deck, in their white nighties, they met Bandsman Ernest Foord and his wife, carrying their blonde infant, Alice. "You're a good swimmer, Major," said Mrs. Foord, putting the child in his arms. "Please try to save my baby."

"Certainly," agreed Major Attwell. But to himself he thought resignedly, "This will be the end of me. I'll never be able to swim, holding both my wife and this baby."

Just then, Bandsman Kenneth McIntyre crawled along the deck, chivalrously took off his own life-belt, and said to Mrs. Foord, "Here, take mine." To Major Attwell's profound relief, Mrs. Foord took back her baby — though he was saddened later to learn that she, her husband, and the child all perished.

As the water began to surge around their knees, Major Attwell turned to his wife and said, "Mama, if it's our turn to die, let us jump together." He tied a life-belt with a broken shoulder-strap around her, kissed her on the lips, and held her tightly by the right hand; and as the ship's boilers exploded under them with a muffled roar, he cried out, "Now, Mama, now!"

They leaped three yards clear into the water; plunged down, down, down; felt the punch-punch of watery fists in their eyes — and were astonished to find themselves shot up to the surface again, holding hands under the moon's pale globe of yellow light. They sank and rose three times, until, in the seething mass of naked bodies, Major Attwell found an air-cushion that he placed under his wife's arms. Then he swam briskly with both arms, while his wife held the back of his night-shirt.

Next, he spotted a life-boat, gasped a lungful of air, and screamed, "Hi-hi-hi-hiya!" As he and his wife were dragged aboard, scraping their shins, he was convinced his nose and toes were touching. "They were the only parts of my body," recalls Attwell, now a spry, silvery-haired recluse of eighty-seven, living with his canary Chummie in Westway Village, Ontario, "that didn't seem frozen lifeless."

Captain George Wilson, the pious and practical horn player of Toronto, also almost lost his life while trying to save a baby. He never did return the stamp he borrowed from Deputy Bandmaster Willy Wakefield, because Wakefield drowned. He never did recover the three hundred dollars under his pillow, because the wallet went down into the sea. He had time only to hurl a black wool overcoat over his pyjamas, and to join the crowd "clogged like a shoal of cuttle-fish" at the end of the companion-way, which "surged me up the vertical stairs as though I were toothpaste".

A woman on the slanting deck threw him her two-year-old infant, while screaming, "Save my baby! Oh, save my baby!" He tried to hand the baby up to the top of the deck to Ensign Ernest Pugmire, his Salvationist friend, who was nude except for a red-flannel lumbago belt around his waist.

Just then, the explosion catapulted Captain Wilson backwards, and he found himself in the water. Kept buoyant by his ballooned-out overcoat, he swam to a wooden plank, gripped it with numb fingers, and sobbed with relief when he saw a heavily loaded life-boat veer toward him. But it passed him by.

"I could see the faces of the passengers in the life-boat as they passed me by," recalls Captain Wilson. "I was not resentful. I knew I would tip them if I got aboard. But I'll never forget the looks on their faces — a mingling of sorrow and embarrassment and regret."

Five minutes later, another life-boat headed toward him, and somebody thrust out the blade of an oar to him; and as Captain Wilson threw himself forward with his last ounce of strength, he blacked out. When he came to, he was sitting on a wooden coal shelf in the *Storstad* boiler-room. He refused a gulp of whisky, pious to the end, saying, "I am a Salvationist abstainer." But he was overjoyed to find Ensign Ernest Pugmire still alive, though blue and shivering in his red-flannel lumbago belt. Captain Wilson wrapped a green chenille curtain and a towel around himself, and gave his chum his overcoat. He was delighted thereafter when Ensign Pugmire exclaimed, "You know, I do believe the shock has cured my lumbago."

Bandsman Herbert Booth Greenaway almost went to his glory while wrapping a sweater around a baby. He was wearing the heavy grey sweater over his pajamas, when he saw on the almost perpendicular deck, "like spectres in the fog", Bandsman Ernie Evans and his wife, holding their chilled baby. Greenaway was just about to place his sweater over the infant's shoulders, when he was hurled down the slope and whammed into the belly of a gentleman in an ornate dressing-gown who was clutching the submerged deck-rail.

"Excuse me, sir," gasped Greenaway, remembering the politeness he'd been taught as office boy to the Salvation Army's founder, General William Booth, "I'm awfully sorry. I slipped."

"Oh, that's jolly well all right," murmured the gentleman. "Accidents will happen, old chap." Then he dived elegantly into the water and vanished, like a figment out of *Alice in Wonderland*.

Greenaway muttered a prayer under his breath: "If you save me, O Lord, I shall help build up your Kingdom." Shortly afterwards, he jumped into a life-boat that was just pulling away, and didn't even wet his white running-shoes.

"I believe I did keep my promise to the Lord," says Greenaway, now retired in Toronto at sixty-eight, after eighteen years with the Salvation Army, followed by serving as Dominion Field Commissioner for the Canadian Boy Scouts. "I always regretted that Evans and his wife and baby perished in a watery grave. But I still remember that experience as a scary dream, played out before grotesque mirrors, and it was as though I'd never wake up."

And Captain Rufus Spooner, the Moose Jaw cockney, who'd played the deck game of "Dead Man", almost went to his glory trying to comfort a honeymooning bride separated from her mate. She was Ensign Margaret Greenaway, the petite, brown-haired wife of one week.

Captain Spooner, in his red-striped pajamas, found Ensign Margaret on deck, shivering in her white nightie and weeping. Spooner asked her to stand on his bare feet to keep warm while she explained. After hearing the tearing of metal and inrush of water, she and Tom had hurried out of their cabin into the passage-way. Tom had returned to the cabin to fetch her wrap. Meanwhile, the lights flickered out, and in the darkness Margaret clutched the arm of a man she thought was her husband. Only after she climbed the stairs with him to the deck did she realize her companion was a stranger.

"Don't worry," Spooner soothed her. "Tom'll be all right. I'll go down below and get you a blanket and life-preserver."

She stepped off his feet, and he groped downstairs to the first cabin on the right that he could see, where he removed a grey blanket from the bunk and four life-belts from the wall. The stairs by now were so nearly vertical, he believes "an angel of mercy must have lifted me up them."

He draped the blanket over Margaret's shoulders, put the life-belt on her, gave the other three life-belts to three other women, and led them all in creeping crab-wise along the upturned, slimy side girders of the *Empress*. Then an explosion rocked the liner, and a column of steam hissed out of a porthole; and the last he saw of Margaret, she was being sucked down into the water.

Terribly scalded and her ankle mangled, Margaret found herself riding on top of a shattered deck chair. Two Swedes on a raft floated by, and as one of the men reached out a broken oar, he shouted: "Are you alive?"

"I don't want to live," Margaret moaned. "My husband's gone."

"Don't be afraid, little girl," said the big Swede, as he hauled her onto the raft. "My poor wife is gone, too." Seeing her tremble in the chill, he opened his coat, drew her up close, and buttoned her inside against his warm body; and she was just mumbling "Thank you," when pinwheels seemed to twirl around in her head, and she blacked out.

Meanwhile, when the *Empress* exploded, Captain Spooner felt himself being sucked ten feet below the water. He struggled in the whirl and plunge of a curling wave, and as he was being turned over and over, he thought to himself, "This is the end. I leave myself to the mercy of God." But thanks to his life-saving training with the St. John Ambulance Brigade, he bobbed corklike to the surface, and swam to a smashed piece of lumber. He crawled on top of it, and lay exhausted and frozen for three-quarters of an hour, until a life-boat from the *Eureka* fished him out and took him to the *Storstad*.

In the engine-room there he slid sheets of newspaper inside his pajamas to keep himself warm, and began rendering first aid to the naked survivors. He was overjoyed to find Ensign Margaret's husband, Tom

20

Greenaway, quite alive. After failing to find his wife on deck, he'd clung to the railing, determined to die as the ship went down. But the suction tore him loose, and he rose to the surface to find a table floating under him.

"I don't think you'll ever see Margaret again," Spooner said gently, as he explained how he'd seen her shot under the water.

"Rufus, I don't want to live without her," Tom sobbed, and Spooner took him in his arms and comforted him.

When they landed at the Rimouski wharf, the two Salvationists rode in an open livery hack to one of the town's many kindly French-Canadian homes that took the survivors in. There, warming themselves before the living-room fireplace, were their fellow-bandsmen, George Wilson, Ernest Pugmire, and Major Frank Morris, all grinning broadly.

"Why don't you go into the bedroom, Tom, and see what you find there?" one of the trio spoke up.

Tom Greenaway rushed into the bedroom and found lying on the bed, black as soot and scalded, but very much alive, his bride, Margaret. They fell into each other's arms and embraced, and then the first thing she asked was, "Where's Rufus, who helped save me?"

Spooner, the cockney bachelor of twenty-seven, shyly came in and said, "Here," and blushed as the bride put her arms around him, too, and kissed him.

"You know, I love the sea," says Spooner, today a retired Salvationist colonel, as he displays the many seascapes he has since painted and hung in his Toronto home. "But I'm so aware of how the sea can be so cruel."

The cruelty of the sea will never be forgotten by Billy Boy Hughes, the jocular sea-going bellhop of seventeen. As the *Empress* went down, the youth sat straddle-legged on the deck-rail, fighting off a hysterical teen-aged girl in a nightie, who was choking him to death.

Already he was hearing a high death-hum in his ears, and her fingernails seemed to be gripping his windpipe like razor-sharp claws, when they both plunged under. Suddenly she let go. The quick rolling movement churned his stomach, and now the sound in his ears was as the roaring and fading of sea shells.

He fingered his signet-ring, a gift from his Liverpool sweetheart, Annie Veronica; and he thought, "Billy Hughes drowned? Billy Hughes drowning? No, no! I must think of Annie Veronica. I must save myself."

He frog-legged to the surface, and saw the stars glittering through the lifting mist. He heard a few faint screams far off, but the ship was nowhere in sight. He turned over on his back and floated wearily in the green water that was so glassy, so calm, except when he bumped with a queasy shock into the dangling arm of a corpse.

He floated by an old man struggling in the water, his white Santa Claus beard hanging over a beer keg, who was yelling, "Help! Help!" Hughes yelled back, "God love you, old man. Hold on," and the old man was dreamily left behind.

He floated by Steward Jack Brown, a husky six-foot ex-cop, who suffered from asthma, and who was puffing and blowing as he hunched over a piece of jetsam. "Billy Boy, take me with you!" Brown called out. "God love you, Jack," Hughes replied. "I can't. I haven't the strength. Good-bye."

Clenching and unclenching his freezing fingers, Hughes struck out in a side stroke, and swam until dawn seemed to be breaking, pink and dove-grey, in the sky. In a daze, he passed by Walt Grey, another *Empress* bellhop, who used to entertain the passengers by singing and dancing, and who was now clinging with a girl to a suitcase. Dimly he could hear Walt holler in encouragement, "Stick it, kiddo! Stick it!" Hughes smiled to himself and whispered, "God love you, Walt."

Each breath intake was a gasping sob now; he felt homeless as a jelly-fish, and the stretch of green water seemed endlessly lonesome and formidable. He was about to go down in despair, the salty taste in his lips too bitter to bear, when he saw a glimmer of red light. Heart pounding, he swam for it, and joyously reached a life-boat full of about fifty people. He grabbed a rope, and hooked his elbow over the side, and pleaded feebly, "Please, pull me in."

A burly passenger in the boat pushed the palm of his hand under the bellhop's chin, and brutally shoved him back into the water. "Go away," he growled. "No room! No room!"

Hughes was stunned.

22

Then an officer stood up in the boat, oar in hand. "I'm in charge of this boat," he said quietly. "And you're a murderer. I sentence you to death."

With one blow, he knocked the burly passenger off the boat into the water, and then offered the oar to Hughes, and pulled the lad shivering aboard. As the man swatted overboard sank screaming, the other passengers turned their heads in silent shame for him, and the life-boat slowly headed toward the *Storstad*.

Hughes is today a lean, grey-haired landlubber, for many years in the import-export business in Montreal. He has long been married to his sweetheart, Annie Veronica, and their son, Gerry, has carried on the sea-going tradition by travelling around the world at thirteen. "But I'll never forget how I couldn't sleep for seven nights when I sailed home for Liverpool from Quebec aboard the *Alsatian*," Hughes recalls. "I asked the liner's chief steward for all his dirty silverware, and I stayed up each night cleaning the silver, as though trying to wash away a secret crime."

Who was guilty of the crime of sinking more than a thousand souls in the St. Lawrence was a mystery unsolved. Captain Kendall was not the last man to leave his foundering ship, but that wasn't his fault. As both her tumbling giant funnels struck the water simultaneously, and the *Empress* lurched, he was hurled off the flying bridge into the sea. He clutched a piece of grating, and dolefully watched his proud liner vanish under two meeting waves; then he was picked up by a life-boat. He unloaded more than fifty survivors onto the *Storstad*, and set out with six volunteers to rescue another batch.

"But everybody I came to on the water was dead," he said of his second life-boat trip. "I felt them myself to see if they had any life in them."

Raging with fury, he returned to the *Storstad*. He stalked up to the bridge to confront the master of the coal vessel that had wounded his pride and his ship.

"Are you the captain of this ship?" he demanded.

"Yes," said Captain Andersen.

"You have sunk my ship," Captain Kendall said. "You were going full speed, and in that dense fog."

"I was not going full speed," glared Captain Andersen. "*You* were going full speed."

"I was *not*," cried Captain Kendall. "If I had been, you would never have hit me."

A river pilot stepped in to hold back Captain Kendall. The young captain of the once-mighty ocean liner staggered into the chart-room of the "coal nigger", and collapsed on the floor.

In June, an official inquiry was held at Quebec City, headed by Lord Mersey. But the legal fog that shrouded the 612 pages of testimony was as thick as the pall over the St. Lawrence. The lawyer for the *Storstad* called Captain Kendall a "cool, deliberate, efficient British master" who had "lost his cool head" in a "feverish, frantic, chaotic act of absolute madness". The CPR lawyer for the *Empress* wasn't so fog-bound in adjectives, but he did get lost in the simile, "It is rather like as if children had two little toy boats in a bath."

Lord Mersey wound up by saying Captain Kendall "would have been better advised if he had given the *Storstad* a wider berth". But the full brunt of the blame was heaped on the shoulders of Chief Officer Toftenes of the *Storstad*. The Norwegian was judged "wrong" for altering his ship's course in the fog; and for "neglecting" to summon Captain Andersen "until the mischief had been done".

(The exonerated Captain Kendall went on to command in World War I the HMS *Calgarian*, which was sunk by German U-boats, with a loss of forty-nine lives. Now retired at eighty-five, after serving the CPR for twenty years as marine superintendent for London and Southampton, Captain Kendall says cheerily, "People seem to think I'm playing a harp. I'm still going strong.")

The Quebec courts immediately seized the *Storstad* "in the name of the British Empire". A marshall tacked the writ up on the ship's bridge, borrowing Mrs. Andersen's shoe as a hammer. Then the collier was sold for $175,000. But wrangling raged for years over the question of who should get paid first out of that sum — relatives, who claimed some $500,000; or the CPR, with a $2.4 million claim for the loss of the *Empress*. The Supreme Court of Canada held that claims for loss of life should be given priority. But the Privy Council ultimately over-

24

ruled that decision in favour of the CPR. The case was further fogged up when a Norwegian inquiry held the *Storstad* blameless.

It turned out that survivors collected not a penny from either of the shipowners for lost baggage or money. Orphans and widows had to depend largely on the Lord Mayor's Funds set up in London and Liverpool, with heavy contributions coming in from King George V, Queen Mother Alexandra, the Prince of Wales, and the London actor, Sir Herbert Tree.

Who was guilty of the mischief done was not a matter of recrimination for the thousands of grieving mourners. As church bells tolled along the St. Lawrence, they came to Quebec City that Sunday to meet the "fairy-white funeral ship", the Government revenue cutter *Lady Grey*, her flag flying at half mast, her deck piled with 188 unidentified coffins. The *habitants* of Rimouski had hewed and hammered rough pine boxes, when coffins ran short, so that the dead might be carried home in respect. They had painted on the crude boxes such inscriptions as *"une femme"*, *"un homme"*, *"une petite fille"*, or "mother on top, child below". Where one pair were removed from the water locked in each other's arms, a French-Canadian fisherman had not the heart to separate them in death. He had simply painted on their joint coffin, "mother and daughter together".

The dead were laid on counters in a crêpe hung shed on Pier 27, and here mourners came to identify their own. Perhaps the most affecting scene was the dual claim made by two bereaved fathers for possession of a boy two years old, with long curly hair, attired only in his night-dress. On either side of the body stood a claimant father — F. W. Cullen, a buyer for the T. Eaton Company of Toronto, and Alfred A. Archer of Mennen, Saskatchewan. The men were brought together by Canon Scott, rector of St. Matthew's Episcopal Church, and they consented to study the child's features again. It was pitiful to see the two fathers, each sympathetic with the other, in turn brushing the curls back from the silent child's forehead seeking evidence to support his convictions.

Since each father continued to cling to his claim, the King Solomon's judgment was laid before Mayor Napoleon Brouin of Quebec. He called in the expert evidence of the Cullen child's nurse, also a survivor, on the theory that she knew the baby better than his own father did. She opened the child's mouth and identified the last milk tooth that little Albert Cullen had cut; and so the body was awarded to the father from Toronto.

The tragedy is commemorated today by a floating red buoy in the St. Lawrence Seaway, marking the spot were the *Empress* went to her grave. On the main highway between Father Point and Rimouski, there is also a small CPR cemetery, ringed by an iron fence, containing the still unidentified dead.

The only mass memorial in honour of the *Empress* victims is held at Toronto's Mount Pleasant Cemetery, in front of a grey stone monument, with a wave at its base and a cross surmounted by a victor's crown. Every year since 1914, the Salvation Army survivors have gathered there to honour the memory of their comrades promoted to glory on Black Friday, May 29. Colonel George Attwell recites from the Forty-sixth Psalm, "God is our refuge and our strength." And a wreath of yellow, red and blue flowers is laid by the orphaned Gracie Hanagan, now Mrs. M. E. Martyn, the daughter of the Army's doomed bandmaster.

They never sing the hymn that was played by her father and the brass band as the *Empress* slid away from the quay of Quebec on her tragic voyage; but they will never forget its words:

> God be with you till we meet again,
>   When life's perils thick confound you,
>   Put His loving arms around you;
>
> .   .   .   .
>
> Keep love's banner floating o'er you,
>   Smite death's threatening wave before you;
> God be with you till we meet again.

_ 2 _

Inferno in Newfoundland

I N WAR-TIME ST. JOHN'S, NEWFOUNDLAND, THAT
Saturday night, it was perfect weather for a saboteur's fire. It was
a raw and bone-chilling fourteen degrees above zero on December
12, 1942. The hilly streets were sheathed in ice, and every window
in every house was blacked out against Nazi U-boats.

By eleven o'clock most of the sixty thousand townspeople were
snug in the parlours of their hospitable homes, tuned in to radio station
VOCM to hear Biddy O'Toole sing that laughing Irish folk ballad, "I
Met Her in the Garden Where the Praties Grow". She was one of Uncle
Tim's Barn Dance Troupe, whose weekly Saturday-night show was being
broadcast from the stage of the Knights of Columbus hostel. The hostel
was the chief amusement centre for servicemen stationed in the heart
of North America's most ancient capital city, in the British Empire's
most ancient colony.

Jammed in the hostel's downstairs auditorium for the barn-dance
show were four hundred spectators, mostly men of the Canadian and
American armed forces and their "Newfy" girl friends. One hundred
other revelers in uniform were jitterbugging to the tomtom beat of a
jukebox in the adjoining restaurant and lobby, or playing ping-pong in
a recreation-room festooned with scarlet Christmas bunting, or thinking
of bunking for the night in the upstairs dormitories of the two-storey,
spruce and fir fire-trap, coloured a rusty cocoa brown, high on Harvey
Road hill.

After Biddy O'Toole had taken her bow, a Canadian soldier named Eddy Adams, dressed in chaps, boots, checkered shirt and ten-gallon stetson, stepped before the microphone. He said "Howdy" to the western fans among the merry-makers, began plunking a tune on his guitar, and started to yodel "The Moonlight Trail".

It proved to be a short trail. Half-way through his song, listeners at home heard a woman's scream cut the gaiety like a dagger.

"Fire!" she shrilled. "Fire! Fire!"

No sooner had her thin scream faded than the master of ceremonies, Joe Murphy, dressed in hillbilly overalls, clutched at the microphone. "Please, folks, no panic," he yelled above the hubbub. To the orchestra he hollered, "For God's sake, boys, keep playing!"

Listeners at home were aghast to hear a series of muffled explosions. Then the radio went dead.

Simultaneously, all the lights in the hostel flickered off. As tongues of orange flame licked across the darkness, a stampede of humans clawed towards the four exits, which were barred and locked against the black-out; and the trapped victims bit and scratched and hammered and prayed for life.

Within five minutes, anybody still left in the flimsy building was a roasted corpse. Ninety-nine persons died in this house of merriment so suddenly transmuted into a funeral pyre. One hundred and nine wounded revelers writhed in agony from burned hair and limbs. Though the St. John's Central Fire Station was a mere two hundred yards away, the $100,000 servicemen's centre was gobbled up by flames until it was nothing more than a gaunt skeleton of white-hot ashes.

This was the swiftest and deadliest indoor fire in the annals of Canadian disasters. It was even more spectacular than Montreal's Laurier Palace Movie Theatre fire of January 9, 1927, when seventy-six children suffocated while trying to escape up the narrow theatre aisles in panic. The St. John's blaze was almost certainly lit by an enemy agent, who used rolls of toilet paper as his torch. Indeed, it was so intrigue-ridden that St. John's District Fire Chief P. J. Wakeham, who "fought the Knights of Columbus inferno from beginning to end", wrote a novelette, *The Flaming Holocaust*, based on the fire.

St. John's at the time was a hotbed of intrigue. The port city was a rallying-point for European-bound Allied convoys; and so it was swollen with servicemen and infested with enemy agents of all stripes. The Americans had taken a ninety-nine-year lease on Fort Pepperrell, a sixteen-hundred-acre military Gibraltar, overlooking Quidi Vidi Lake. The Canadians had set up military bases at Torbay and Gander. The Newfoundlanders — who, stubbornly, were not to confederate with Canada until seven years later, in 1949 — had their own Newfoundland Militia billeted at Shamrock Field.

Squabbling among all three Allied groups was often sharp. The Newfoundlanders, proud of their tradition of being a separate British colony for 450 years, regarded the new-comers as "foreigners". They resented the smart-alecky Americans, who called them "goofy Newfies", and their island "a piece of rock entirely surrounded by fog". They resented the moneyed Canadians, and reminded the interlopers that Newfoundland had overwhelmingly voted against joining Canada as a province as far back as 1869. Above all, the Newfoundlanders resented both Americans and Canadians for flirting with their daughters.

On their part, the Canadians and Americans resented the exorbitant prices charged them by the merchants of Water Street. This St. John's "fishocracy" had reputedly ruled the 320-mile-long island with an exploiting hand. For cheap labour, according to the historian, Dr. C. R. Fay, the merchants used to ship in thousands of illiterate immigrants from Ireland, "making a trade of importing paupers in the spring as a substitute for ballast". As long ago as 1818, a disenchanted settler named Stewart had written, "All the people who have made large fortunes in the trade of our Island have risen from low situations in the fishery. They were all at one time either codfish planters or boat-keepers. Having risen 'from the cod-hook', they make severe masters."

The Newfoundlanders continued to prefer their Water Street merchants and their illusion of colonial independence to union with the "foreigners". "We'll rant and we'll rave like true Newfoundlanders," began one of their chauvinistic folk songs. And their anti-Confederation ballad warned defiantly, "Come near at your peril, Canadian Wolf!"

All this friction, of course, was catnip to enemy agents. As a result of their secret information, a Nazi U-boat was able to surface right off Bell Island and sink two British freighters loaded with Newfoundland

29

iron ore. Another German submarine, even more audacious, torpedoed the gates guarding the very entrance to St. John's Harbour, and sneaked off in the night.

Inevitably, the saboteurs began considering ways of setting fire to the tinderbox of a port town, overcrowded with Allied servicemen. In the phrase of Dr. Fay, "St. John's has two claims to distinction: it is the oldest town in North America, and it has been burnt more often than any other capital city in the world."

But the fires of the past devoured the whole town's houses rather than human life. In the Great Fire of 1846, a glue-pot boiled over in a George Street cabinet-maker's shop; then a gale skipped the flames across vats of seal oil throughout Water Street and Duckworth Street. By nightfall, burning seal oil covered even the water in the harbour, and the town was no more than a forest of crumpled chimneys. Though twelve thousand people were left homeless, reported a contemporary insurance salesman, J. J. Broomfield, "the merchants all appear in good spirits and have already begun erecting temporary buildings of wood to house the fish."

The Great fire of 1892 started in the barn of a merchant named Timothy O'Brien, a mile north-west of the wharfs. One of O'Brien's drivers, Tommy FitzPatrick, tumbled in the barn with a lighted pipe in his mouth. The ashes ignited the hay, and another powerful gale swept the flames raging for sixteen hours. Two-thirds of the city was ravaged; eleven thousand were left homeless; and the fire caused a $20 million loss, including the melted gold coins that merchants had hoarded in their cellars. "Firemen were compelled to work without water," reported one observer laconically, "as the pipes were under repair, and the supply had not been restored."

But the saboteur on that December Saturday night in 1942 had his eye on mass murder, not on the mass gutting of buildings. He couldn't have picked a better fire-trap than the Knights of Columbus hostel. The wallboard building, faced with imitation brick and set on one of the loftiest points in the centre of town, had been erected just twelve months before as a servicemen's "home away from home". It was a tragicomic compound of errors.

First of all, the builders — an organization called the Knights of Columbus Canadian Army Huts — broke the law by not bothering to

30

submit any plans or specifications to the St. John's town council. In fact, the red-faced city officials couldn't produce a blueprint at the official inquiry later conducted by the Supreme Court justice, Sir Brian Dunfield.

Secondly, the builders broke the law by installing doors that opened inward. The auditorium had just two emergency exits — both on the left side of the room — leading immediately to the open air. Each of them had a wooden door with three vertical panes of glass in the upper portion, and a screen door — also opening inward — covered with plywood as a black-out. Even this did not satisfy the building's staff; in their zeal to comply with black-out regulations, they took one further precaution — they locked all the doors! The place was like a double-barred rat-trap.

Thirdly, the builders broke the law by blocking the way from the auditorium to the street — the only exit left open. People wanting to leave had to make their way through a restaurant and a lobby before reaching the exit, which consisted of an inner and an outer door, with a small vestibule between them. The restaurant was usually jammed with dancers, as well as with tables and chairs; and the lobby was also likely to be filled with dancers.

Finally, the builders fumbled by not installing a separate emergency lighting system. The hostel auditorium did have lights at the emergency exits; but they and the auditorium lights were controlled from the same panel, which was in the movie projection booth at the rear of the hall. When flames raced through the booth, melting the fuses in this panel, all the lights went off, and the crowd groped toward the exits like blind men in a bedlam.

The saboteur must have known about these weaknesses. He used this knowledge ingeniously to touch off what Sir Brian Dunfield called "a classic case of the kind of flash fire which is built around a low-grade gas explosion. That, in my view, accounted for the great rapidity of the fire. It certainly looks as if an enemy agent was about."

About ten-thirty that night, the enemy agent lit a match to a trail of toilet paper leading to a storage cupboard on the second storey. The plywood cupboard adjoined one of the dormitories, and was built within the loft over the downstairs auditorium. Cardboard cartons of toilet paper and paper towels were stored in the cupboard, piled one upon another; and one package had been broken open.

The burning toilet paper formed a sort of torch. It swiftly burned through the seven-eighth-inch wallboard above it. Then it threw its flames along the interior of the loft, licking along the sun-dried and resinous rafter timbers, feeding on the roof trusses and the insulation of tarred felt, and consuming all the oxygen. The plumes of bluish flames burned slowly that way over the auditorium for at least half an hour, producing a huge ovenful of carbon monoxide gas — clear, colourless, without taste or smell, but lethally poisonous.

"By the time the fire made its first public appearance at 11:10 P.M.," Sir Brian Dunfield later deduced, "all the extensive lofts of the building, tight and unventilated as they were, had become a gas-holder filled with inflammable and explosive gases — an immense bomb over the heads of the people in the building and unknown to them."

The people had other things on their minds. Girls were on the mind of two RCAF sergeants from Toronto, who had a Saturday-night pass from the barracks at Torbay, eight miles from St. John's, and were ready for a pick-up. One was Sgt. Max ("Goldy") Goldstein, a twenty-three-year-old physical-training instructor, with intense brown eyes, a narrow black moustache, and a powerful forty-four-inch chest spread. Back in Toronto, he had won national weight-lighting championships for the Young Men's Hebrew Association. He was particularly proud of being able to lift a 280-pound bar-bell in a "clean and jerk" movement, and to hoist a two-hundred-pound man aloft with one hand. As a body-building fresh-air enthusiast, keenly sensitive to smells, he didn't smoke or drink; but he was not averse to female company. Just a few days before, he had written his father, Samuel Goldstein, owner of a Toronto slipper and shoe factory, "I plan to attend a dance Saturday night, Pop, and maybe meet some nice girls."

His buddy, Sgt. Bill Collis, was an easy-going fellow of twenty-five, also with black hair, black moustache, and liquid brown eyes. Before enlisting, he had been a professional musician, playing a saxaphone and clarinet with Hal Hartley's Band in Montreal and Stan Williams & His Blue Marines out of Cobourg, Ontario. His father, David Collis, owner of a furniture store in Oshawa, Ontario, knew that Bill had been corresponding with a girl back home. "But after all, I'm not serious now about marriage," his son had written, "because you never know what will happen in a war."

At 10 P.M. the two air-force sergeants, bundled up in their blue greatcoats, black leather gloves, goloshes and parkas, trudged up icy Le Marchant Road toward the "K. of C. hut", past houses green with the patina of time and sea air. Occasionally they dodged an army truck, its headlights painted black except for a tiny permissible slit of dim yellow light.

Overhead, planes buzzed angrily, as though trying to pierce a hole through the obdurate fog-bank. The mist crawled in from all the outlandishly named Newfoundland outports, looking from overhead like a wrinkled elephant's hide. The fog crept out of Bumble Bee Bight, Nick's Nose and Pick Eyes; swooping over Hole in the Wall, God Almighty Cove and Horse Chops; weaving like a drunken sailor through Come by Chance, Seldom Come By, and Blow Me Down; rolling across Ha Ha Bay, Witless Bay, and Leading Tickles; skirting Famish Gut, Great Pinchgut, and Maggoty Point; and wrapping its gray wraith around Heart's Content, Heart's Delight, and Heart's Desire.

The two Torontonians cursed the near-zero cold.

"Ah, well," said Max Goldstein philosophically. "You know what they say in this town: 'If you don't like our weather now, come back in ten minutes.'"

"Yes," said Bill Collis. "And whatever you say about the bootleggers here, with their iodine-tasting 'screech' and rolling you for your last dime, you can't beat the folks of the outports for hospitality. It's 'Come in, my boyo, for a cup o' tea by the fireplace.'"

The two climbed up the treacherously snowy four front steps of the Knights of Columbus hostel. They checked their hats and coats, admired the Christmas streamers strung from the ceiling, and ordered coffee and doughnuts for five cents. Then they inspected the supply of army and air-force girls. Goldstein decided to decline the doughnuts, "because I've got to watch my weight". But he was impressed with a few beautiful girls he spotted, regrettably attached already to males. Collis thought the female pickings that night were just so-so.

Goldstein had a dance with an air-force girl, and Collis played a game of checkers, and then both decided to play a game of ping-pong.

33

But no ping-pong balls were available, and Collis didn't feel like asking the sailors at the next table for the loan of a ball. "I'm too tired to make battle with the navy tonight," he told Goldstein. "Let's forget it."

They paused for a moment, debating whether to join the crowd seated in the auditorium on collapsible steel chairs, waiting for the barn-dance show to begin. Goldstein's passion for fresh air saved them both.

"It's too hot and sticky in there," Goldstein said. "Let's blow."

As they put on their coats to leave, Collis also noticed the smoky, humid atmosphere. "Look at the plywood black-out shutters they've got stuck against the windows," he observed. "Isn't that a hell of a thing, Goldy? You'd think they'd use dark window blinds instead, and let a little of God's air inside this sweat-box."

No sooner had they stepped outside than they bumped into two comely girls they had met before. Goldstein took the blonde by the arm and strolled back toward the "sweat-box", calling over his shoulder, "See you later, Bill."

"Sure thing, Goldy," said Collis, as he stayed behind to talk to his brunette charmer. "It looks as though we'll have a hot time in the old town tonight after all."

That evening an old shirt was on the mind of Private Reginald J. Holwell, a very youthful-looking nineteen-year-old, who had joined the Newfoundland Militia. Frugality had been dinned into his head when he was brought up at Herring Neck, a small fishing settlement on the north-east coast of Newfoundland. He had just finished high school the year before at St. John's; and though he looked so young, with his light brown hair and brown eyes and his slender five-feet-eight, the Newfoundland Militia had accepted him. When Shamrock Field was taxed to capacity, they had billeted him in one of the 350 beds at the Knights of Columbus hostel.

Holwell had been stricken with mumps for three weeks. As soon as he was discharged from the hospital that Saturday, he made his way back to the hostel at 6 P.M. to look for a shirt he had left under his mattress while billeted there in the tiers of metal bunks. Though his Newfoundland buddies had since been moved back to Shamrock Field, his shirt was still there.

The young lad stayed for dinner, and chatted curiously with some of the exotic men still bunking in the hostel dormitories — the Fighting Free French, quartered in what was called "the French Room"; and some Chinese merchant seamen, rescued from the waters off Newfoundland after surviving an enemy torpedo attack.

Holwell knew the barn-dance show was being staged that night, but was undecided whether to stay around for the fun. He flipped a mental coin, and his good sense won out. "I'm not feeling up to the mark after three weeks in hospital with mumps," he told himself. "Better I should visit my uncle and aunt."

About 11 P.M., leaving the home of his uncle Albert Miles, Holwell made his way back to the barracks at Shamrock Field in the frosty night. After checking in, he suddenly noticed that the whole sky over St. John's was lit with a reddish glow. Heart pounding, he eluded the barracks fence patrol and ran for three breathless minutes toward the hostel. He heard a furious crackling, and met women with children in their arms fleeing in hysteria from their homes. Remembering his decision not to stay for the show, he thought: "The mumps have saved me from being burned to death."

The radio performance of her father and brothers was on the mind that night of Margaret Ryan, a pretty, twenty-eight-year-old St. John's housewife. She and her civil-servant husband were listening to the radio in the parlour of their three-storey wooden home on Harvey Road, its windows immediately facing the Knights of Columbus hostel across the street.

She was particularly interested because her father was the Uncle Tim who conducted "Uncle Tim's Barn Dance". His real name was William Patrick Duggan, and he was a fifty-five-year-old barber, with jovial blue eyes and a face like the map of Ireland, who loved entertaining on the side. He had recruited for his barn-dance troupe his three sons: Mickey, a pianist of thirty-two; Gus, a twenty-year-old dancer; and Derm, a sixteen-year-old drummer boy.

Mickey, however, had accepted an engagement to play at the Caribou Hostel that night. His substitute in Uncle Tim's band was a Canadian Navy musician, Ted Gaudet. Margaret was curious to see how this stand-in's playing would compare with Mickey's sure touch on the keyboard.

35

As soon as Margaret heard the chilling scream of "Fire" over the air, she jumped to her feet. She and her husband raced to their front door, where red-hot cinders were rocketing across Harvey Road and the panes of glass in the adjoining clapboard houses were already cracking like rifle shots.

"I shall never forget the scene as long as I live," she recalls. "The whole Knights of Columbus building, from end to end and from top to bottom, was one golden mushroom of flame. I saw men diving from the twenty-foot-high upstairs windows, their pajamas blazing, as though they were human torches. And over and above the roar of the flames, I could hear the pounding of the trapped victims."

A rumpus raised by three boozy sailors was on the mind of Joe Murphy, known professionally as "Barry Hope, your genial, live-wire emcee of Uncle Tim's Barn Dance". When the fire broke, the newly married master of ceremonies was in the wings backstage; he was dressed in overalls, white shirt and ten-gallon stetson, a pair of ear-phones clamped to his ears.

Just a few minutes before the show went on the air over VOCM, Murphy had been on stage to warm up the audience. This time, however, three sailors seated in front, exuberant from tippling too much, kept interrupting his spiel. No sooner would Murphy spin a yarn than one of the three would stand up and cap it with his own funny story. This ad-libbing drew laughter and cheers from three St. John's teenagers seated right behind the sailors — Douglas Furneaux, son of the very learned veterinary, Dr. J. H. Furneaux, and his two chums, Hedley Tuff, Junior, and Herb Noftall.

Murphy didn't really mind these unsolicited antics, as long as the tomfoolery got the audience in a happy frame of mind. But now that the show was on the air, he was annoyed to hear an unaccustomed crackling noise sputter through his ear-phones.

"Damn those sailors," Murphy swore softly to himself. "I had an idea those boys would start something before long."

The thought occurred to him that the special military police, present in the hall from the various armed services, would soon quell the unruly sailors making the commotion. Actually, this crackling was the noise of the flames in the air-tight lofts above, seeking oxygen, and meanwhile building up an unevenly heated gas reservoir poised ominously over the heads of the people. Doug Furneaux and his friends in the stuffy auditorium below thought the noise sounded like "the scratching of rats in the attic", or "peas thrown along the floor", or "the drumming of hailstones on the roof".

The sound that stung Murphy into action was the woman's unearthly scream of "Fire". Flinging his ear-phones aside, he dashed out on the stage. He was horrified to see rapiers of mustard-yellow flames slashing out of the slots of the movie projection booth at the back of the auditorium. Amid the *boom-boom-boom* of muffled explosions overhead, he clutched at the microphone and pleaded with the crowd and the performers to avoid hysteria.

As a blast of searing-hot gas hissed down from the ceiling, and the stage curtains flashed into purple flame, and his own hillbilly overalls caught fire, Murphy thought of his bride listening to the show from the radio at home. He wondered how she was reacting to her husband's unexpected performance.

"I found out later," Murphy recalls. "My wife keeled over in a cold faint."

A final puff of oxygen touched off this erupting chain of fire-gas explosions. This fillip of air was provided by an anonymous Newfoundland Militia man who opened the door to the paper storeroom, apparently supposing it to be a toilet.

The unknown man was spotted by Signalman Maurice Weldon, a twenty-two-year-old Torontonian, who had been on corvette convoy duty with the Royal Canadian Navy for the past year. He'd gone to the hostel dance that Saturday night to celebrate the wind-up of three weeks' exams he had written for his leading-signalman's papers. Weldon was preparing to hit the sack early, in the rear dormitory on the second floor. He was already in his underclothes. Then he saw the Newfoundland Militia man open the door of the storage cupboard, packed with the smouldering toilet paper. A sheet of flame coiled out of the cupboard, and the stranger left the door open and ran for the stairs.

Weldon raced across to the door and glanced inside. Fire of an incredible, white-hot intensity filled the top of the cupboard, and oozed out as if under pressure of a forced furnace draught. Beneath the fire,

Weldon saw unburnt cartons and read the words, "Toilet Tissue". The whole cupboard seemed as if ready to explode; and Weldon ducked behind the door, and in his second attempt managed to slam it shut. As he did so, a jet of bluish flame knifed over the top of the door. In astonishment, Weldon smelled flesh burning, and realized his own arm and shoulder were painfully burned.

In his underclothes, not looking behind, Weldon tried to shake up the sleepers in the dormitory — four RCAF men and two Americans — and ran on toward the stairs. Blue flashes of fire pursued him closely, as if a maniac with a flame-thrower had run amok. When he got to the stair well, it seemed to him that the heat was so fierce he could hardly stand it, for now the tails of the flames were snapping like bull whips. Only at the foot of the stairs did he emerge into a pocket of cooler air; and then he stumbled wearily into the outer lobby and blacked out, and remembered nothing more until awaking in the hospital.

Now disaster swung like a flaming sword all over the hostel. On the stage, Joe Murphy burned his hand and right heel badly, but kept his self-control. He realized he could do nothing with the crowd; people were stampeding toward the front exit in the savage heat, tripping over the clattering metal chairs in their panic, and dropping like flies from the deadly darts of carbon monoxide gas. Just before the lights all flickered out, he tried to shepherd his troupe of performers to a window backstage.

Four members of his troupe refused to be shepherded. The guitarist, Hector Woolley, a Canadian Navy signalman, had been courting a girl singer in the cast. When he saw her jump from the stage into the auditorium, Woolley followed her to try to save her. A heavy piece of flaming timber fell and pinned him to the floor. Murphy later identified Woolley at the morgue by his flawless set of white teeth. "Hector was so completely covered by heavy soot and grime," he said afterwards, "I thought at first he was a dead Negro."

The girl singer was horribly burned, but she was rescued. Two sailors picked her up and tossed her out of a window to safety. She wandered about dazedly laughing, like Ophelia, a little mad.

The dancer, Gus Duggan, Margaret Ryan's twenty-year-old brother, lost his life trying to save others. He saw that panicky spectators were

38

trying to climb over the heads of each other to reach the locked doors. So he jumped down among the audience, and with members of the Newfoundland Militia, heroically attempted to form a human chain, while others battered down the barriers. Rescuers later found the scorched bodies of Gus and the Militia boys in a pile, their hands still clasped together in death.

The same fate almost befell Margaret Ryan's brother, Derm Duggan, the sixteen-year-old drummer boy. Jammed vise-tight against a wall, Derm felt himself suffocating. Then, as the trapped mob gave a convulsive heave outward, he was shot over their heads toward a broken-in window. There an American soldier, yelling, "Snap out of it, kid," sustained his flight by flinging the drummer boy, gored by broken glass and his hair aflame, out to the snow. Derm was hospitalized for two months, and forever after refused to talk about his grisly flight "in any way, shape or form".

Margaret's father, William Patrick Duggan ("Uncle Tim"), was one of the twenty members of the troupe who scrambled with Joe Murphy toward the black-out-shielded window backstage. The jovial barber ripped down the plywood shutters, and then his saxaphone player, Michael Frelich, vainly tried to smash the window-pane with his fists. Murphy then stepped forward.

"I took up a steel chair," he now recalls, "and threw it with all my force against the window. Glass, window-sashes and the chair went hurtling to the snowy ground ten feet below. Uncle Tim Duggan was the first to leap out the window. Since he was in his fifties, it was a miracle he didn't hurt himself in the fall. The wonderful old fellow got up, and caught the others as they jumped, and managed to break their falls."

Murphy waited until all members of his barn-dance gang had dived to safety through that window. Just before he jumped, the ceiling over the stage exploded down and the piano plummeted, flaming, through the floor. He could hear the wails of the people still trapped in the crematorium of the hall, "like something out of a really evil nightmare". Murphy leaped sobbing into the waiting embrace of Uncle Tim Duggan. Later, Uncle Tim vowed that he would never be a barn-dance entertainer again.

Doug Furneaux, the teen-ager seated with his chums behind Murphy's hecklers, behaved in a chivalrous manner that would have made his veterinarian father proud. His chum, Herb Noftall, was trampled to death in the pandemonium. His other chum, Hedley Tuff, ran to the exit on the west side of the auditorium, which was locked tight and blocked with bodies piled six feet high. "By the time I was swept out," said Tuff, "even the framework of the door was plumed in flames. Two girls, with their hair and coats ablaze, tumbled out behind me."

Doug Furneaux raced toward another exit — on the east side of the auditorium. He was horrified to find it locked. He tried to kick it down, but was prevented by the surging crowd from getting solid blows at the door. In the tumult and the darkness, someone turned on a flashlight, and Furneaux was able to break down the door.

This landed him in the lobby, and he was appalled to find that yet another locked door barred the way to the open air. As a crazed airman knocked himself out by hurling his body at the shuttered door, Furneaux took in the eerie spectacle. "Many were blessing themselves and praying aloud," he recalls. "Others, with hair ablaze from the dropping Christmas decorations, kept running around in circles until they dropped dead on the floor."

Even when the second door was finally battered open, Furneaux helped others before making his own escape. He helped rescue the dozen survivors who escaped through this exit. He dragged out a navy rating, unconscious from the poisonous gas. Together with three air-force men and two sailors, he hauled a Chinese merchant seaman from the lobby out into the open. His legs amputated by fire, the seaman was unfortunately already dead.

The last man Furneaux rescued was an airman. The flyer had torn out the black-out shield from the window; but the exertion had been too much, and now he stood limply inside on a radiator, his face leaning against the glass, too weak to smash it. Furneaux and the others broke the pane and hauled the inert air-force man through, as though he were a tailor's dummy.

As burning brands whizzed by his face, Furneaux admired the gallantry of Clarence Bartlett, a burly St. John's constable. The cop carried through the smoke and the flame two men and two girls, all four with their hair completely burned off, and the girls naked except for their panties. The constable foraged in the smoke near Furneaux for the fifth time and found a huge man, weighing about two hundred and twenty pounds, all his clothes gone, apparently dead. The policeman was trying to drag the mammoth gentleman clear, when a violent gas explosion sent his helmet careening twenty-five yards away — and Bartlett most of the way with it.

From his cot in the hospital, Furneaux said, "I'll never forget how so many people suddenly remembered their prayers in their time of crisis."

Prayers for each other were now being silently recited by the two Toronto air-force buddies, Sergeant Max Goldstein and Sergeant Bill Collis, neither knowing whether the other was alive.

Inside the hostel recreation room, Goldstein had separated from his blonde dancing partner and was walking around the crowded floor, when he heard a piercing female scream. In an instant, the mob caught him up in its torrent of panic, and he was swept toward one of the locked doors. His physical fitness came in handy, because with three other servicemen, he rammed the door open, causing his shoulder to be sorely raw for four days after.

As the crowd poured out of this passage-way, which was ringed with flames, Goldstein stood in the frosty cold, physically petrified. He wondered whether Bill Collis was trapped inside, and he still remembers how grateful he felt for his escape; how he was excited by the danger, yet saddened by the tragedy.

Meanwhile, Collis was worrying about Goldstein. He was still talking outside with his brunette friend, when suddenly he was startled to see the four corners of the hostel engulfed in orange flames. He immediately sprinted to the side of the building, thinking of Goldstein's good-bye: "See you later, Bill."

Hearing the shrieks and the pounding of the trapped victims inside, Collis twisted the knob of a side door. It wouldn't give, so he kicked it. As the door wrenched open, a blast of furnace-hot air licked out and then sucked back. Then a needle of blue flame streaked out and just missed

41

his cheek. "My flesh shriveled at the heat of that flame," he recalls. "I tell you, it was a hell of a shlemozzle."

Only six people managed to scramble out of the entry he had broken open. The last was a young air-force man, the sleeve of his uniform wreathed in fire. "Hit the snow!" yelled Collis. When the young fellow stood dazed, Collis rubbed snow on his coat, and for good measure, helped him roll in a snowbank.

A cordon of military policemen then held Collis back, and he stood in a trance, trembling as he stared at the mushrooming flames, and thinking of his old pal, Goldy. "I felt so sad and so helpless," he recalls.

Each involved in his own melancholy, unaware of the others, Collis, Goldstein, Margaret Ryan, and Reginald Holwell stood and watched. They were part of a crowd of ten thousand who came racing to the scene and stood in the snow, while army searchlights stabbed into the blacked-out night and illuminated the port town's most ghastly fire.

An attempt to sound the fire alarm was made at 11:11 P.M. by John St. John, a local free-lance journalist, who earned his keep as book-keeper and clerk for the hostel. He was last seen seated in his office, at a desk circled in flame. He was trying to phone the alarm to the Central Fire Station, located only two hundred yards up the road. The fire was faster than the notoriously slow night service of the telephone operator; his call never went through. A brave man died at his post, his charred fingers gripping the phone receiver.

At 11:15 an alarm was finally rung in by a policeman from a traffic box half a mile down Harvey Road hill, at Rawlins Cross. Constable S. Reynolds could only tell the sergeant at Central Police Station, "There's a vivid light in the sky, somewhere in the direction of Shamrock Field."

This message was flashed to the black-out-shuttered Central Fire Station, so heart-breakingly near the hostel, at 11:17. Fire Captain David Mahon had his men on the scene within two minutes, the fire pumpers spinning like coins as they skidded on the ice. It was too late, for as Sir Brian Dunfield later said at the official inquiry, "I think everyone who was still inside the building was dead by 11:15."

Soon lines of fire hoses were linked to hydrants and laced across Harvey Road, Long's Hill, Carter's Hill, and Parade Street. Four

42

thousand gallons of water a minute hissed and arched into the night, and the water pressure was raised so high, the firemen could scarcely grasp the nozzles. Their helmets became so sizzling hot, despite the cork linings, that they had to stop at intervals and pour water into them. The heat was so intense, they could not get within fifty feet of the hostel, and many firemen had the very clothes burned from their backs.

It was obviously useless to throw water on the hostel. So Fire Captain Mahon devoted his men's efforts largely to preventing the spread of flames to the scorching-hot clapboard houses on the south side of Harvey Road. They swifty doused the big blazing buildings to the immediate east and west of the hostel, the Catholic Cadet Corps Armory and the Church Lads' Brigade Armory. (Later, when the city morgue became crammed with corpses, both armories were hastily put into service as emergency morgues.)

By now, orange flames geysering high in the night were carrying burning fragments over the whole eastern section of St. John's, and lobbing them as far away as Bannerman Park. Happily, not a breeze was stirring now. Dr. Fred Rowe, later Highways Minister in the Newfoundland government, was among the spectators; he recalls that when he lit a cigarette, the flame of his lighter burned evenly and straight up. Had there been one wisp of wind, St. John's would surely have been reduced to an ash-heap again.

To help control the scattering fireworks, the Americans dispatched to the scene a thousand-gallon pumper from Fort Pepperrell. The American servicemen jumped into action by joining hands and forming a human chain that encircled the inferno and held the crowd back at a safe distance. Indeed, the military police were so zealous that they kept forcing the city's plain-clothes Assistant Chief of Police and District Inspector to identify themselves, and even ordered the embarrassed fellows off the danger zone.

Not until two-thirty on Sunday morning did the fury of the flames die, leaving of the once jolly hostel no more than a tall chimney, sticking out naked and obscene among the charred ruins. The embers were so hot, though, that the firemen had to continue playing water on the chaos until 8:30 A.M. Ironically, a snowstorm then began raging and continued all day, its white mantle in bitter contrast to the black

43

cinders; and the rescuers pried through the ashes with picks and shovels and bare hands, and separated the bodies frozen together in death.

Sergeant Max Goldstein and Sergeant Bill Collis left for Torbay late that Sunday morning by different buses, and their joy at seeing each other at the barracks was something to behold.

"Gee, Maxie, you're alive," said Collis, grabbing him, and hugging him, and whacking him on the shoulder to make sure his old buddy was no phantom.

"Gee, Bill, it's swell to see you breathing," said Goldstein, returning the embrace. "The gods were sure good to both of us."

For the next two days, Goldstein was commanded to stand guard over the white-shrouded bodies laid in rows on the cement floor of the Catholic Cadet Corps Armory. As relatives came in, he had to lift the shrouds and let them try to identify the corpses. The identity discs of some servicemen were so deeply embedded in scorched flesh, they could barely be seen. The bracelets and watches of the women were so badly melted that chemicals had to be used to uncover engraved initials. the stench of the decaying bodies was so ghastly to Goldstein that he could not eat for two days. To make matters worse, the decomposing flesh attracted dogs, and Goldstein was ordered to shoot them with his revolver.

At the end of two days, when another air-force sergeant from his squadron was finally instructed to take over, Goldstein "almost went hysterically mad", and he played a prank that still makes him feel ashamed today. He regarded this sergeant as a "mean lead-swinger and gold-bricker", and he thought up a practical joke that would both relieve him of his repugnance for his onerous duty and also let him take revenge. Goldstein had a corporal show the sergeant how to remove the shrouds from each body. When the ornery fellow undraped the last shroud, Goldstein was lurking underneath, and startled him by leaping out and emitting spooky howls.

"That sergeant didn't know whether to laugh or cry," says Goldstein, today a prosperous Toronto real estate broker, his name changed to Gould. Shaking his head at the memory, he adds, "You know, whenever I have a barbecue with my wife and child in our back yard,

44

and I smell wood burning, my mind immediately goes back to that St. John's fire, and I get the funniest shameful feeling."

For a week after the calamity, St. John's reeled with shock. Prime Minister Mackenzie King wired his condolences. Mayor Maurice Tobin of Boston cabled that he wanted to rush blood plasma and surgeons expert in the treatment of burns. (Only two weeks before, these same surgeons had treated victims of Boston's Coconut Grove night-club fire, when 494 merry-makers died in a similar panic among blazing ceiling decorations.) The bereaved were reminded of their tragedy daily, as one funeral procession after another rolled like tumbrils through the port town's icy streets to bury the nineteen dead civilians.

Sergeant Bill Collis will never forget the mass military funeral conducted in honour of the eighty servicemen and merchant navymen — Canadians, Americans, and Newfoundlanders. The slow, measured beat of muffled drums and the skirling lament of Scottish pipers playing "Flowers of the Forest" sounded throughout the entire town, as the flag-draped caskets were borne on the shoulders of pallbearers from the three allied services. As the cortège wound through the ancient streets, the cathedral bells tolled mournfully, and a cruel wind swept down from John Cabot Tower on Signal Hill, where Guglielmo Marconi had received the first transatlantic wireless message in 1901. As the band rendered "Nearer My God to Thee", and coffins were lowered in the craggy ground, Sergeant Collis was among the party who fired three rifle volleys into the raw air, before the bugler sounded the last post.

"Ever since that barn dance, I have never had the inclination to play my instruments," says Collis, today the owner of a successful furniture store on Bayview Avenue in Toronto. He points to his saxophone and clarinet, hanging unused on the wall of his fire-insulated recreation room, and adds, "And whenever I go into a theatre or a night-club, I always take note of where the emergency exits are located."

Reginald Holwell, having served brilliantly in the Mediterranean war theatre, is now a thirty-five-year-old employee of the telecommunications division of the Department of Transport at Corner Brook in Newfoundland.

"My most vivid recollection will always be of seeing so many charred bodies covered with sheets, and grieving for the poor Newfoundland Militia boys who enlisted the same time as I did — guys like Private Cyril Hicks from Bonavista and Private Llewelyn Snooks from Curling and Private George Lambert from Fortune," he says.

A month after the tragedy, Sir Brian Dunfield examined 174 witnesses in the St. John's court-house. He guardedly concluded that the fire was of "incendiary origin", possibly "a case of sabotage". In retrospect today, as Newfoundland's most urbane and literate Supreme Court justice, he freely uses the more forthright phrase, "enemy agent".

Sir Brian dismissed arson for profit as a possible motive, owing to the hostel's ownership by the Knights of Columbus. It wasn't an accident, caused by a cigarette-smoker carelessly tossing away his match, because the cupboard was too small for anybody to stand up in. Moreover, another hostel cupboard was observed, with its door open and rolls of toilet paper on the shelf, their ends pulled out and trailing down to the floor — "an unnatural and suspicious state of affairs".

Most suspicious of all, Sir Brian noted, St. John's was afflicted with a rash of fires while his inquiry was still being conducted. A few weeks after the Knights of Columbus fire, dozens of rolls of toilet paper were discovered cunningly packed in the loft of the YMCA's Red Triangle hostel, as though arranged for a blaze. "The toilet-paper connection is instructive," Sir Brian pointed out. "A criminal often repeats a method which has been successful."

A fire broke out soon after in the St. John's U.S.O. building — "a place where one would not have expected to find it". Four lives were lost when, in the early morning, this fire consumed the wallboard-constructed Old Colony Club in the city's suburb. "The club was much resorted to by the forces," Sir Brian said, "and on the night before, many of the army officers in St. John's would have been there but for the postponement, caused by bad weather, of an intended party." Finally, the saboteur evidently extended his activities to the Knights of Columbus hostel in Halifax, inserting a lighted cigarette into a letter-box at 11:00 P.M., while servicemen were watching a movie show.

"These coincidences are at least remarkable," Sir Brian summed up. "One cannot help suspecting a concerted design against buildings frequented by the armed forces."

46

Margaret Ryan, the daughter of Uncle Tim, does not have to be convinced that the barn-dance catastrophe was caused by an act of sabotage. She is sure.

The shock of the experience still lives with her. She is today a widow, collecting the baby bonus for five of her six children. But she still lives in the same house on Harvey Road. Her bedroom on the second floor faces the spot where the Knights of Columbus hostel once stood, and she is haunted by all its ghostly memories.

"Even now, before I go to bed, I always make sure the shades of my bedroom window are up, so I can see out," she says. "I can't bear to go to bed if they are down. Still my sleep is often broken by dreams in which I hear the screams of the trapped people, and I see the flames of their funeral pyre lighting up the December skies. Then I wake, and I say a prayer for the soul of my dead brother Gus, and for the souls of all the other cheerful people whose lives were ended in the saddest barn dance ever held in Newfoundland."

_ 3 _

The Tornado That Blew Down Regina

O N DOMINION DAY, JULY 1, 1912, THE DAY AFTER the tornado scooped up flying canoes and bathtubs and people and their parlours and skimmed them through the prairie sky to their doom, the newspapers in Regina published curious advertisements.

The capital city of Saskatchewan had just been flattened by Canada's most vicious twister of the century. Like genies uncorked from a bottle, the demons of the winds had come howling and screeching over Regina at a velocity of five hundred miles an hour. They blotted out the red sun, and left a string of havoc in their trail.

These dancing dervishes of the atmosphere, spinning in the shape of a green funnel, had sucked up into their whirlpool at least twenty-eight Reginans and killed them outright. Thirteen other victims died of wounds, three hundred were scarred or maimed, and three thousand were left without a roof over their heads.

The advertisers in the Regina newspapers the next day seemed more concerned about the six million dollars' damage wreaked by the freak tempest on five hundred buildings than about the human victims. Real-estate operators vied in peddling new business lots at $35,000, and houses at $12,000, in the areas just razed so cruelly by the tornado.

"Do not let the House Problem prevent your coming to Regina," advertised J. K. McInnis & Sons in the July 2 Regina *Standard*. "We will build you a residence and sell it to you on an easy payment plan."

48

On July 3 the Regina Board of Trade went so far as to place a full-page real-estate ad in the Winnipeg *Free Press*. It trumpeted the devastated city as a haven for safe investments: "The Eyes of the World Are Upon Regina . . . The Capital and Wonder City of This Mighty Province . . . The City of Destiny Whose Growth Can No More Be Stemmed Than the Waters of the Sea."

Thus did the land speculators hail Canada's most remarkably commercialized disaster. It was a disaster in which the city's business men were not content with trying to hush up the catastrophe; some survivors claim the city even tried to exploit the misery of the victims for a profit.

Homeless Reginans, whose roofs had been blown away, found shelter in Albert Public School and in 250 Mountie tents erected in Dominion and Broad Street Parks. But the city fathers insisted on charging twenty-five cents a night for the cots rented out to the refugees. The city organized clean-up crews to remove the rubble strewn over shattered homes. But the city also billed each ruined home-owner stiffly for each job of "mercy" done.

For fear their "sensational" headlines might put a blight on business, the city allegedly tried to refuse to mail out of town any copies of the Regina newspapers containing news of the tornado. Instead, the city business men issued their own one-dollar souvenir picture booklets. These discreetly referred to the tornado as a "cyclone"; glossed over the numbers of dead and wounded as trifling; and soared into a paean about the "unquenchable optimism" that would "build from the ruins the bigger and better Regina that is to be . . . The Queen City of the West".

There was a simple reason why the merchants tried to camouflage the havoc that had erupted from the summer skies and blitzed the Queen City with such atomic suddenness. Regina was in the throes of a land boom. It was rather embarrassing to concede that a mere caprice of nature might impede business progress. The development of Saskatchewan's Number One hard wheat was luring Ukrainian, German and Norwegian immigrants, and they were pouring in by the hundreds to become "sod-busters". Regina was aswarm with Scottish and American real-estate agents, and these hustlers were outdoing each other in the imaginative prose they confected to sell subdivisions.

49

"The most wonderful and most magnificent offer ever made in the history of Canada," rhapsodized one full-page advertisement of Eastern Annex property. "Free Church, Free Teacher, No Taxes . . ." (and in much smaller print) ". . . for two years." An eastern visitor at the time, according to the historian Earl G. Drake, observed with awe, "Every other office in your city appears to be either a bank or a real-estate office."

Yet though Regina had increased its population to thirty-one thousand — the biggest prairie metropolis between Winnipeg and Calgary — it remained little more than a raw frontier town. Its sidewalks were largely wooden planks, and its few $3,500 de luxe Ford automobiles became bogged in the sticky clay gumbo that mired the streets. The town's militant Social and Moral Reform League deplored the gambling and opium dens run by Chinese in the Germantown section on the East side; the "naughty books" borrowed by young ladies from the new Carnegie Public Library; the vogue for suffragettes' baggy pantaloons ("If women are to remain refined, they must stand by skirts!"); and the sale of liquor in dance halls, which was advertised by gaudy signs proclaiming, "Whisky is the best Minister for the Interior." Above all, the reformers frowned on Regina's annual bonspiel, when convivial visiting curling teams replayed the "last end" at midnight by whirling innumerable chamber-pots down the town's hotel corridors.

The Regina newspapers only occasionally aided the moral crusaders in their attempts to make "mud town" a "culture town". When a police raid nabbed twenty-two trollops from bordellos, the *Standard* piously charged, "Vice is rampant in Regina." The *Leader*, bewailing the public's love for a risqué play about adultery while shunning a concert of the Regina Orchestral Society, moaned, "The public today prefers filth to art."

Actually, Reginans in 1912 preferred such visiting entertainers as Sophie Tucker, Barney Oldfield and his race car, and Buffalo Bill and his circus. However, when the celebrated baseball pitcher, Rube Marquand, appeared there in a stage act, he was booed: "Your name's all right in a box score, but in the theatre you're a bore." Pauline Johnson, touring the Canadian West, declined to recite her poety in Regina, because "My manager would see himself in hell before he would play me in such a dead town at such a low percentage." And the touring evangelist team of Crossley and Hunter only drew large audiences when they sermonized on the subject of sin and fulminated: "You may dance your soul into hell."

For all their piety, the Presbyterian and Methodist merchants, ensconced in the prosperous West End, had no compunction about squeezing higher rents — as much as fifty dollars a month — out of immigrants renting the filthy hovels they owned in the East End slums. The average worker, lucky to earn $71.20 a month, kept the family chickens and pigs in his back yard and even in his kitchen; he was appallingly overcrowded, with ten double beds often being shoe-horned into five-room houses.

Yet a prominent Regina clergyman intoned, "Working men have no right to organize to force their masters to pay higher wages. Servants, obey your masters, for it is right." An early potential CCF socialist taunted back, "We object to a lot of Sky Pilots telling us how to live, while they go through our pockets."

When the Regina government was so businesslike with its tornado disaster victims, it was running true to form; the city business men had always been profiteering. This tradition dated right back to when Regina was called Pile O' Bones — so named by Indians after the buffalo bones heaped bleaching in the sun beside Wascana Creek. A local merchant of the 1880's, Pascal Bonneau, tried canning twenty tons of the buffalo meat and peddling it to the métis half-breeds at exorbitant prices; but the flesh of the beasts was apparently too strong and the tins of the stuff exploded in his face. A more astute trader, Fraser Tims, collected cart-loads of the buffalo bones, and shipped them off east to be sold as fertilizer. And when the half-breed rebel, Louis Riel, was hanged in Regina, another merchant was even more enterprising. The insensitive fellow advertised foot-length souvenirs of "the rope that hung Louis Riel" — and had to import nearly a ton of hemp from Winnipeg to meet the rush of business.

The tight-fistedness of the Regina civic government was notorious. When the city fathers finally decided to hire the first town constable — ex-corporal James Williams from the nearby Mountie barracks — they gave him fifty dollars a month and just *one* free uniform. "It's a trifle uncomfortable," Chief Williams reported morosely to town council, "when my one suit gets wet." After promising to bathe the dark tank

51

town in "a flood of illumination", the city compromised by installing ten street lights — and then only turned them on for Saturday nights.

The city fathers were induced into occasional spurts of generosity by the derisive wit of the "Regina bald aigle", Nicholas Flood Davin. He was a master of Irish blarney, a whisky-drinking poet, and founder of the Regina *Leader*. It was he who manoeuvred a death-cell interview with Louis Riel by disguising himself as a priest. He became an M.P. by calling his opponent a "double-faced, ear-wigging huckster of calumny" and silencing hecklers by wrapping his rich brogue around a recital of Kipling's "The English Flag". Davin was described in the House as "the Honourable Member for Assiniboia, who has a bare face, a bald head, and rooms to let". Davin retaliated: "The Honourable Member, like myself, has no hair on his face. His head, like mine, is bald. He, like myself, has rooms to let. But there is this difference: mine are furnished and his are not."

Davin mocked Regina's muddy sidewalks and its sharp real-estate operators with one devastating phrase. "Last week we had a nice rain," he wrote in the *Leader*," and everybody who walked down Broad Street took a homestead on one foot and a pre-emption on the other." The CPR's Regina service, extravagantly praised by the local merchant boosters, was annihilated in another editorial witticism: "The CPR have ennobled and elevated Canadian fiction by publishing, at their own expense, the purest edition of fiction in the Anglo-Saxon language, *viz.* their time-table."

Despite this sniping, Regina's mercantile boosterism continued rampant. The high-pressure land agents pointed out to easterners the eight-foot-tall Gaspard Beaupré, a giant of 310 pounds from nearby Willow Bunch, who required a whole deerskin to make himself a pair of moccasins. "That's the sort of man we're raising in Regina," they bragged. And when a multi-storeyed "skyscraper department store" was erected by the Regina merchant R. H. Williams, a jokester pointedly reminded a rival merchant it was time to expand. On the windows of the poorer merchant's squat premises, the booster scribbled, "Elevator boy wanted!"

All this earthly vainglory was shaken to its very foundation by the big wind that blew from out of the heavens on the Sunday afternoon of June 30, 1912.

52

A temperature of one hundred degrees wrapped the whole city that day in a blanket of oppressive torpor. The sun hung large, crimson, and burning in a sullen pink sky. The air was a steamy and sultry bath. The streets were decked out with flags for the Dominion Day celebration on Monday, but by 4:30 P.M. the Union Jacks everywhere drooped listlessly on their poles.

Celluloid collars wilted and were removed in the Regina Theatre. There bandsmen, preparing for their holiday concert, were practising the tune, "Saskatchewan":

> Saskatchewan, Saskatchewan,
> There's no place like Saskatchewan.
> We sit and gaze across the plains,
> And wonder why it never rains,
> And Gabriel blows his trumpet sound,
> He says: "The rain, she's gone around. . . .

Women that day fainted in the sticky humidity of St. Paul's Anglican Church. A crowd was packed there to hear the Bishop of Qu'Apelle, and Canon Hicks of London, England, deliver fire-and-brimstone sermons.

Romantic couples sweated as they paddled canoes in Wascana Lake, the shimmering blue man-made lake beside the new Legislative Building. Families sweltered on the verandahs of their wooden houses beneath the shade of silver willow trees. The men sipped iced lemonade, and the women fanned themselves with palm leaves, and sighed at the prospect of going in to cook Sunday dinners on their coal-burning stoves. A few puffs of wind began stroking the long stalks of wheat, baking in the scorched prairie fields on the fringe of town.

At 4:30 P.M., people looked up at the sky and saw two swarthy grey clouds racing rapidly toward each other, one from the south-east and the other from the south-west. There was an ominous rumble of thunder, the sky glowed an eerie green, and—according to an eyewitness account—blue-red flashes of lightning snaked across the surface of the earth.

Saskatchewaners were accustomed to summer dust storms, and had even devised their own ways of gauging whether it was safe to venture into them. According to the story of D. B. MacRae, a successor to

53

Davin as editor of the *Leader,* a prairie dust-bowl farmer would stand at the door when a storm threatened, and toss a gopher into the air. "If the gopher came down," he maintained, "the farmer knew the day was safe for farming. If the cussed beast began to burrow while still six feet up, it was obviously no day for field operations."

But Reginans, unlike Kansas dust-bowl farmers, had never before experienced a tornado, and did not recognize the classic symptoms of an oppressively hot and humid atmosphere, accompanied by tumbling clouds.

A tornado is formed by a layer of cool, dry air aloft riding the back of the heated, moist air near the ground. Being lighter, the hot air rushes upwards into the stream of cold air above with a fantastic gyration of energy.

A turbulent ring of wind is formed, rotating counter-clockwise at a velocity up to five hundred miles an hour. A vacuum in the centre of this whirling funnel sucks up dust and tumbleweed, giving the condensed vapour on its rim a dirty grey-green sheen. When this boiling area of low pressure surrounds a house in its path, it causes the building literally to explode, for the higher normal atmospheric pressure inside the house must have an immediate outlet. The path of the churning twister is about a quarter of a mile wide and perhaps fifty miles long; and after a few minutes, as though spent by rage, it dies in short gasps of bitterly cold rain and hail.

At 4:50 P.M., the two malevolent clouds collided with a roar right over Regina's Legislative Building, near the west end of Wascana Lake, and formed a tornado, shaped like a colossal funnel. Eyewitnesses variously described it as "a greasy ice-cream cone, with the tip of the cone pointing toward the earth", "a mammoth elephant's trunk", "an awful cornucopia", and "a black hand of God, with finger tips clutching down for us poor mortals".

Writhing and shrieking like a thousand wailing banshees, the thing bounced into the heart of the city like a giant lawn-mower and vacuum cleaner combined. It slashed a six-block-wide swath of death and violence northward right across town, zigzagging erratically. It sliced down entire blocks of prosperous houses along Smith and Lorne Streets, sheared away whole rows of merchants' emporiums on both

54

sides of Eleventh Avenue, and somersaulted heavy freight cars, with their loads of farm implements, across the tracks in the CPR yards. It even stripped all the bark off the elm trees in Central Park, and then sucked the very trees up into its smoky vortex.

It played odd tricks — content with just smashing the windows of the King's Hotel, yet picking up the enormous Winnipeg Grain Company elevators on the outskirts of the town, and flinging them into the prairie sky as though they were tiny kernels of wheat. Telephone and trolley poles snapped like sticks, plank sidewalks were tossed confetti, and the whole city's lights were snuffed off in a twinkling.

First to feel the fury was Wascana Lake, where the whirling winds formed a monstrous waterspout, drowning five people. Sucked into the tornado's mouth was a real-estate salesman, Vincent H. Smith, paddling in a canoe. He and his craft were scooped up into the air for a half a mile, and then rammed through the third-storey window of the Kerr Mercantile Building, where the salesman met his death. Another boater, thirteen-year old Bruce Langton, was sent flying through the air in his canoe for three-quarters of a mile. He was gently deposited in his boat in the north-east corner of Victoria Park, his paddle gripped in his fingers though his forearm was broken; and he still lives today to tell of his curious flight.

The Provincial Legislative Building — newly built of light-dressed stone for the forthcoming visit of Canada's Governor-General, the Duke of Connaught — reeled under the tornado's impact, but didn't topple. Eight carloads of cement at its base were blown through the air and, mixed with the tornado's rain, plastered the hair of people for miles. The suction ripped strips of copper from the parliamentary dome, crumpled office partitions, and sucked out papers from metal filing cabinets. The examination papers for all Saskatchewan school grades were piled on long tables in the Department of Education, and the tornado scattered them to the four winds. Teachers had to pass or fail pupils just on their own opinion of the year's scholastic work.

Next the turbulent wind barrelled northward, crunching Regina's richest residential section. At Fifteenth Avenue, the south wall of the Williamson Apartments blew out clean, and through the air came sailing pianos, a yelping terrier flung about like a rag, and a nude woman astonished in her bathtub. Slashed as though by a razor was the Lorne

55

Street mansion of Honourable Walter Scott, Premier of the province. Flattened as though by cannon-balls was the Smith Street residence of H. C. Lawson, manager of the Regina Exhibition. On Victoria Avenue, Judge John Lamont was just putting up his hand to close the sash of his bathroom window, when the whole brick wall of his mansion crashed away. After waiting several minutes, the judge cautiously opened the bathroom door, went downstairs, and walked out the gaping hole that was his front door.

At Victoria Square, the Presbyterian and Methodist churches were demolished, and the big cupola of the Baptist church was yanked off and rolled like a marble two blocks away to McIntyre Street. The only undamaged church was also the only one occupied by a congregation — St. Paul's Anglican. It was jammed with people listening to the visiting canon from England. This escape gave rise to a good deal of crowing afterwards: "God protected the Anglicans, because only they are of the true faith."

After making a junkman's dream of the new Carnegie Public Library, the winds tore off a stone wall and whirled away the roof of the new four-storey YWCA Building. Most of the sixty girls inside escaped into nearby Central Park and hid under the bushes; but the Y secretary, Miss F. Morton, dragged several girls into a closet, and they knelt and prayed.

Eight girls were entombed when the south wall of the Telephone Building shuddered violently in the wind, which then crushed the three-storey brick-and-stone structure into an ant-heap. Three of the telephone operators plunged from the second storey to the basement with their fifteen-ton switchboard. Miraculously, the three girls burrowed through the flying bricks and glass, and wriggled out of a basement window. They were the first to stagger to the Regina *Leader* Building to give a first-hand account of the disaster.

The tornado seemed to reserve the brunt of its fury for a pulverizing attack on the mercantile and warehouse district along South Railway and Cornwall Streets. The brick stores along Crapper Block were flattened as though by a steam-roller. The winds disdainfully ripped to tatters the land deeds in the Western Construction Real Estate Company, geysered up a shower of knick-knacks from the shelves of the P. T. Evans Five-and-Ten-Cents Store, and papered the prairie sky with designs unfurled from the establishment of Mr. F. M. Crapper, vendor of wallpaper.

The steel girders supporting the four-storey Donahue Building twisted like taffy. Dewdney Street was wrapped in $150,000 worth of horse blankets, sucked out of the tumbling four-storey Ackerman Building. Fifty live horses in a stable were plucked up from Mulligan's Livery on South Railway Street and deposited on the buckled CPR tracks. A bookkeeper, doing some overtime Sunday work in the Advance Thresher Company Building, walked into the steel vault to put away the ledgers, and when he stepped out, was bewildered to find himself "in the middle of the bald prairie".

The whirling dervishes were not content with venting their spleen by flipping up the rows of grain elevators on the city limits. The wind pirouetted at least eleven miles south-east of Regina, kicking over each farm-house in its path. It caused an involuntary strip tease by whipping away every bit of clothing — even her shoes — from a newly married farmer's wife from Whitby, Ontario, Mrs. Walter Stephenson, caught milking her cows. And miles away from Regina, in the Saskatchewan hamlet of Govan, the tornado enjoyed its last dying fling. It playfully ripped away the awnings from the Hub Meat Market, blew in the plate-glass windows, and peppered the strings of sausages with hailstones as big as baseballs.

After the tornado had passed, the people of Regina seemed to be in a state of shock. At 4:55 P.M., the siren atop the power-house sounded the "all clear". Citizens whose homes had not been in the path of the hopscotching whirlwind rushed out into the cold rain to examine the wounds of the city. They found the gay bunting and flags for the Dominion Day celebrations were now wet shrouds.

With their bare hands men began digging through the rubble, urged on by the moans of the wounded trapped below. Until the arrival of 150 Mounties from barracks two miles west of Regina, volunteers were sworn in as special police. The town's two fashionable undertakers, Jim Wright and George Speers — with their spans of black horses, in black robes with dangling tassels — now sweated unstylishly. They hauled loads of the wounded to the General and Grey Nuns Hospitals, and corpses to the fire hall. Because the town's telephone service was wiped out, Boy Scouts served as messengers. Because the electricity was blasted away, volunteers dug through the ruins under a balefully dark sky by the flicker of oil lamps held aloft by thousands of women.

The rescuers worked away in dazed silence, and the survivors recited their tales of escape with a mingling of humour and incredulity, as if the victims couldn't quite believe the grotesque thing that had struck them from the skies.

Dora Hudson, a fifteen-year-old girl, escaped with a scratch behind her ear, but saw her Cornwall Street house crash in and kill her brother Fred, and pin her father wounded against the cement cellar floor. "The silence was what got you," she recalled later of her search through the shattered house for her family. "The hurt ones were so hushed. No one wept, much less screamed in pain. Nobody who died did so noisily. Not even the children cried. It's the loneliest, most lost feeling in the world, when your landmarks are suddenly gone. When you met anybody that had life in them, you just wanted to grab them and love them. Even your worst enemies were your good friends then."

One of the first to tour the embattled area was George F. Dawson, then a fourteen-year-old assistant, at two dollars a week, to the City Building Inspector, H. D. Mathias. Dawson, today a municipal-affairs administrator in Regina, recalls, "The inspector came to our house, looking pale as a ghost, and surprised to find us still standing. After a quick cup of tea, he, my dad, and I made a swift tour. The city smelled earthy, as it always does after a deluging rain following a hot, humid summer afternoon. As usual, those peculiar little black beetles covered the sidewalk in front of the fire hall on Hamilton Street. The stench around the railway yards — where the train-loads of bawling cattle were piled up pitifully on their sides — was just too-too. We didn't loiter there. On Dewdney Street, in front of the wrecked Liquor Board warehouse, a straw hat was blown clear through a telephone pole. And I was most astonished to see a rooster, perched on a fire hydrant at the corner of Market Square. It was naked, except for a couple of tail feathers, and crowing as though it were early morning instead of around 6:00 P.M."

The Beelby family were never to forget how the tornado sliced their home in two, flying each half of the truncated house in different directions. One infant was in the upstairs half, and one in the downstairs half.

58

When the wind slashed at their white frame house on Smith Street, William Beelby, the manager of a grain elevator, dashed upstairs with his wife just in time to wrap a sheet around their sixteen-month-old son, Norris. The tornado whirled them, top storey, crib and all, 150 feet across the road. It deposited them all safely in a neighbour's yard, where they crawled out through the attic window.

When the wind struck the bottom storey, William Beelby's eleven-year-old daughter Marion and his twenty-one-year old brother Wilfred were standing by the kitchen stove. Wilfred managed to pick up little Florence Beelby, aged two and a half, but the tornado snatched her from his arms. The wind whirled the whole bottom half of the house fifty feet away, crumpling the walls. Marion landed flat on her stomach on the kitchen rug in the street, and Wilfred landed bleeding on his back. Groggily, he looked for the child. He found Florence safely blown inside the oven of the stove — a little flesh torn off her legs, but otherwise amazingly unruffled in her pink summer dress.

"I remember seeing a cracked platter of my mother's tumble from the top shelf in the kitchen pantry," says Marion, now a Regina housewife. "We found it on the sidewalk, with no more than the same old crack in it."

And Wilfred Beelby, now a hardware-store manager, remembers vividly "the perishing cold of the tornado rain", and "the wet cement embedded in my hair for two weeks," and a bottle of brandy that bounced out of the Beelby medicine cupboard. It landed on the street — cork out, standing straight up, glass unbroken, and brandy intact. "In our shaken-up state," he says, "believe you me, we needed a drink of brandy."

The grim humour of the tornado's aftermath is recalled by Dorothy Hall, at seventy-four now a retired civil servant "and very much alive-o". "Our home suffered broken windows and some flooding from the terrific downpour," she says, "but we were certainly not terror-stricken. I simply arrived home from a walk on the prairie, airing my young cocker spaniel Peter, and I refused to be alarmed by the sight of a funnel-like cloud."

Though a man came rushing by, shouting "All Regina is wrecked but this part!", Miss Hall imperturbably continued her walk through the city to see the excitement. "I spotted a Ford motor car, being used in emergency rescue work, with a large two-foot splinter wedged through the hind tire," she says. "I was fascinated to learn later that it had run for several hours before becoming flat."

A friend of hers saw two men assisting out of a wrecked house a third man, whose left pant leg hung empty.

"Oh, dear," said Miss Hall's friend. "That poor fellow has lost his leg."

"No, ma'am," said a fourth man, following the three. "A beam fell on his leg and broke it. But it was a wooden leg."

Judy Anderson, now a Vancouver housewife, recalls some of the tall tales told. "One man said he was taking a bath when the big wind hit, and the bathtub was picked up and went sailing through the air," she remembers. "His listeners asked in horrified tones, 'What did you do?' He answered, 'I just took hold of the faucets, and steered it, and landed on top of the Wascana Hotel, and phoned down for more water.'"

The freak pranks played by the tornado stand out in the memory of many survivors still living in Regina today.

Dr. David Low, a pioneer physician living on the edge of Victoria Park, pointed out to Mrs. Marguerite E. Robinson a huge, square-cut wooden rafter; it was jammed into the second floor of his home "like a toothpick being put into a cake to test it". Miss Violet McGillivray remembers a man blown through the roof of the livery stable; at the first-aid station, "they found the imprint of a horseshoe on his head."

Carl B. Pearen saw a flying piece of two-by-four lumber driven through a brick wall in the gable of a house. "It was driven in so tight," he says, "that when workmen tried to remove it with a sledge-hammer, they found they'd have to damage the wall. So they sawed it off even on both sides, and painted it, and left it, and there it still rests."

Mrs. Ina P. Bird recalls a woman friend in a devastated home, who was concerned chiefly about her precious wedding lace that was whooshed out of the attic; and a young man, who was extraordinarily modest when the whirlwinds picked him up. "He'd been lying on the bed in his underwear," Mrs. Bird says, "and he grabbed a frock-coat on his way out."

60

Mrs. Avera Bertell Fraser remembers how her newly engaged twenty-one-year-old friend, Stella Dawson, was playing the piano for her mother in the parlour when the tornado struck. As the floor heaved under them like a ship's deck at sea, overturning the piano and flinging debris, Stella and her mother found themselves in each other's arms.

"I love you," Stella's mother said, "and whatever happens, Stella, let us cling together." Even at this moment of crisis, though, Stella instinctively felt for her diamond engagement ring, and was aghast to find the wind had sucked it off her finger. "Happily," recalls Mrs. Fraser, "both mother and daughter suffered only a few bruises, and Stella detected her diamond ring two days later under her wrecked home."

Other survivors today recall their first automatic response to the disaster — feelings ranging from hysteria to pity to religious exaltation.

A sense of wonder filled Miss Lilian Smith, then a dark-haired, brown-eyed English immigrant of twenty-one, clerking in a Regina insurance office. She was standing alone at her window on Robinson Street, just about to go downtown to supper, when a tent outside swooped through the air like a magic carpet. She instantly thought to herself, "If there is anyone out on the prairie, they will be blown to pieces." Then she went to the YWCA, where she calmly helped load a wounded girl on a stretcher, and then to the Grey Nuns Hospital, where she held a lantern all night, so doctors could perform their surgery in the black-out.

A fear of God's wrath overwhelmed another English immigrant, George Hodgson, then a seventeen-year-old printer's devil working for the Regina Caxton Press. He was lying on the cool grass of the city-hall grounds with his chum, Bill Goldthorpe. Then they observed the approach of the "herculean-looking funnel of smoke" and the "terrible flashes of lightning that were running along the ground like a red snake".

George exclaimed, "Oh, my God, it's Judgment Day! Quick, Bill, let's go." The two youths jumped to their feet and dashed to Bill Goldthorpe's home, a second-hand furniture store, on the north-west corner of Broad Street and Eleventh Avenue. Bill managed to scramble in, but George had a nightmarish moment, trying to escape the clutch of the wind that hurled him against the shed.

When he finally crawled inside the store, George tenderly picked up under each arm his chum's two little sisters, Ada, eight, and Emily, ten. He wiped away their tears, and comforted them: "Don't be scared of those sign-boards and chimneys flying outside the window. It's just God's handiwork." To himself, he later murmured, "But I hope to God I never see another one."

A compulsion to run to her Scottish mother tugged at Lindsay Barclay McGall, then an eighteen-year-old employee of the Department of Education, with long golden curls, so beautiful that she'd won first prize as the "Hindu Princess" at the Regina City Hall fancy-dress ball. She and her friend Peggy Smith were strolling on their way to cool off at Wascana Lake, when the tornado whirled toward them. Laughing as though it were a joke, they scurried into Peggy's home on Smith Street. No sooner were they inside than the whole house began dancing, the floor crashed in, and the girls tumbled down into the basement, not suffering a single scratch. "This experience is happening to *me* in such a short space of time," Lindsay thought. "Just like a flash. I must get home."

No longer laughing, she saw a glimmer of light shining through the rubble; and she climbed up the basement wall and squeezed out. So desperately worried about her mother that she didn't even think of her friend Peggy, Lindsay began running through the freezing rain toward her home on Lorne Street. But the road was unpaved, and she was appalled when the sticky gumbo clenched at her pumps with an octopus grip. She jumped out of her shoes and raced through the mud in her stockinged feet.

When she came close enough, Lindsay could see that the whole back of her home was blasted away. But her mother and father were standing on the shell of the verandah, and beckoning to her. "Oh, Lindsay, where have you been? Praise the Lord, lassie, you're all right." Lindsay was so relieved, she dropped where she was in the muck, and her eldest brother, Graham, had to pick her up and carry her to shelter.

Lindsay, who is today a pretty little housewife of sixty-five, Mrs. Robert Stewart, married to a breeder of Holstein cows at a Boggy Creek ranch near Regina, has suffered a guilt complex all these years. "You know, I often think how very thoughtless I was about my girl friend when I climbed out of the basement," she says. "I'd forgotten that Peggy was there. But, you see, I was so keen to see my dear mother."

Those trapped under debris for hours seemed to accept their doom with a fatalistic composure that was remarkable.

Kenneth Dunn, a boy of five, was buried under a Dewdney Street house for five hours, bearing the pain of a broken leg without a whimper. When rescued, he said "Sure, I had the creeps something bad. It was awful. But I kept saying to myself, 'I am a Boy Scout, and I must not cry.' Then I felt cool as a cucumber."

Walter Ingram, a travelling salesman for the Tudhope, Anderson Company, was consulting in the office with the company manager, John Bryan, when the big warehouse fell in like pasteboard. After being released four hours later from the ruins, Ingram said, "I could feel that Mr. Bryan must be lying on top of me. Reaching up my hand, I could feel his limp body. I said, 'Mr. Bryan, help me — I can't walk.' His arms seemed broken, and he said, "I cant help you, but I'll stay with you. If you can crawl, I will guide you.' Talk about cheer! That helped me more than anything — just what he said, 'I'll stay with you.'"

Mrs. Frank Ferguson was cheered up by her husband for five hours, when they were trapped together under their Fourteenth Avenue kitchen. "After we keeled over on the floor," she said, "all I could think about was how I must get used to the fact of being a widow. I even imagined the funeral we would hold for my husband. Then I could hear Frank beside me, pinned on top of the stove. Oh, gosh, I was so gleeful! Frank kept joking, "Ha ha ha! Imagine me sitting on a stove! And just think, sweetheart, of the ruined meat loaf in the oven. Isn't it a hell of a time to have a silly old cyclone — just when we were having meat for a change, instead of a can of baked beans?' I began laughing with him, and we both began saying our prayers, blessing the Lord for sparing us both."

And at seven o'clock next morning, Harry J. Potts, of the Lorne Street firm of plumbers, Potts & Smith, was discovered sitting on a piano stool amid the ruins of his house, reading a book. All his worldly goods had been blasted away, except for the piano stool; but he seemed to brim with elation. "Here is a funny doggone coincidence," Potts said. "I found this book blown into my yard. It is entitled *Business Hints for*

63

Beginners. Providence must have delivered it to me, for this loss means I'll have to start my business life all over again."

Despite their heart-breaks, the same spirit of commercial optimism seemed to radiate throughout the city the next day. The first of many special trains arrived from Regina's traditional business rival, Moose Jaw, bringing ten doctors — as well as two enterprising undertakers. While thousands of tents were set up on the lawns of more fortunate neighbours, Mayor Peter McAra, Jr. ordered immediate construction of emergency shacks on McIntyre Street North — which would be sold to the homeless "on easy terms". More than seven hundred carpenters streamed into the city from Winnipeg, and the newspapers commented, "Though sixty cents an hour is being paid, even at that awesome figure, enough carpenters are not to be got."

The 95th Saskatchewan Rifles were swiftly brought back to Regina from their Manitoba summer quarters at Camp Sewell, and martial law prevailed. They guarded the trestle tables set up in Victoria Park Square, where the homeless came to identify lost property; and they patrolled the warehouses, with orders to shoot any looters on sight. Six men were arrested for stealing a bottle of beer each. To discourage other vandalism, for this mild offense each of the six was sentenced to a year of hard labour.

Along with its headline, "Estimated Monetary Loss Is Over Three Million", the Regina *Standard* came out with some odd items. The paper announced on the front page that its "great $10,000 circulation contest, which is in progress, will be indefinitely postponed." At the Roseland Theatre, advertised as "the safest and coolest spot in town today", however, Rev. D. C. McGregor of the Presbyterian Church would deliver an address on "The Problems of the Modern City". The visiting American theatrical troupe, the Albini-Avolo Company (including an unknown actor called Boris Karloff), had taken a boating picnic to the top of Wascana Lake that hot Sunday, and had returned to Regina at sunset to find the city in ruins. Now, the actors published a heart-warming ad: they would stage a benefit performance of the comedy, *The Real Thing*, at the Regina Theatre, and "one-half of the gross receipts will be donated to the relief of the sufferers."

The *Standard* also gave solace to the "stricken and humble labour class who will now rise to the occasion" — not with financial aid, but by publishing a series of mawkish and lachrymose poems. One began: "Keep not your kisses for my dead, cold brow! The way is lonely, let me feel them now!"

Another editorial poem lauded the "soothing sap of human kindness" that had checked the city's "grasping greed". Quoting (not very accurately) from Macaulay's "Horatius", it called for a Utopian brotherhood under which

> None were for the party,
> But all were for the State;
> When the rich man helped the poor one,
> And the poor one loved the great.

A wit at the Regina *Leader* took a more realistic attitude. "The poetry fiend has tuned his lyre," he announced. "Get the gun! This thing must be stopped before it commences."

And the journalist quoted the far more poetically earthy comment of a slum mother, bereft of her family:

"Sure, I get the willies, whenever I see a storm cloud now. I want to dive into a cave, for fear all the bitty walls are fixing to fall in on me. The storm didn't hurt us poor folks — we never had anything anyway. We know you can always get dollars and cents, but lives you can't. These rich folks who died, they must have made God angry. They must have provoked Him to wrath. We had lots of folks here who got so high up in the world, they thought they owned it. Yep, it takes something like this to bring them down equal."

Survivors today, with their varied memories, differ strongly on just about every aspect of the tornado's aftermath: the degree of the onslaught, whether the government was generous and, indeed, on the precise number of people wiped out by the catastrophe.

An old-time Reginan, James Quigley, holds out for twenty-eight "officially" dead. He maintains that the city fathers were "most generous"; and he observes that thousands of dollars were donated to the sufferers by the province of Alberta, the city of Calgary, the CPR, and the Governor-General, the Duke of Connaught. Another veteran, Mrs. L. McK. Robinson, has lived in Regina since 1919; she observes that the city has grown so handsomely due to the selfless work of men like her husband, an alderman on Regina's City Council for seventeen years. "Regina civic leaders have never been money-grubbers," she maintains.

Others, however, differ. Mrs. A. W. Carlson remembers how her immigrant father from London, England, T. Mansell, was outside putting up a drain pipe for rain-water when the storm struck his Edgar Street house. "As poor immigrants, the condition of my father and mother was pathetic," she recalls. "They met with little sympathy from the tight-fisted city fathers, whose attitude was 'Immigrants are here for what they can get.'"

Still a Regina city administrator today, survivor George F. Dawson continues to be indignant about the measly financial assistance provided to victims by the city fathers who preceded him in office. "I am also reasonably certain that, in addition to the hush-hush of events by the merchants and real-estate agents," he says, "there must have been a real hush-up job enforced on the undertakers. I maintain the published figure of thirty-one deaths is ridiculously low — especially when one considers there were twenty-eight bodies taken from one building *alone*."

Others point out that the full extent of the damage was not reckoned until months later. Mrs. C. Boehmer, now of Balgonie, Saskatchewan, recalls that the house, stone barn, granaries, pigpen and buggy of the John Zinkham farm, five miles east of Regina, were annihilated. Norman R. Taylor, now of Minden, Ontario, remembers, "They never did find the third storey of my house at the corner of Fourteenth Street. I myself was just walking upstairs, and I must have rode the staircase for about two hundred feet, and was buried in debris unconscious."

Newspapers of the day were certainly cavalier in their treatment of the facts. The correspondent for the Toronto *Star*, W. D. McBride, estimated that forty-five bodies were dragged out of the ruins, and listed the victims as "two Chinamen . . . a third Chinaman . . ." Not that the brave people of Regina drew racial distinctions in aiding the Chinese victims. Mrs. Ina P. Bird, now of Broadview, Saskatchewan, recalls that her husband, then working for the city government, was sworn in as a policeman:

"A Chinese man came up to him and told him he had seen his friend come out of the building across the street and run as fast as he could. The whole front of the building came out and followed him a short distance and fell on him. He was so sure his friend was under the wall, now flat on the ground, that it was lifted up. Sure enough, there was his friend as flat as a pancake."

Perhaps the surest record of the wreckage was made by George Watt, a pioneer Regina gardener, who kept a diary every day of his life, according to the book *Pioneers! O Pioneers!* by Jessie Bothwell. On July 1, the diarist faithfully wrote: "Result of yesterday's tornado is appalling — sixty-five dead and hundreds wounded. Three churches, YMCA, YWCA, library, telephone buildings, hundreds of other buildings razed to the ground. Started men cleaning up debris around grounds of Government Bldgs."

The city's mayor decreed that henceforth, to make sure the great tornado would always be commemorated, the flag must fly at half-mast each Dominion Day in Regina. It is a supreme stroke of irony, however, that the fates decreed that the city would remember the date for almost the next half-century as a money disaster.

After much financial haggling, the city fathers at the time managed to borrow $500,000 from the somewhat stingy Saskatchewan provincial government, at a rate not to exceed 5 per cent. As a guarantee of repayment, the city had to mortgage $2 million worth of its property to the provincial government. The city did nothing to compensate the tornado sufferers for their financial loss; but it did loan them the half-million dollars to rebuild their stores and warehouses, with payments spread over a long period of time.

As the tight-fisted city fathers fell behind in their repayments, the equally tight-fisted provincial government insisted that Regina sell its debentures to cover the arrears. Squawking vehemently, the city had to keep opening its reluctant purse strings.

At last, in February, 1959, the Regina *Leader-Post* was able to run a headline: "Cyclone Account Finally Closed." Regina today is a truly beautiful and prosperous Queen City of one hundred thousand people; but it had to pay dearly for the giant wind that blew its merchants down and scooped is real estate up into the prairie skies.

"The city's cyclone debt was expensive," concluded the *Leader-Post* financial writer, Jack Schreiner. "In forty-six years, the interest payments alone exceeded one million dollars — twice the value of the original loan."

_4_

When Hurricane Hazel Hit Toronto

A S HE STEPPED WARILY ACROSS THE WOODEN swing bridge over the Humber River that Friday evening, Joe Ward cursed himself for forgetting his umbrella. Not that he was worried about the headline in the afternoon Toronto *Telegram:* "Hurricane Hazel Heading Here." That, of course, was ridiculous. Hurricanes never happened to Toronto.

But he should have remembered his umbrella, because rain had been cascading down steadily over Toronto's suburban Weston for the past three weeks. And now, at six o'clock on October 15, 1954, hurrying home from his job as a sheet-metal worker at the De Havilland Aircraft plant, Joe Ward was already soaked to the skin.

Gale gusts of wind sledge-hammered the rain hard into his ears. The fury nipped his turned-up nose, sluiced into his bright blue eyes behind his rimless spectacles, drenched his grey hair soggy, and made his teeth chatter with the cold.

Joe Ward turned up the collar of his plastic rain-coat, and tried to run down winding Raymore Drive. His feet stuck. Without sidewalks, the riverside street was a quagmire of yellow chewing-gum.

Never had he seen the Humber River in such a rage. He and his Nottingham childhood sweetheart, Annie Evelyn, had honeymooned on the Humber River in England thirty-five years ago. They had decided to spend their autumnal years on the banks of Toronto's Humber, be-

68

cause it was such a pretty Tennysonian brook. Now, the babbling brook was a boiling cauldron of coffee-coloured brown, flecked with angry froth of cream, and rising, rising, rising.

Joe Ward cheered up as he sloshed toward his stucco bungalow, painted white and robin's-egg blue, at 141 Raymore Drive. He was always warmed by the sight of his dream cottage. He and Annie had scrimped and saved for fifteen years to pile up the ten thousand dollars they had paid for it. He loved the bird-bath, the willow tree arching over the neatly manicured lawn, the hedges of white spiraea, and their lovely garden of red roses, peonies, and climbing morning glories, envied even by their next-door neighbour, Ted Jeffries, the professional gardener at the Lambton Golf Club.

"Just imagine," Joe Ward thought, "only two more payments due on the cottage. We'll have a bang-up party this Christmas to burn the mortgage."

As Joe dripped puddles into the house, he was greeted by Annie. Like many old married couples, she and her sixty-three-year-old husband looked strikingly alike. "For goodness sakes, Pop," she exlaimed, "change quick into some old things!"

He slipped on a baggy pair of grey work pants and his brown carpet slippers. She chattered of how she'd helped Mrs. Jeffries carry a cardboard box full of old clothes through the rain to St. Matthias Anglican Church a quarter mile away, on Scarlett Road, for Saturday's rummage sale. "And, ducky," she said, "you know what I told Elizabeth Jeffries? I said we didn't have to go to Niagara Falls to see the sights. All we had to do was watch the water squirting through the ditch sewer pipes in Weston."

After a hot supper of fish and chips, Joe Ward smoked one of his two nightly White Owl cigars, and they both sat in the living-room and laughed at the antics of Gorgeous George, the wrestler, on the television set.

Suddenly the lights went off at 9:00 P.M. But neither panicked. Annie lit a candle, put on her white night-dress, and decided to go to bed. Joe yawned and dozed off in the living-room easy chair, his feet stretched out on the hassock, his blue budgie bird, Joey, perched on his shoulder.

69

At midnight, Joe woke with a start. In the darkness, he put his feet down — and was chilled when they plunged into water. He splashed across the floor, opened the front door, and was dismayed at what he saw and could not see.

The wooden swing bridge he had crossed earlier had torn loose, and was now a monstrous battering-ram pitching drunkenly in a roaring sea. His beloved bird-bath and white spiraea hedges had vanished, and his willow tree, uprooted, was now flailing its limbs like a harpooned whale. Far off in the black night he could hear what sounded like the dying screams of Mr. and Mrs. Jeffries.

Joe Ward shut the outside storm door, and ran to open his cellar door; and his black-and-white English terrier, Lassie, swam toward him. He dried her with a towel, rolled her in eiderdown to keep her warm, and clutched her as he waded through knee-deep water to arouse his wife in the bedroom.

"Wake up, Missus," he said, as the flood oozed up within one foot of her pillow. "We've got water inside. But don't worry, Missus. We'll be all right."

Annie slipped on a spotted blue silk dress, grabbed a small flashlight, and fought back her fear as she felt the whole bungalow heave and rip loose from its foundation. Her husband rammed a hole through the ceiling, and helped her shinny up to the blue shingled roof; and they both spun down Raymore Drive on it as though on Huck Finn's raft.

Three lots down, their cottage roof bashed into the stationary roof of a neighbour, Jack Anderson, who had already escaped in a motor launch. They both entwined their fingers, and as they leaped in the dark toward the Anderson roof, Annie murmured, "If we die, Pop, we'll die together." As soon as they landed, their own roof shattered into splinters.

For the next seven hours, the elderly couple stood on the sloping roof, clinging to a TV aerial. They prayed as they watched their screaming neighbours being washed down Raymore Drive one by one to their doom, and as they saw the dirty brown water churn up to within two feet of their own perch.

70

Joe Ward tried lying on top of his wife to keep her warm, and he vainly flicked the flashlight on and off until its battery died, and his hopes died with it. Annie tried to remove her panties to wave them as a flag, but she was too numb. She buoyed up her hopes by thinking of what her married daughter, Greta, had once said in a speech at St. Matthias Church: "If we ask for help, we usually get it." "Oh, Father in heaven," she prayed, "help us, help us!"

At last, in the violet dawn, help came in the form of a red Hydro helicopter, piloted by Bruce Best. All night it had been used as an air hearse, carrying corpses strapped to its bright pontoons. Now it hovered over them like a giant dragonfly, and scooped up Joe and Annie Evelyn Ward to safety.

That Sunday, Joe returned with tears in his eyes to where his dream cottage had once stood. He found in the sucking silt a few unbroken cups, and their copper-colored Eaton's carpet swept a half mile away. His wife, who got some free sheets and pillow slips from the St. Matthias Church rummage sale, to which she herself had earlier donated, also wept. She stared at the sodden chesterfield and chairs, which had been turned into upholstered sponges, and said, "It looks as if the devil got hold of an egg beater and used Raymore Drive as a mixing-bowl."

And yet, the Wards were lucky. They were one of the seven families who got out alive from Raymore Drive. Thirty-eight persons were drowned on their street of death. Thereafter, it was called the "Calamity Crescent of the most horrible hurricane that ever hit Toronto".

Altogether, eighty-three persons were killed by wind and water driven by the evil hurricane bearing the gentle-sounding name of Hazel. Born in the Caribbean, on October 6, 1954, the cruel storm tortured half a continent before reaching Toronto nine days later; and though her breath was nearly spent by then, she still managed to blow up gales of seventy miles an hour. Three hundred million tons of water were dumped from her witch's cauldron onto Greater Toronto — a history-breaking record of four inches of rain within twelve hours. Before she died over the Hudson Strait on the morning of October 17, she had ravished the face of southern Ontario as it had never been scarred before.

71

In suburban Toronto alone, forty bridges were pounded to shreds, three thousand people were forced to flee from their flooded homes, and $25 million worth of property was turned into sludge-covered junk. Suburbanites living on the banks of the meandering Toronto creeks known as the Humber, the Etobicoke, the Highland, and the Don woke in the night to find a torrent battering at their doors.

The tiny streams that crease the outlying Ontario countryside—the Nith, the Grand, the Credit, the Saugeen, and the Conestogo—became swollen, angry torrents; and the tiny communities of Woodbridge, Beeton, Brampton, Bolton, and New Hamburg became as the Everglades of Florida.

Holland Marsh — seven thousand acres of rich, black farm soil, thirty-five miles north of Toronto, which had been reclaimed from the swamp by Dutch market gardeners — became as the legendary Atlantis. One thousand Dutch farmers had to escape in a flotilla of boats to the sandbag dikes at Bradford. They left the gulls to preside over their $10 million worth of onions, cabbages and pumpkins, now rotting and reeking and bobbing in the Holland River waste land.

For Toronto, the disaster was notable for two reasons. Canada's second-largest city, often called "Hog Town", had always been known as Canada's most emotionally cold city. Yet, though the hurricane immobilized trains, buses and planes, Torontonians proved that in a crisis they could respond quickly with acts of heroism and kindness.

The disaster was also notable for the way it proved to Toronto's some 1,500,000 citizens that they were not immune to the malignant perversities of nature. Indeed, it was because they refused to believe that the elements could blot out their lives that so many died. Hurricanes, after all, happened in far-away places like Cuba or the Carolina coast, but never in Toronto. Dozens of protesters had to be carried piggyback by police out of their wallowing homes by force.

Fred Turnbull, Chief Ontario Meteorologist at Toronto's Malton Airport, was one man who believed in hurricanes. This Saskatchewan-born Cassandra of a weatherman knew it all the time. Defying the scoffs of his superiors, he personally made four radio broadcasts warning that the hurricane would lash Toronto that Friday evening. Today, years after the calamity, Turnbull hates even talking about how his warning went unheeded that day.

72

Ever since it was spawned off the Caribbean Windward Islands, Turnbull anxiously charted the path of Hurricane Hazel from his Dominion Government weather-forecasting headquarters at Malton. Here a dozen teletype machines chatter away, twenty-four hours a day. Every three hours they brought him fresh reports from six hundred weather stations dotted across the width and breadth of North America.

A hurricane is a doughnut-like ring of tropical winds spinning around up to 125 miles an hour. It spins counter-clockwise in the Northern Hemisphere, clockwise in the Southern. At the centre of the doughnut is a fifteen-mile-wide hole of calm low air pressure. This hole is the vicious "eye" of the hurricane. Immediately around the eye are dense cumulus clouds towering to heights of thirty thousand feet. Surface winds suck up moisture from the steamy tropical seas, and as they near the dry storm centre of the doughnut, they spiral upwards with turbulent energy. When they cool off in the wall of clouds, they release a deluge of torrential rain.

Turnbull watched with foreboding the progress of this whirling harridan called Hurricane Hazel. She went wild in Haiti, tipsily grabbing up the entire banana crop. Along the South Carolina coast, she tore thousands of beach homes to tatters in a drunken orgy, then continued her spree by reeling into Virginia, and on toward Pennsylvania. Since hurricanes seldom climb mountain ranges, the United States Weather Bureau predicted she would bump her head against the Allegheny Mountains, and faint away cold sober into the seas.

But Turnbull was convinced the United States weather experts were wrong. His forecasters predicted that dying Hazel would get a sudden pick-me-up, move up from Buffalo, and twirl north-east across Lake Ontario in gusts of up to seventy miles an hour. Turnbull knew the weakening hurricane would be rejuvenated in this way, because it was bound to clash with a stormy mass of cold Arctic air which he had observed pushing south-east across Ontario toward it.

"It was like two billiard balls colliding," recalls Turnbull's senior forecaster, John Knox. "Hazel No. 1 smacked into stationary Hazel No. 2, getting up enough energy to carom up north through Ontario. Put another way, it was like two pitchers of water crashing against each other, mixing their wet contents, and finally dumping it all. The icy Arctic air suddenly cooled and condensed Hazel's vast cloud load of tropical water vapour. So Hazel wept buckets of rain from Windsor to Kingston, and particularly over the mouth of the Humber River."

With restrained professional pride, Knox adds, "Meteorology is an inexact science. But our three special-bulletin predictions for that Friday, warning of record rain and gale-force winds of forty to seventy miles per hour, hit it right on the nose."

Why didn't the weather men warn of the havoc that would follow in Hazel's wake? "Because it wasn't our function," says Knox. "Our job is to forecast weather, not floods. By wicked coincidence, southern Ontario had endured unusually heavy rain all during October. Hazel's super sluice of rainfall made Ontario's already swollen rivers overflow their banks. It created a disaster the likes of which I hope never to see again, thanks to the Ontario Conservation Department's new flood-warning system."

Wondrous strange were the sights to be seen as the hurricane swept its two-hundred-mile-wide swath of destruction across southern Ontario.

Up above, a Trans-Canada Airlines North Star plane, bound for New York, was struck by a bolt of lightning as it was flying at four thousand feet over Clear Creek, Ontario. Then, tempest-tossed by the tail-end of the storm, it limped back to Malton Airport.

Down below, the New York Polonia Opera Company troupe, trying to plow their way in a Greyhound Bus from Buffalo to Toronto to sing two Polish operas in Eaton Auditorium, got mired in muck up to their hub-caps. They had to spend the night singing their Polish arias to the Irish bus driver.

In other Ontario spots, the show went on. At Breslau, the forty-first International Plowing Match continued soggily, though gales of sixty-five miles an hour plucked up the farmers' two hundred tents and turned them into a sky carnival.

At Ottawa, the Rough Riders gamely tackled the Toronto Argonauts, though the Lansdowne Park gridiron was a morass of mud, and the score-board was walloped down, and the fence was whirled away, thus allowing "the biggest crowd of free-loaders on record" to sneak in.

At Oakville, in the face of seething Sixteen Mile Creek, sixty strikers stuck to their picketing posts beside the Ford assembly plant;

and Fred Chiles, president of Oakville's United Auto Workers local, boasted, "If we can picket through Hurricane Hazel, mister, we can picket through anything Ford can throw at us!"

And at Vineland, the Garden Centre Theatre players earnestly persisted with Oscar Wilde's comedy, *The Importance of Being Earnest*.

Death unveiled its face in unexpected ways. It came to a seven-year-old schoolboy named Wayne Hodgson of London, Ontario, as he was hurling stones angrily at the turbulent Thames. He lost his balance, and was sucked to death in his one-time play-stream, so suddenly grown arrogant.

It came to twenty-seven-year-old Gerald Auger of Hull, Quebec, in his neighbour's back yard. Like a good neighbour, he picked up a loose wire that the storm had flung into the flooded yard, and it electrocuted him in one second.

It came to Canadian National Railways fireman Stewart Nicholson after he lay trapped for two hours under the locomotive he had ridden so often on the Palmerston-to-Southampton run. The washed-out tracks gave way like ribbons near Southampton, and the train flipped over into the flood-clogged ditch. Nicholson was breathing his last by the time rescuers sliced their way through to him with acetylene torches.

Death came to an elderly Orillia recluse named Willis Hopkins as he sat in his inundated barn, keeping his pet rabbit company. When they found him dead of a heart attack, he was slumped on a floating rocking-chair beside the rabbit hutch, his bunny clutched in his arms.

It came to a waitress named Mrs. Nora Wicks in Catfish Creek. The forty-five-year-old mother phoned up from the Aylmer RCAF station, where she worked on the night shift, to tell her son Bob, "I'll be home in a few minutes." She never came home. Three days later, at noon, Bob found her sprawled near her car, which, along with the Catfish Creek bridge, was crushed beyond recognition.

In a flooded corn field death met a twenty-two-year-old insurance-company accountant named Irwin Joyce, whose folks in Beeton were keeping supper waiting for him. He sprang out of his Studebaker, which was twirled away like a chip of wood by the torrent pouring over the Boyne River bridge. The insurance man waved his flashlight to warn off the approaching car driven by Otto Haugh of Cookstown, with his family of three. In the end, the corn field drowned all five of them.

And brave Warren Lanning of Oshawa was carrying his ten-year-old son Warren on his shoulders over the rising waters on the Eckhard Bridge. He was aghast when the death torrent wrestled with him and snatched the boy from his grasp. The boy's fingers were reaching out from the mud when they later found his body near Markham.

And yet Hurricane Hazel provided a few lighter moments. That Friday night, the marquee of the Elmwood Theatre on South Avenue in Syracuse read: "Now Playing — Gone With the Wind." The sign went with the wind.

That Friday night, Mrs. Helen Thompson of Nobleton was expecting a baby any moment. A neighbouring nurse, Mrs. Percy Lewis, waded to her home and got her into a panel truck; and after a hazardous roundabout trip over flooded roads, the mother arrived at Humber Trail Memorial Hospital at 9 P.M. She was delivered of her child by an interne at precisely 9:16. "You can bet," said Mrs. Thompson, "that my baby daughter definitely won't be named Hazel."

That Friday night, humour and pathos mingled as householders battled the flood. They were not unlike the classical case of Xerxes, who scourged the Hellespont, or the Mrs. Parkington who tried to fight a tidal wave with a mop. There was, indeed, an incorrigible housekeeper at Pickering who refused to be carried to dry land by the Royal Canadian Navy sailors, until she had swept the mud from her kitchen — a slimy coat of Rouge River silt that was four feet deep.

There was the case of Ken MacKinnon and his twenty-two dollars' worth of groceries. That Friday night, MacKinnon had loaded up with groceries at the supermarket, and carried them through the rain to his riverside home on Clarence Street in Woodbridge. Since his wife is badly crippled, he cooked dinner, and comforted her as she sat in her chair. "Old girl," he said casually, "it looks like we're going to get plenty of water tonight. It's up to the corner of the house."

Just as he was serving the stew, the cat jumped off the flooded kitchen floor into his wife's lap. MacKinnon's crippled wife sat in her chair, with brown water eddying about her ankles, her eyes widening in fear.

"I thought it was time we got out of there," MacKinnon remembers. "So I waded up the road through waist-high water to the telephone. But when I tried to put through the call to my brother, the operator said, 'Sorry, sir, the lines are being kept open for emergencies only.' Well, I thought of my wife sitting back there helpless in her chair with the cat, and the deluge rising, and I guess I got nettled.

" 'If this isn't an emergency,' I yelled, 'I don't know what the hell is!' "

Happily, a farmer named Russell Rowntree backed his high-wheeled tractor to the door of the MacKinnon home in time. Mrs. MacKinnon was loaded aboard, still seated on her chair, the cat purring on her lap, to be fed and billeted at Rev. Joseph Hodgson's United Church parish hall. After toiling with the other flood-fighters through the night, the red-eyed Mr. MacKinnon returned to see the water almost touching the ceiling of his bungalow. The house he had taken such care of for seven years was utterly ruined; yet all he seemed worried about was his twenty-two dollars' worth of groceries.

"It was my whole week-end shopping," he said, pointing dolorously at a floating orange. "Now look at it."

There was the case of Johannes De Peuter and his son's twenty-five-dollar jalopy. The De Peuters had emigrated from the Netherlands six months before. That Friday night, Mr. and Mrs. De Peuter and their dozen children — ranging in age from William, twenty, to two-year-old Deo — were seated in the kitchen of their two-storey white frame farm-house in the Holland Marsh. They had eaten their dinner of pork chops, and like good members of the Dutch Christian Reform Church, they were listening to their nightly chapter from the Scriptures, read aloud by Mr. De Peuter.

Then the whole house began to groan and crack atop the six oaken poles supporting it in the saucer of reclaimed loam that is the Holland Marsh. William looked out the window, and pointed at his black 1934 Frontenac, with its two flat tires, which he'd recently bought third-hand for twenty-five dollars.

"Hey, Dad," William exclaimed. "My car is floating away!"

His father looked and said, "That's not your car floating away. That's *us* floating away."

For the next three hours, the De Peuter family endured a weird voyage by candlelight. They huddled on the brass beds in the second storey of their uprooted home, while the enraged Holland River swirled up to the ceiling of the first storey, and tossed them around as though they were aboard a modern Noah's Ark. Using an axe handle, Papa De Peuter fended the house away from Hydro poles looming ahead in the black night, and from the top branches of red sumach trees bearing strange fruit of celery and cauliflower.

Occasionally the hurricane's force would rock the house to one side. Then all the children would be told to run to the other side to keep it balanced. It was, recalls William De Peuter, absurdly like the scene in Charlie Chaplin's movie, *The Gold Rush,* where Charlie and his fellow sourdough teeter-tottered their old shack on the edge of a precipice.

Mrs. Catherine De Peuter gathered the younger members of her flock into her arms, and hushed up their tears by whispering, "*Stil en kalm zyn, kinderen.* (Keep calm and quiet, children.)" Papa De Peuter was serene because he had survived four floods when the Maas River knocked over the dikes in his native Brabant in the Netherlands. Gently, he had his children recite the Lord's Prayer: *"Onze Vader die in de hemelen zyt . . ."*

At length, the floating house anchored five miles away on top of the gravel service road running parallel with Highway 400. Rescuers in a canoe carried out a rope from dry land, threw it to the second-storey window, and the Dutch family De Peuter was heaved floundering to safety. The family today lives on John Street, on top of the highest hill in Bradford. And William De Peuter, amused at the memory of how he sold his jalopy for fifteen dollars, loves citing the emphatic words of his father, Johannes, "It's so good to live on this high hill. Because all Bradford would have to drown first, before the De Peuters will drown."

That Friday night, when Hurricane Hazel struck Greater Toronto, thousands slept through it all, unaware that their fellow-citizens were drowning. They were untouched, because the storm wrapped its deadliest grip on the Humber River Valley, to the west of Toronto, and on the rivulets like the Etobicoke Creek that interlace the Humber as tributaries.

The Humber rises in the Peel Plains, about seventy miles north of Lake Ontario. The plains are packed with a tough clay base, which is like a duck's back in flicking off rainfall. Consequently, the brunt of the hurricane's deluge sluiced down the saturated Humber Valley, which winds toward Toronto like a trough with steep banks. The boisterous waters were forced over the banks, sometimes rising as high as thirty feet, sometimes racing ahead at a speed of forty miles an hour.

The flood struck at Thistletown, north-west of Toronto proper, where two drowned, and where seventeen incubator babies had to be evacuated from the unlit and unheated Hospital for Sick Children. It struck in suburban Long Branch, where seven drowned, and where fifty fleeing families had to be rescued from the Pleasant Valley trailer camp, as the Etobicoke Creek swept away their trailers. It struck at West Hill, where seventeen young married couples saw the wild Highland Creek bowl their cottages off their props like tenpins. It struck in Weston, near the Humber-drowned Elms Golf Course, where the screams of a woman echoed over the water for hours. And it struck in Islington, where the Black Creek became blacker, and where the Islington firehall was turned into a morgue, stacked with twenty-four bodies. It was felt in York Mills, where the law library in the home of Toronto's most prominent libel lawyer was left a shambles of mud. It was felt in the Don Valley, where paintings in the club-house of the Don Valley Art Club were mired in grotesqueries madder than any dreamed of by Dali. It was felt in Schomberg, where a Main Street housewife wailed that the six-foot torrent "came in one door and went out the other".

And yet, except for their umbrellas being blown inside out and their cars being drummed by rain in creeping traffic, most Torontonians did not feel the flood's fury that Friday night. It was certainly not felt by the hundreds who turned out in glittering evening gowns and tuxedos at Simpson's Arcadian Court on Queen Street, for the "Night in Nassau" ball to aid the Canadian National Ballet Guild. Nor was it felt by passers-by, puzzled when they saw the transported searchlights, which usually light up the sky for the Canadian National Exhibition grandstand show, being shone over the Bloor Street Bridge. They didn't know the lights had been carried there to help rescuers search for bodies in the Humber.

Frank Peppiatt, scheduled to get married that Friday night, knew nothing of the disaster until next morning. Peppiatt, then writing and co-starring with John Aylesworth on the CBC-TV comedy show "On Stage", was marrying Marilyn Frederickson, the blue-eyed, blonde singer on the "Wayne & Shuster Show". It was to be a real TV wedding at St. Timothy's Anglican Church on Ridley Boulevard in North Toronto — with Jackie Rae, the TV emcee, as best man, George Murray to sing "I Love You Truly", and Wally Koster of the "Cross-Canada Hit Parade Show" as usher. After the 7 P.M. ceremony, a reception was to be held at the North Gate restaurant on Yonge Street; it was to be filmed as a wedding gift by Harry Rasky, producer of the "Newsmagazine Show", who had borrowed two cameras and his CBC-TV camera crew for the occasion. Since both the bride and the groom had television rehearsals next day, they were going to spend a one-night honeymoon at the Grange Hotel on Lake Ontario, in Scarborough.

That Friday morning, Peppiatt groaned nervously as he saw the rain gusting down in broad sheets. His superstitious Scottish mother tried to cheer him up: "Rain before seven, fair by eleven."

While Marilyn, close to tears, was putting on her white formal bridal gown, her bridesmaid, Pat Patterson, the CBC commentator, tried to cheer *her* up, too.

"I knew your wedding was going to be a big production, Marilyn," she joked. "But I didn't know you were going to call on the biggest producer of them all. Tell Him to stop already!"

Peppiatt, his best man, and the minister were at the church promptly at seven o'clock. But they were the only ones. There were no guests, no ushers, no bridesmaids, no bride. Not until an hour and a half later did they straggle in, the pink hems of the bridesmaids wet, the golden slippers of the bride dripping.

Things perked up at the reception. Johnny Wayne and Frank Shuster arrived, jestingly kissing Peppiatt and shaking hands with the bride. Young Rasky and his camera crew shot a one-hour movie of the festivities. Friday was usually a dull evening at the CBC, and Rasky

80

was unaware that his television news bosses at the network were frantically phoning all over town to round him up, with his two cameras and his crew, to cover the mounting disaster. Not until close to midnight did he learn that the year's biggest news story was unfolding under his nose.

By then, Peppiatt and his bride were having a bottle of champagne in their suite at the Grange Hotel on Lake Ontario. They didn't turn on their radio then; nor did they next morning, when they had breakfast in their room. Only at 10 A.M., when they were driving along the lake shore, did they switch on their auto radio. As they heard Mickey Lester on CKEY graphically detail the calamity, they were petrified. They stopped the car to listen.

"We were dumbfounded," Peppiatt recalls. "Both of us shared the one selfish thought: we were glad we had driven east instead of west along the lake shore at midnight, or else we might have drowned on our wedding night. We thought gratefully how Someone had been mighty kind to us."

To show his gratitude, Peppiatt performed with his partner, John Aylesworth, on the four-hour telethon staged by the CBC to raise donations for the Ontario Hurricane Hazel fund. Wayne and Shuster were masters of ceremonies, and the singers included such TV stars as Juliette, Shirley Harmer, Joan Fairfax, and Phyllis Marshall. They raised $137,000 that night of the total five million dollars ultimately received by the fund. Donations ranged from ten thousand dollars from Pope Pius XII, to ten dollars from three little girls in Hamilton, Ontario, who got their mothers to bake cookies, which the girls sold from door to door.

The flood water acted in hypnotic fashion on a Weston widow, who stared at the rising Humber until 4 A.M., as though mesmerized by a serpent. Mrs. Ella Louise Norman takes in boarders at her two-storey, red-brick home at 27 Little Avenue, which sits high on a bank immediately facing where the Lawrence Avenue bridge crosses the Humber River. Mrs. Norman, a cheerful, snowy-haired ex-school-teacher of sixty-five, had lived in her house since 1922; she was determined not to budge.

81

That Friday afternoon, she fought her way through the stinging rain up the black-top road to the grocery store. "Haven't you any more brains than to go out in weather like this?" demanded the shopkeeper.

"I need something to eat for my boarders," Mrs. Norman retorted.

The only boarder who came home for supper, however, was Gerry Lewis, a twenty-five-year-old Londoner, working as an inspector at the A. V. Roe aircraft plant. His comment on the flood was almost a Noel Coward parody of English understatement.

"It is a bit of a shock to see houses floating over the top of the bridge," Lewis remarked at eleven o'clock; then he went upstairs to bed.

Mrs. Norman wrapped a blue-and-red motor rug around her shoulders, sat on the couch in the glassed-in sitting-room on the front verandah, and watched the tormented river. She wasn't alarmed when a naval officer from HMCS *York* pointed at the gnarled old elm growing out of the embankment in front of her house and warned her, "When you see that elm tree move, madam, you must escape out of your back door." She was merely stupefied.

"I was in a frozen trance," she recalls. "Even when the electricity went off, I just sat there in the dark, fascinated. I couldn't believe that my itty bitty Humber was growing into this frothing monster before my eyes. I watched the firemen lower life-preservers from the edge of the Lawrence Avenue Bridge with ropes, in the hope they might be clutched by victims being washed down-stream from Woodbridge. Then I watched the bridge itself crack and crumble away. I watched the heads of people and squealing pigs and pianos sweep by in the current like logs. And still the river was rising. I watched until I fell asleep, at 4 A.M., sitting up on the couch."

Mrs. Norman woke at 7 A.M., aroused by the ringing of the alarm clock. She didn't even glance outside, because the electricity was back on again, and her radio was blaring: "Weston is now a disaster area. If you live there, you must report to the Town Hall immediately."

She hurried upstairs to her boarder's bedroom, and shook his shoulder. "Wake up, Mr. Lewis," she said. "You're in a disaster area. You've got to report to Town Hall."

82

Lewis blinked his eyes open, and regarded her quizzically. "I think you are a trifle upset, Mrs. Norman," he murmured. Then he sat up, and told her to look out the bedroom window.

She did so, and she noticed that the cement pier, fifty yards north of the Lawrence Avenue bridge, had vanished in the night. She was fond of this landmark, where each spring a religious zealot painted on the cement pier, in huge tomato-red letters, "Jesus Saves".

All Mrs. Norman could gasp was, "Jesus Saves is gone!"

Lewis looked at her and shook his head. "My dear Mrs. Norman," he said, "I think you had better go downstairs at once and put the kettle on for tea."

Today, Mrs. Norman and her restrained English boarder continue to live at 27 Little Avenue, and she says, "I often look at the Humber creek wriggling placidly by my front verandah, and I wonder if the night I saw it swell into a brute snake wasn't all a dream."

The flood was felt chillingly by Walter ("Watty") Harwood, who lived at 149 Raymore Drive. A philosophical and somewhat sardonic assistant editor of an engineering trade magazine, Harwood had lived for eleven years in his two-storey clapboard home. He shared it with his wife Ruth, an attractive, articulate Manitoban of forty-one, and his mother-in-law, Hope, a tiny ash blonde of sixty-three, who used to perform in Gilbert & Sullivan operettas in her native Brandon. There was also Mickey, the deaf old cocker spaniel, and their two gray cats, Patty and Susie, adept at catching the abundant river rats.

That Friday afternoon, Hope reread in bed a short story that Harwood had once written for *Weird Tales* magazine, inspired by the Humber's rats. It was called *The Trap*, and was about a mad inventor who had made an electric-eye device for guillotining river rats, but who wound up being eaten by his intended victims. Ruth set out one hundred tulips in their river-bank lawn, the way she had been taught by their gardener neighbour, old Ted Jeffries, and after dinner typed out a letter to her twin sister in Pittsburgh, describing Toronto's pelting rain storm. Watty himself, after the electricity flickered off at nine o'clock, read by the oil lamp one of Max Brand's paper-back western melodramas.

There was no hint of melodrama in the air at eleven o'clock when Watty snapped a leash on Mickey, and took the fat old cocker spaniel for his nightly walk to the river, one hundred yards away. The rain had stopped abruptly, and the wind's gusts had dropped into calm.

"How's the river?" called out a neighbour, Sidney Jameson. Watty knew him as an Eaton's elevator operator, who wrote sentimental Edgar Guest-like poems for the *Weston Times & Guide*.

"The water's high and ferocious, like it usually is in spring," sang out Watty. "But I've seen it worse."

By 11:30 Watty and Hope were in their bedrooms upstairs sleeping. Ruth stayed in the living-room to finish typing out her letter by the light of the oil lamp. At midnight she walked to the door, and was alarmed to see that their yard, which sloped down to the river, was a surging sea. She ran upstairs, yelling, "Wake up! We're flooding."

Hope threw on a blue crêpe dress, with no undergarments beneath, and ran downstairs to open the front door, crying, "Where are my darling cats?" The bedraggled cats raced in, yowling like demented humans, and flew upstairs to the bedroom. Watty came downstairs fully dressed; his only thought was to remove their new television set from its stand and put it on the couch. Ruth wondered aloud, " Should I call up the Jeffries to warn them?"

"Not at this hour!" protested Hope.

But Ruth persisted, and heard the last words she was ever to hear from Ted Jeffries: "Thanks, Ruth, for calling."

The brown water was now boiling up three feet high on the bottom floor. Watty tried to reach out from the staircase to pluck a hundred-dollar bill tucked away in his mother-in-law's Bible in the bookcase, but couldn't make it. Ruth saw the letter she had written with such pains floating away in the flood, and was helpless to retrieve it.

They all went upstairs and sat on a bed in Ruth's room. This bed, which in the past had shown an annoying tendency to shift about, was bolted to the floor — a fact for which they were to be profoundly thankful. Presently Ruth, feeling somewhat stunned, walked over to the bedroom window — just in time to see their front verandah tear away. Then the Jeffries' uprooted house was flung right against the Harwood house. Ruth punched her fist through the window-screen of her bedroom, and bloodied it by breaking the attic window in the Jeffries' house.

"Mrs. Jeffries!" she cried. "Oh, Mrs. Jeffries!"

There was no answer.

"I had a wild hope of trying to pull the elderly couple through the attic window," Ruth recalls. "Instead, I saw their home whirl away in the roaring night. I felt so sad. I thought of how Mrs. Jeffries always had a hot cup of tea brewed for him when he came home, and of how in summer he'd call out to me, 'Gardener, had your beer yet?' and how at ten o'clock sharp each night he'd have his bottle of beer and cheese sandwich, and of how Mrs. Jeffries had planned going back home to England but couldn't bear it because of her one phobia — fear of crossing the water."

As these thoughts flashed through Ruth's mind, she felt her own house shiver and sway. The top storey cracked loose from the bottom storey, and began to float down-stream. Ruth, Hope and Watty clung to the box-spring of the bed, while the water gushed through the window, ripped off their shoes, crashed away the walls, and swept away the mirrors and bureaus. The torrent left only their naked bed on the tossing floor of the bedroom.

Watty folded his arms and sat up in the bed. "I love you both," he said philosophically. "But this is the end, and we're going to die. Life, after all, is the only nightmare that is real."

His wife had been calm until then, but these words stabbed cold fear through her stomach, and now she began to tremble all over. "I'm not going to die!" Ruth shouted. "I'm not going to die!"

His mother-in-law crouched down on her knees and, somewhat ashamed of showing her emotions, began to pray, "O God, save all us sinners."

Their miracle came when their raft-like bedroom washed onto the ledge of the flat roof of a neighbour, Thomas Wakeling; he had already escaped, leaving only his two budgie birds behind. Watty and Ruth helped Hope crawl onto the roof, and they shivered in the night air there until 7 A.M., as the flood swirled up to within eight feet of them.

Ruth pummelled and massaged Hope to keep her warm, but her mother kept thinking of her clinging wet crêpe dress. "If we're rescued," Hope thought absurdly, "will a hotel let me in — with me in my bare feet and my shrinking dress?"

Watty removed his trousers and underwear. He put his underwear on the roof and his trousers back on again, and he stood on his underwear to protect his toes against the chill. Suddenly exhilarated, he began dancing an Indian dance on his underwear and whooping wildly, "We're alive, folks! We're alive!"

At last, firemen tied two aerial ladders together, and thrust them from the river bank to a maple tree and from the tree to the Wakeling roof. The marooned trio straddled the ladders, and then were carried on the shoulders of the firemen through neck-deep water to safety.

As Hope was thus borne piggyback through the rushing current, she moaned, "We've lost our little dog tonight."

She was abashed as her rescuer gritted his teeth and said quietly, "*We've* lost two firemen tonight, lady."

As soon as a blanket was wrapped around her shoulders, Ruth said, "All I want is a drink and a cigarette." Rescuers poured her out a paper cup of rye and handed her a cigarette; and then her courage ebbed and she dissolved into hot tears.

Today the Harwood family lives at 98 King Street, three blocks from the Humber River, as if they were impelled to stay near the scene of their distress.

"A week has not gone by since that I have not dreamed of Hurricane Hazel," says Ruth. "I dream of eighty-year-old Mrs. Helen Brough, who used to hear ghostly tappings on her door, but who refused to accept them as a warning, and who drowned. I dream of Mrs. Irene Gould, who escaped carrying her Bible. And I dream of John McGarvey, who couldn't look into the eyes of his son Tom, because both knew that his mother Wilhelmina, and his sister and brother, were all blotted out. Mostly, though, I dream of the grey set faces of the firemen who rescued us so heroically, and who refused to complain when their fellow-rescuers died like heroes."

86

The heroism displayed by the rescuers and comforters was indeed herculean. To be sure, some ghouls ripped rings off the fingers of corpses; and Toronto's then candidate for Mayor, Nathan Phillips, labelled the city's fifty-thousand-dollar contribution to hurricane victims "a niggardly drop in the bucket". But Torontonians that Friday night gave of themselves, not niggardly but valiantly.

Valiant was the word for the Salvation Army of Metropolitan Toronto. Brigadier Norman Buckley, its soft-voiced and grey-eyed welfare director, was aroused from his bed around midnight Friday to be told by Weston's Captain James Morrison: "There's trouble here with the river." From then until Monday morning, Brigadier Buckley got no more than three hours of sleep.

He took over Weston's two-storey, red-brick town hall as a refugee centre, and gave coffee and comfort to the grieving survivors of Raymore Drive. "I don't believe in consoling the bereaved with such trite phrases as 'God knows' and 'God understands'," Brigadier Buckley says. "I had to inform one man he'd lost his son and daughter and six grandchildren in the hurricane. I simply sat down beside him to give him company, and prayed, 'I hope you and your wife will receive the strength from God to bear it.'"

On Sunday morning, Brigadier Buckley was sleepily attending a Salvation Army rally in Mutual Arena to hear General Wilfred Kitchen deliver a sermon. But he wasn't listening. All he could think of was the urgent need of a place to collect clothes and food for the refugees. He was inspired to think of the vast Seaforth Armories on University Avenue. Soon that capacious centre was heaped with a Himalaya of supplies, and Brigadier Buckley's pockets were jammed with dollar bills pressed on him. And he was deeply moved by the generous offers pouring in — a barber prepared to go anywhere to cut hair free; a brewery offering its trucks to deliver milk instead of beer, a Six Points Plaza cleaner volunteering to clean and sterilize victims' clothes free; even a business man donating three cemetery plots.

Valiant was the word for the Toronto Red Cross. Its executive secretary, Don Brandt, an earnest fellow of forty-one, was also aroused from bed by a midnight phone call on Friday and did not get to bed until Sunday night. He immediately alerted the Red Cross disaster chairman, a lawyer named Brigadier Ian Johnston, and its president-elect, R. Dale-Harris. They held a rendezvous at the Red Cross headquarters at 460 Jarvis Street, aroused other workers, and then hurried to the stricken Black Creek area near Jane Street, where they bedded down flood refugees in the class-rooms of the public school. When they returned to Red Cross headquarters at dawn, the phones began ringing. They never stopped.

"It was a nightmare," Brandt recalls. "Nobody was in the office but the three of us. The local radio stations flashed announcements that people wanting to help should get in touch with the Red Cross. And relatives began flooding us with calls from all over North America. We grabbed the calls as they came in. We finally got organized, when eleven telephone lines were installed in our board-room, and our around-the-clock service handled over two thousands offers of assistance. They ranged from that of the head of a big firm, who said, 'My whole factory is at your disposal,' to the offer of a steno who told us, 'I'd like to come down and type for you.'"

In this hour of need, the disciplined corps of grey-uniformed Red Cross women volunteers performed prodigious feats. At the Dundas Street firehall in Islington, converted into a morgue, they volunteered to wipe off the mud clinging to the faces of the drowned. "It was like an act of religious dedication," recalls Roy Edwin Davey, a paper sales-man, who donated the three thousand paper cups he had in the trunk of his auto that Friday night. "I was so touched by it that I joined the Red Cross." (He is now president of its Ontario division.)

Valiant was the word for Mrs. Aileen McLaren, head of the Toronto detachment of the Red Cross Corps. This statuesque volunteer of forty-four, with cool blue eyes and caramel-coloured hair, worked in ankle-deep water all night at the Long Branch municipal building, tending waifs of the storm. Most solemn of her charges was a ten-year-old boy, deserted by his parents. They had gone off to a movie, and left him in their trailer without a baby-sitter.

Most helpless was a four-months-old premature infant, Nancy Thorpe, nicknamed the "Hurricane Hazel baby". At the height of the hurricane her mother, Mrs. Clifford Thorpe, handed her to Long Branch Fire Chief Albert Houston. He ferried the infant across the racing water that was once Island Road, and put her in the outstretched arms of a neighbour. He tried to return for her mother, father, little brother, and grandmother. But they were all sponged away by the flood. For the next five hours, baby Nancy, along with thirty-two other refugees, perched on the slanted gable roof of Mrs. Edna Jones's cement-block home.

As the Red Cross officer in command, Mrs. Aileen McLaren was later confronted with a prickly problem: who was to get motherless Nancy? Her uncle and aunt? Or her paternal grandparents? Mrs. Mc-Laren's good natured husband Joe, already trying to feed milk to four squalling infants, made the decision: "First send her to St. Joseph's Hospital, where they'll keep her alive with a preemy baby's special formula." Ultimately, Nancy Thorpe's grandparents were awarded this genuine orphan of the storm.

Valiant was the word for Constable Ronald Nuttley, of the Long Branch Police Force. This twenty-four-year-old cop, a muscular 205 pounds, spent seven hours that Friday night in icy, chest-high water on Island Road. He pulled a dozen stranded people in a rowboat to safety with a plastic clothes-line, carried a crippled nude lady on a broken-down door as a stretcher, slapped a suicidal wife out of her hysteria, nearly electrocuted himself, and escaped drowning by the skin of his teeth. He got home at 5:30 A.M., and was back on the job at noon Saturday.

"The thing that stands out in my memory was how I felt when the current dragged me under, and yanked me toward death in Lake Ontario," Nuttley recalls. "I felt for sure my goose was cooked. My whole life didn't flash in front of my eyes, as they say in fiction. I was just damn scared. I thought to myself, "If I ever get out of this, I'll never worry about anything again. Is this my time for dying? No, I'm too young. I intend marrying Dianne this March. I must struggle. I must grab at something.' Just then, I cought a clump of bullrushes, and was saved."

Valiant was the word for Superintendent George Regan's Toronto Harbour Police, who saved eighty-four lives that Friday night.

One of their two most hair-raising rescues was performed by Third Officer Ernie Norrey, a black-moustached Englishman of forty-one. He was despatched to Leaside, where a man had been washed off the Pottery Road Bridge, and was standing on the roof of his black Ford in the middle of the implacable Don River.

89

That man was Jack Bates, a two-hundred-pound truck driver of twenty-seven, who had been driving home. By the time Norrey arrived, Bates's car had turned topsyturvy. He had been "swivelled around like a propeller" a hundred yards down-stream, and was screaming as he clutched a clump of green willows. Rescuers were trying to fire a light line to him by a rope gun, but each time the wind hurled the line away.

Norrey calmly had the rescuers tie a stout rope around a lamp-post; then he and Patrol Officer Doug Sheppard got into a rowboat, and the rope held them steady as they were fed out down-stream toward Bates. A miniature Niagara was pounding the truck driver; the current ripped off his dungaree pants, and he was sobbing for his last lungful of air when Norrey tossed him a line and hollered, "Tie this around your waist and we'll try to pull you."

As soon as he slip-knotted the line under his armpits, Bates stopped struggling and felt blissfully serene. "It was the happiest feeling," he says. "I thought of my wife and baby girls, Darlene and Linda. I thought, 'Maybe this is the end of this here family man.' I didn't care too much any more. 'I've fought hard enough,' I thought. 'Now it's up to Old Dame Fate.' Then I felt the back of the boat with my fingertips."

Norrey reached down, and said gently, "Okay chum, hang onto me." Just then, Bates's Old Dame Fate walloped an oak tree at them, which ruptured the boat, capsized it, and sent them spilling like puppets. But Norrey was able to get up strength to throw a line to shore, and all three were pulled choking to safety. Today, whenever Bates takes his family driving by the Don River, his daughter, Darlene, points and says gravely, "Look, there's the river that almost did Daddy in."

Valiant, too, was the rescue made by Harbour Police Patrol Officer Max Hurley, a chunky fellow of forty-one, with iron-grey hair and soft blue eyes. Hurley had been a champion six-day bicycle rider in the nineteen-thirties, riding against Torchy Peden. In his spare time, he was now trainer and pilot for Shirley Campbell, and that Friday evening he had dinner with her to plan her next marathon swim across Lake Ontario. He was called in by the Harbour Police near midnight, and told to rescue a man perched in the fork of a willow tree in the rampaging Humber, beside the Old Mill night-club.

Hurley put life-saving equipment in his small dinghy, but found no truck available to take him to the scene. He spotted a dazzling new black Cadillac parked in the Harbour Police garage, and began lashing the dinghy to its roof. By coincidence, the Cadillac had been parked there by his old friend and rival, Jack ("Hot-shot") Russell, who a few weeks before had piloted Marilyn Bell in her successful all-night swim across Lake Ontario. In fact, Russell had just enjoyed a steak-and-liver dinner that evening with Marilyn Bell. He had driven her home in the Cadillac belonging to her patron, Dr. Bernard Willinsky, surgeon of Mount Sinai Hospital; and after dropping her off, Russell had come down to the harbour to make sure the doctor's yacht, *Mona IV*, was safely moored.

"What the hell are you doing Max?" Russell demanded, when he saw Hurley in the Cadillac.

"I've commandeered your Caddy for adventure," Hurley grinned. "Hop in, Hot-shot."

Russell flexed the red dragon and schooner he'd had tattooed on his left arm when he was a merchant seaman in Shanghai. "Let's go, Max," he said.

On their arrival, they found a mob of 250 rescuers — firemen, Hydro men, St. John Ambulance men — helplessly standing on a steep bank beside the washed-out Old Mill Bridge. One hundred feet away, sitting in his incredibly sturdy willow, was Gerald Elliott, a thirty-three-year-old telephone lineman, whipped blue and cold in the torrent. By the yellow glare of the searchlights, he looked to Hurley like "a ghost face" poised in a blob of seaweed. Russell said, "I've seen bloated bodies floating down the yellow Whangpo River in China, but I've never seen any river so wild as this."

Hurley tied a life-line around his waist and tried to shinny along a fence rail jutting into the water; but the forty-mile-an-hour current was too violent, and he had to be pulled back after venturing out five feet. Policemen fired a rocket with a rope at the end of it toward Elliott, but the hurricane gusts flung it into the torrent. Firemen crept toward him along an extended sixty-five-foot ladder, but it was too shaky and they wriggled back. Even a Hydro helicopter, caught in the snarl of nearby shrub branches, couldn't make it.

Around 3:30 A.M., Hurley in disgust rigged a long line to the dinghy, and he and Harbour Police Officer Al Morton got ready to

91

paddle her out. However, two other Harbour Policemen, Ike Pond and Gene Brushett, suggested: "First get out of the boat, feed it out with the line, and then see what happens."

Hurley complied. No sooner was the empty dinghy a dozen feet out from the bank than the current sucked it far below the surface. Hurley shuddered, for it took fifteen men to haul it back up.

Dawn was breaking, and Hurley kept running up and down the muddy bank, fretting aloud: "Elliott's willow will break any minute now. We've got to do *something*. He's put up such a battle to live, he *deserves* a fair shake now."

At length, Hurley turned to the other Harbour Policemen. "I'm going to try to make it in the boat without a life-line," he said. "I'll try to circle around to him by pushing myself forward along the curving fence rail with a paddle. Then I'll pull myself from shrub to shrub until I reach him. I'm going it alone. I'm a bachelor, after all. You guys are all married. Okay?"

The others agreed quietly, "Okay."

A York Township cop stepped forward and pleaded, "Don't do it, buddy. You're nuts. It's suicide!"

As Hurley embarked in his tiny egg-shell of a boat, he called cheerfully over his shoulder, "Mister, you drive your cruiser. I'll row my rowboat."

Three times the current whiplashed Hurley back. At last, as he clawed his way forward within thirty feet of the clinging Elliott, tears ran down the strained faces of the men on shore. "I bawled like a baby," says Hot-shot Russell. "The only other time I wept like that was when Marilyn Bell made it across Lake Ontario."

While Hurley bucked and plunged beneath the swaying willow, he threw Elliott a life-jacket and told him, "Jump into the stern of the boat, quick!"

Elliott, numb from having clung aloft for five hours, croaked hoarsely, "Thank God, I've got someone to talk to."

He jumped, and they were eddied down-stream. "You married?" Hurley asked.

"Yes. Got four kids."

"Well," joked the dauntless Hurley, "it's a good thing your wife doesn't know where you are now." They were both laughing hilariously, as though it were the funniest joke in the world, when they reached the ambulance ashore.

And perhaps the most valiant of all were the men of the Kingsway-Lambton Volunteer Fire Department. By a twist of fate, five of these rescuers became the victims of the Humber River they had swum so often as boys.

That Friday midnight, these volunteers (paid fifty cents for dousing a grass fire and seventy-five cents for putting out a house fire) heard the siren wail at the volunteers' firehall on Kingdom Road in Etobicoke. Volunteer Fireman Jim Britton, who lived two short blocks away, raced to the hall. He was wearing just his brown house slippers and blue leather windbreaker.

"It was our third rescue call that evening," recalls Britton, an intense, brown-eyed adventurer of twenty-seven, who worked as flying instructor at the Toronto Flying Club. "Three youths were reported stranded on a roof-top in Humber Boulevard, which runs parallel with the river."

The Humber road was dry when their six-ton red fire engine turned onto it from Dundas Street. About a mile south of Dundas, though, the pumper's headlights picked up oozing muck. Fireman Frank Mercer had been following the fire-reel in his own car, and it stalled. The eight volunteers pushed Mercer's car aside and tried to back up the truck, but the flood water was foaming up to their hub-caps.

"I radioed our position from the radio in the fire truck," recalls Britton. "We were told to stick it out and try to save the rig."

For three hours, the men were stranded on top of their fire-engine, exchanging wisecracks and singing "Home On The Range," but inwardly frightened as the torrent surged relentlessly higher. When the headlights blinked off, leaving them in darkness, and the hose on the back of the truck began circling away like a worm in the water, they realized it was no time for laughter. They all shook hands solemnly and said, "It's every man for himself."

Ashore, one hundred feet away on Kingsway Crescent, stood twenty-nine-year-old Detective Frank Greer of the Etobicoke Police Department. He cried out, "Please hold on! Please!" He tried to row a boat out to them while clinging to a wire fence that ran fifty feet into the water, but the pulverizing current was too strong.

Just then, Detective Greer heard the volunteer firemen shriek, "Our fire-engine is turning over! She's going!"

"For God's sake," Detective Greer hollered, "dive toward shore!"

Volunteer Fireman Britton dived from the top of the pumper, cursing fiercely. "I was mad as hell," he recalls. "I was sore as a hornet that we had been told to try to save the truck. I thought, 'To hell with the truck! Better to save the lives of this brave bunch of boys. And we could have saved ourselves hours ago when water was just creeping up. Damn the bloody fool who made the mistake! This ain't no Charge of the Light Brigade. Oh, damn the bloody fool!' "

In his wrath, Britton rolled over on his back and tried to float in the black current. The knitted waistband of his zippered-up leather windbreaker saved him by preventing the escape of the air that was trapped inside the garment. Then, miraculously, his fingers grasped the branch of a slender maple, and he heaved himself onto the tree, forty feet from shore. He heard a moan, and there, six feet away, was hanging Fireman Frank Mercer. He had a death grip around a limb of the tree, his knuckles showing white.

"Hang on, Frank," Britton whispered. "Hang on."

Detective Greer, on the end of a human chain and up to his neck in water, tried to reach out his hand to Mercer. Both he and Britton were too late. With infinite sorrow, they saw Mercer slowly unclench his fingers and sweep down the river, one of the five firemen vanquished by the Humber.

Detective Greer tossed a block and tackle to Britton, and pulled him ashore. All the detective could say to Britton was, "It's damn cold," and the trembling volunteer fireman said sadly, "Yes, it's God-damned cold."

Britton today is the paid captain and acting district chief of the Etobicoke Fire Department, and he says, "A day doesn't go by but I

94

look at the Humber nearby, and I think of the catastrophe, and I ask myself, 'If only we had done this? If only we had done that? Then maybe those five poor brave souls would not have drowned.'"

A brass plaque honouring the death of the five Hurricane Hazel firemen has been erected on a square cairn on Prince Edward Drive, not far from the shore of the Humber River. Every October, survivors parade there to lay five wreaths of red roses. Among the mourners are Joe and Annie Ward, the gray-haired couple who were rescued by helicopter from their roof on Raymore Drive.

After the ceremony, the Wards stroll down to where Raymore Drive used to be — now a green playground, with swings and teeter-totters, and nothing but incongruous fire hydrants remaining to tell the story of the street that vanished.

Like so many of the other Hurricane Hazel survivors, the Wards now live on a pleasantly shaded street just five hundred yards from the Humber River, as though they were obsessed with the scene of their disaster. They keep a canoe and a motor launch in their garage — just in case. But they also keep a poem, which they pass along to any other survivor they meet who endured tragedy at the hands of Toronto's unforgettable Hurricane Hazel:

> When some great sorrow, like a mighty river,
> Flows through your life with peace-destroying power,
> And dearest things are swept from sight forever,
> Say to your heart each trying hour:
> "This, too, will pass away."

_ 5 _

Alberta's Avalanche

P LATO ONCE DESCRIBED A SOLDIER WHO COULD not resist the impulse to stare at the corpses heaped on the scene of a disaster. The soldier finally scolded his own eyes, "There, you wretches, look your fill!"

The same morbid fascination impels thousands of tourists every summer to take a conducted horseback ride up seven thousand feet of hairpin bends to the broken peak of Turtle Mountain in the Alberta Rockies. Over near the British Columbia border, the tourist looks down the narrow gorge that is the Crow's Nest Pass at the monstrously scarred mountainside. And he stares with awe at the pile of rubble heaped in the valley that was once the legendary town of Frank, Alberta.

White limestone boulders, as huge as locomotives, are strewn on top of each other, as if hurled there by an angry god. Only a few spears of thick-stemmed grass, clumps of blue lupins, and tough poplar trees have managed to grip a limpet-like toe-hold on the rocks of this vast landslide. With a sense of wonder, the tourist realizes he is staring at the scene of Canada's most fabled avalanche.

In 1953, half a century since "the day the mountain shook", pioneers of Frank gathered under the shadow of Turtle Mountain to unveil a metal shield commemorating the event. This official plaque perpetuates the myths that have always shrouded the Frank Slide in hokum, for it contains three glaring errors. It reads:

Disaster struck here at 4:10 A.M. April 29th, 1903, when a gigantic wedge of limestone, 1,300 feet high, 4,000 feet wide and 500 feet thick, crashed down from Turtle Mountain and destroyed the town of Frank. Seventy million tons of rock swept over two miles of valley, taking 66 lives, burying numerous homes, the entire mine plant, railway sidings, and 3,200 acres of fertile land to a depth of 100 feet, in approximately 100 seconds.

First of all, it's pure humbug to say the avalanche "destroyed" the town of Frank. It's true that, in one hundred seconds, the cascade of rocks obliterated the rows of miners' houses on the north and eastern fringes of town. It cut a two-mile swath across horse barns, mine tipples, and CPR tracks, and dammed up the entire Old Man River. But the fact is that three-quarters of the frontier mining town remained standing.

It's also untrue to say the disaster "took sixty-six lives". That's just as inaccurate as the sentimental claim in "The Ballad of the Frank Slide" that the sole survivor was a "little weepin' babe". In fact, at least one hundred of the town's population of one thousand were killed. Some of the other thirty-four victims were carelessly written off in obituaries at the time as "unknown immigrant Slavs"; their sporting-lady friends were listed as "concubines". Others were western adventurers, scalawags, and fugitives from rapacious wives; they had taken pains never to disclose their true identity.

The official plaque's third error is one of omission. It fails to reveal that the landslide entombed seventeen coal miners inside the bowels of Turtle Mountain for thirteen hours. Their epic struggle for survival is perhaps the most legendary aspect of Canada's most legend encrusted avalanche.

The spinning of tall tales is the favourite outdoor sport of Albertans in the Crow's Nest Pass region. Undoubtedly their big mountains inspire this elephantiasis of the imagination. Even today a tourist on the Trans-Canada Highway or the Canadian Pacific Railway, winding sinuously around seven-thousand-foot peaks, is startled to see road signs near Frank shaped like a huge thumb and pointing aloft: "Look up! The cleanest sky in the world is above you."

Albertans in the area have always drawn on their provincial bank of superlatives to coin picturesque names. Two miles north of Frank is the coal town of Blairmore. Originally, it was to be named Blair, after the then Minister of Railways, Hon. A. G. Blair of Toronto. But local giantism envisioned a place bigger than anything suggested by the name of a mere man from Toronto. Consequently, a "more" was tacked on to "Blair".

To the south of Frank is the town of Pincher Creek. It was named after a pair of prospector's pincers, scooped up from a gold creek by the North West Mounted Police in the 1870's.

To the east of Frank, not too far from the Belly River and right on the Old Man River, is Fort Macleod. It was so named by Scottish Mounties, because they refused to pay $25,000 for the Americans' more gaudily named Fort Whoop-Up near Whisky Gap. But the Mounties did keep nearby Medicine Hat, named after a Blackfoot Indian medicine man, who allegedly tossed both his plumed war headdress and his argumentative squaw into the river, on the theory it would be "heap good medicine" for both.

And to the west of Frank is British Columbia's rugged Kootenay region, named from the Kootenay (or Kootenai) Indians. Its name was adopted by Alberta's first homesteader, an Eton and Oxford swashbuckler with long locks like Buffalo Bill Cody's, prosaically christened John George Brown. He married a Cree squaw called Chee-Nee-Pay-Tha-Qho-Ka-Soon (Flash of Blue Lightning), and insisted that she be addressed as Mrs. Nellie Brown; but for himself he assumed the more vivid Kootenai Inuspi (Long-hair) Brown.

Indeed, the Cree, Blackfeet and Crow Indians were the original weavers of fables surrounding the avalanche area. The Crow's Nest Pass itself got its name from the Blackfeet. A war party of Blackfeet massacred a party of Crows at the foot of Turtle Mountain. A scout of the Blackfeet then found that the main camp of the defeated Crow Indians was hidden on top of the mountain. He reported it as the "Crow's Nest".

After this, all the Indian tribes refused to camp at the base of Turtle Mountain. They gave it its name because it was shaped like the back of a sleeping turtle, with an overhanging slab of limestone as a head. In springtime, when lightning did a dance along the mountain's spine, when huge fissures cracked wider, and rocks plunged down with a rumble, the Indians would whisper ominously among themselves.

"The sleeping turtle is waking again," they would say. "Some day the moving turtle will nod its head, and the whole mountain will come tumbling down."

All this was dismissed as infantile fantasy by the white men. One October day in 1900, a prospector, Sam W. Gebo, kicked at a clod of limestone on the foot of Turtle Mountain. He uncovered a seam of black soft coal seven feet deep. Gebo staked his claim, and sold the coal-mining rights in the Crow's Nest Pass for thirty thousand dollars to a bearded banker from Butte, Montana, named H. L. Frank.

Envisioning a Pittsburgh of the Canadian West, the Montana capitalist launched the Canadian-American Coal & Coke Company with himself as president and Gebo as general manager. A settlement of three hundred miners grew up around Tenth Siding, in the wilderness of pine and fir and howling mountain wolves. Soon the shaft at the base of Turtle Mountain was producing a thousand tons of steam coal a day, and it was decided to incorporate the frontier community into a town.

This extraordinary formal debut of a boom town was held on September 10, 1901. It was to be named after Frank, and Gebo was dubbed mayor. A showman with flair, the Montana banker persuaded the Canadian Pacific Railway to bring hundreds of visitors to the christening on special trains from Fort Macleod, Pincher Creek, the Kootenays, and Blairmore. Among the speech-making guests were Sir Frederick Haultain, Premier of the Northwest Territories (Alberta, though a separate district, was not to become a province officially until 1905), and Sir Clifford Sifton, Minister of the Interior in the current administration of Sir Wilfrid Laurier.

Lots were offered for sale in the new townsite, but everything else was offered free for the splashy celebration. Whisky flowed, there was street dancing accompanied by the firing of muzzle-loaders, and gold medals were given to winners of foot races. A Blackfoot Indian chief offered one of his plumpest wives to Premier Haultain, but the gift was politely declined. When he was told that the new régime would not sanction polygamy, and that he would have to give up all his wives but one, the old chief said, "But I love all my squaws equally. Which one, sir, shall I retain?"

By the spring of 1903, Frank had bourgeoned into a flourishing, roistering frontier town, with a population of one thousand. Its one street, Dominion Avenue, looked remarkably like the set for a Hollywood cowboy movie. Ranchers on horseback would come thundering down the wide dirt road and pull up at the plank sidewalk, probably on their way to the saddlery and general store operated by the Scottish merchant, Alexander Leitch. The town boasted three churches, a two-room school-house that also served as a theatre for touring players in the Pass, and a sulphur-spring sanitarium that sold ice-cold health baths in wash-tubs.

But social life was centred in the saloons and gambling casinos inside the town's four hotels. They did a roaring trade on mine pay-nights. Then the town's two North-West Mounted Police constables would break up the festivities by firing their revolvers into the air. The branch of the Union Bank of Canada paid out more than a 125,000 silver dollars each monthly mine pay-day. The bank manager, J. H. Farmer, an *hombre* of caution, kept four loaded pistols in his apartment above the vault.

Mark Drumm, publisher of the four-page weekly Frank *Sentinel*, was all for genteel law and order. But he was an even more fervent exponent of commerce. He boosted the trade in liquid refreshment by the town's four hotels. Yet he ran quaint ads like this one for the Samaria Remedy Company: "A Wife's Gratitude! Her husband got drunk twice a day. She gave him a tasteless Samaria prescription. He now brings his wages home — doesn't take a single drop!"

Drumm deplored the "hussies, adventuresses, and parlour sporting ladies" who flaunted their bosomy charms in the gambling casinos. Yet his newspaper accepted from the Madame Thora Toilet Company ads that displayed pictures of buxom wenches, and read: "The secret of a perfect bust and form! Madame Thora's French Corine system of bust development is a simple home treatment, guaranteed to enlarge the bust six inches. It also fills hollow places in neck and chest, and cures 'female weakness'. It has been used by leading actresses and society ladies for twenty years."

Drumm was quite aware that the CPR, "two streaks of rust across the wilderness", was the financial mainstay of Frank. A short branch rail line, the Frank & Grassy Mountain Railway, was under construction to link Frank with the coal town of Lille, six miles north in the Rockies. But the CPR stopped only at Frank. People from the other mining towns in the Pass area — Blairmore, Coleman, Bellevue — took a livery rig down to Frank to await the big event when the CPR passenger train pulled into the Frank depot, and spewed out its newest cargo of homesteaders stricken with Alberta land fever.

On its part, the CPR had an insatiable need for Frank's cheap steam coal for its locomotives. To get cheap labour for the mine, the railway put on a strenuous campaign to lure Ukrainian, Welsh, Czech and Galician immigrants to Alberta — called "the Last Best West, beyond which one cannot dream of anything better". The immigrants (many nicknamed "Sifton's sheepskins" because of their custom of wearing sheepskin coats) responded enthusiastically. "Come to Alberta and go into partnership with the Canadian Pacific," ran one early CPR slogan.

"Since we can't export the scenery, we shall have to import the tourists," said the CPR's great colonizer, Sir William Van Horne; and he devised his own catch phrase, "Wise Men of the East, Go West by the CPR." An English immigrant in Ontario who succumbed to this siren call, W. C. Pollard, author of *Life on the Frontier*, remembers being seduced by the slogan: "All aboard for the West. If you can't get a board, get a slab. Everyone must go to the Promised Land!"

On their arrival in the Crow's Nest Pass region, though, several pioneers found the Promised Land wasn't all as promised. A disillusioned malcontent wrote to the Frank *Sentinel*, "It's cold enough to freeze the hair off a dog's back. The sun sets over Turtle Mountain — Gebo's Lonely Mountain — no later than 3 p.m., leaving us in a shadow blacker than a cow's inside. And we're a hundred dollars from anywhere."

A historian from Blairmore, Mrs. T. E. Mudiman, wrote that things were indeed quite primitive in Frank. "The Frank coal company had an electric light plant, and sold power at twenty-five cents for each drop light. The miners wore lamps with open flames on their caps, and sparks from these ignited the powder into a great many explosions. The railway had accidents, too — mud slides, blizzards, collisions. Most of the food was shipped in, though a few folk had a pig in the garden. In fact, there was a Frank town by-law against perambulating porkers. And one time, a Pass lady told the woman who brought her cream each week that the cream of late had not been up to par. The cream lady replied, 'Well, it certainly is as thick as usual — because the mice ran over it all last night.'"

Faced with these harsh conditions, the pioneers derisively said the CPR stood for "Can't Pay Rent, Can't Promise Return". Inevitably, they sought escape in boozing; and they were fleeced by gamblers and con men who poured into the Pass from Montana. "Those Americans can steal a hot stove from you," the phrase ran, "and come back for the smoke."

The Mounties, who tried to quell the rambunctiousness of the miners, were a special target of scorn. They were derided as "Yellowlegs", after the yellow trouser stripes of their uniforms. A frontiersman named Roger Pocock wrote of them mockingly in 1903, "Why, these fellows would ride all day for the Government, then all night for a bottle of whisky, and spend the whole of their leisure devising devilments. Yet, by the trickery of an oath and a uniform, Romance has created the frailest of them into perfect constables of the peace."

These peacemakers had a handful of trouble, despite the anguished plea by the Frank *Sentinel* to the town's trouble-makers, "Raise less hell and more coal!" The pluckiness of the peacemakers is suggested in Judge Peter O'Reilly's admonition to miners whooping it up at nearby Wild Horse Creek: "Boys, I am here to keep order and administer the law. Those who don't want law and order can 'git'. But those who stay with the camp, remember on what side of the British Columbia line the camp is. For boys, if there is shooting in Kootenay, there will be hanging in Kootenay."

Illustrating how the formalized understatement of policemen never changes, a Mountie corporal of the time wrote this classic report of an arrest: "On the seventeenth instant, I, Corporal Hogg, was called to the hotel to quiet a disturbance. I found the room full of cowboys, and one Monaghan, or Cowboy Jack, was carrying a gun, and pointed it at me, against sections 105 and 109 of the Canadian Criminal Code. We struggled. Finally, I got him handcuffed."

By April, 1903, the miners in the Pass were conducting a union wage dispute with the Frank coal-mining company, and violence flared. "Knives flashed on Frank's wooden sidewalks," wrote the historian, Mrs. T. E. Mudiman, "and there was an occasional murder. A young

102

constable of the N.W.M. Police was the victim of a shotgun in the hands of an unknown assailant. He had not been long out from the Old Country, and was a likeable lad. General sorrow was felt at his untimely demise. A fellow-countrywoman — who had not even known him — called at the Frank morgue to offer up a prayer."

On Tuesday, April 28, 1903 — the blustery night before "Old Turtle nodded its head" — one of the remaining Mountie constables in Frank set out for Pincher Creek to return a stolen horse. The stallion had been sold by some cowboy horse-thief to James Graham, a New Brunswick pioneer who had set up a dairy-herd ranch on the slope of the hill opposite Turtle Mountain, to sell milk to the Frank townspeople.

Though a bitterly cold snowstorm was raging in the foothills, James Graham had spent the day buying a cow and a calf from a settler named Ned Morgan on the adjoining Goat Mountain. The two men drove the animals on roads sheathed in ice, and arrived at the Graham ranch, a half mile east of Frank, after dark.

"Spend the night with us, Ned," said Mrs. Graham. "You know our two sons, Joe and John. They're back from South Africa, where they served with the Baden-Powell Constabulary. The boys'll be glad to bunk up with you."

"No thanks, ma'am," said Morgan, with a reluctant sigh. He explained his team of horses had been left with harness still on, tied beside a shack a mile to the east. Just before midnight, he shook hands with the Grahams; and as he trudged back to his team, he noticed that Turtle Mountain seemed to be discharging ominous rumblings into the dour wintry sky.

The faint rumbling was noticed by a gnarled old trapper named Andy Gresack. Just before he retired for the night in his tent beside the Old Man River, on the brow of Turtle Mountain, Gresack mentioned it to John McVeigh. "It must be the old man of Old Man River up to his usual tricks," he said.

A young fellow in his thirties, McVeigh headed the construction crew of Poupore & McVeigh, railroad contractors. They were building the new spur line to Lille. His construction crew — wild men, many of them only indifferently identified on the pay-roll — were camped in shacks in the valley immediately under the Turtle head, with their earth-moving equipment, their bottles of whisky, their unmentioned secrets of families abandoned.

McVeigh, however, had only temporarily abandoned his family. He had been due for a holiday with his wife and child in Lethbridge, but was delayed. So, at the last moment, he'd sent them ahead on the train, planning to join them the next day. "I miss them already," McVeigh told his friends. "I'll dream of them tonight."

Dreams of Wales filled the minds of Alfred ("Jack") Dawe and his two Welsh mining friends that night as they ate a late supper of baked beans and ham. Their cabin was beside the coal company's livery stable containing fifty horses, just north of Frank's outskirts. The three Welshmen had pledged themselves to start back to Wales the day before. But when they could not get the steamship date they wanted, they'd agreed to work one more week. Just before they went to sleep, Jack Dawe observed that the terrier pup was whining strangely in the barn, and had set the horses whinnying and stamping their hoofs. "The poor critter must have caught our homesickness for Wales," he said.

At midnight, Joe Chapman — curly-haired, husky, with cool blue eyes — led his gang of sixteen coal miners one mile deep into Turtle Mountain for the overnight graveyard shift. Old Charlie, the mine horse, neighed nervously as he pulled the coal carts within the tunnel. Chapman's right-hand man, Evan ("Halfpint") Jones, remarked, "I don't like the way the timbers are groaning tonight. You mark my words, when Old Charlie perks his ears like that, you can expect a mine squeeze."

Joe Chapman laughed. "Don't tell me, Halfpint, you take these scary Indian tales seriously, too? Inside a mountain like this, you've got to expect a certain amount of rock friction and eruption from the earth. Why, the whole town of Frank has got all hell for a cellar."

In the icy cold above, the town of Frank was pretty well fast asleep. By 4 A.M. the saloon-keepers were giving the fishy eye to the last straggling drunks still nursing their drinks. In the Hotel Imperial, the night men on duty were busy waking and making ready the travelers for the British Columbia-bound passenger train, the Spokane Flyer, an hour and a half late out of Lethbridge. But in the rest of the town's sprawl of stores, houses and shacks, nestled at the foot of Turtle Mountain like a toy village, the lights were snuffed out.

On the eastern fringe of town, perched beside a creek, lay a neat row of white cottages called Manitoba Avenue, later nicknamed "Suicide Row". Seven unsuspecting families slept serenely here: the families of Leitch, Ennis, Clark, Ackroyd, Bansmier, Watkins, and Warrington.

Alex Leitch, the Frank general-store merchant, stirred in his sleep uneasily. His seven-month-old baby, Marion, was crying in the next room, and one of his two daughters was coughing. Samuel Ennis, a miner, smiled in his sleep; he curled his arm around his baby Gladys, cradled on the pillow between himself and his softly breathing wife. Mrs. Alfred Clark slept fitfully, worried about the eldest of their six children, Alfreda; she had been working in town at the miners' boarding-house, and that night, for the first time in her life, did not return home.

In the cottage closest of all to the mountain, Mrs. William Warrington slept with her seven children. She was slightly concerned because she had left their newly laundered clothes hanging outside on the line. Now the diapers were frozen stiff, bearded with icicles, and swaying in the eerie pink light of the mountain dawn.

At ten after four, a CPR brakeman named Sid Choquette was one of the few men awake to see sleeping Turtle Mountain leap into death-dealing life. He was in a freight train that had just shunted twenty-eight empty coal cars on a siding west of the mine tipple. He stepped out of the caboose, glanced up, and saw hell break loose.

With an ear-splitting din, a mile-wide slab of white limestone ripped free of its shoulders of shale, sandstone, and coal beds. The convulsion gave off a noise that was a blend of a low roar and a high-pitched whistling — "a weird double-bass-and-piccolo-flute duet." Seventy million tons of rock began cascading down the slope of Turtle Mountain — just as lumps of white flour slide down a slanted pastry-board.

Boulders as big as hotels bounded over each other, belching sparks when they clashed in midair and convincing people that this was an erupting volcano. Buildings twenty-five miles away in the Rockies trembled and swayed, as if on a merry-go-round, convincing other people that it was an earthquake. The earth's tremor was felt by Wallace T. Eddy, a homesteader miles away in Burmis, whiling away the chilly morning by reading detective stories with his feet in the stove oven.

105

The most formidable havoc was wrought by frontal columns of compressed air that preceded the landslide at a speed of a hundred miles an hour. Like invisible battering-rams, these giant fists of air ravaged the mine's sawmill. They uprooted the electric plant, twisted two miles of CPR tracks into fantastic shapes, and flattened people as though they were upset chessmen.

After these hammering blows the coup de grâce was delivered by the torrents of snowy rocks. Like a foaming Niagara Falls, they buffeted and buried all that was left in their path. The waves of devastating limestone fanned out across the valley of the Crow's Nest Pass for two miles, and poured five hundred feet up the opposing mountain slope, engulfing everything in an enormous white sepulchre.

The town of Frank jolted awake, as if suddenly struck over the head. It was two minutes before the saloons, stores and houses stopped swaying. The first shattering tumult reverberated into relative quiet, punctuated by the crashes of still tumbling boulders. A blinding shroud of limestone dust hung over the valley. A drunk staggered out of the Hotel Imperial saloon into the darkness, wailing, "Wiped out! The Lord has visited us for our sins," and he was never seen again.

But the first positive action was taken by Sid Choquette, the brakeman. "My God!" he shouted to his fellow brakeman, Bill Lowes. "The Spokane Flyer — its passengers will crash into the rocks, unless we flag it down."

Choquette ran one mile across the hot, jagged rocks of the avalanche. He groped his way through the pall of dust, ducking the showers of boulders, and silently praying that the snowstorm would delay the train just one more minute. With a sob of relief, he was able to swing his lantern in the headlight of the Flyer just in time.

> A CPR freight came puffin'
> Along the railroad track.
> The wall of ol' Turtle Mountain
> Tossed the echo right back.
> Tossed the echo right back, right back
> Into the shiverin' mornin'.
>
> The brakeman he was in the caboose
> On a day he'll never forget.

It's a good time now to mention
That his name was Sid Choquette.
His name was Sid Choquette, Choquette
There in the shiverin' mornin'.

Sid crossed the sea of flyin' stones.
He busted a leg and an arm.
But he flagged the Spokane Flyer,
Before she came to harm.
Before she came to harm, to harm
There in the shiverin' mornin'.

The other townspeople of Frank, digging through the debris on missions of rescue, were not so fortunate.

James Graham, the New Brunswick dairyman, his hospitable wife, and their two sons from Africa, were sealed dead under fifty feet of rock. The only thing left alive in Graham's ranch was the cow he had just bought, its horns completely ripped off its head.

Andy Gresack, the trapper, was found wrapped in his shroud-like tent beside the dammed-up Old Man River. He was clutching an iron frying-pan, and looked alive in his gnarled way; but when they touched his hair, his scalp peeled off like a Frenchman's beret.

John McVeigh, the faithful young husband, who went to sleep dreaming of his wife and child in Lethbridge, never woke from his dreams. He and his motley construction crew, in their shacks, with their bottles of whisky and their secrets, were crushed into smithereens.

Nor did Jack Dawe, the Welshman, ever fulfil his dreams of return ing to Wales. The advance blast of the avalanche hurled him and the livery stable of horses one mile away. They said his lips were contorted into a jolly smile when they found him, rather like a happy man in a Breughel painting. His terrier pup was still alive, shrill in its melancholy.

The avalanche played a capricious game with the families in the cottages of "Suicide Row". People sleeping in one room of a house were mashed to pulp. Yet people sleeping in the next room were flung to safety.

Though the Bansmier cottage was ripped off its foundation and somersaulted twice, the family was left without a scratch. Charles Ackroyd and his wife were pulverized. But his thirteen-year-old stepson, Lester Johnsen, escaped with little more injury than having the feathers from his pillow forced into his chest by a flying bed slat. Dr. George Malcomson plucked out the feathers as though the lad were a chicken.

The girl, Alfreda Clark, who stayed away from home for the first time in her life, now wept with mingled feelings of agony and thanksgiving. Her father, her mother, and all her brothers and sisters were now lifeless bodies.

Samuel Ennis woke, pinned under his collapsed house, with a smashed hip. His wife beside him was also pinned into bed, with a broken collarbone. Both immediately fumbled in the dark for their infant daughter Gladys, who had been cradled on the pillow between them.

"Sam," gasped Mrs. Ennis, as she touched the feebly stirring child, "Gladys is choking to death! Do something!"

With quivering fingers, her husband managed to scoop out a blob of mud corked in the infant's mouth. He thumped her back, and was rewarded by a loud "Da-da!" Soon, with what was called "superhuman strength", Ennis also managed to pry out from the rubble eight-year-old Delbert, with both legs broken, and young Marion and Hazel, without serious injury.

Faint cries led Ennis to his brother-in-law Jim, who had been asleep in another room. His features twisted in pain from a broken hip, Jim moaned, "Keep digging. I can feel a soft hand beneath me."

Under the rubble, the rescuers freed Mrs. John Watkins, who had been flung, asleep, from the cottage next door. Though she was a human pincushion, her skin needled by piercing rock, she managed to groan, "How's my family?"

"Safe," they told her.

"The Lord be praised for His infinite mercy," she said.

Fate dealt more capriciously with the Scottish merchant, Alex Leitch. He, his wife, and four sons, ranging in age from four to fourteen, were all killed. But the three Leitch daughters escaped. The youngest, seven-month-old Marion Leitch, caught the fancy of the public. She was hurled from her family's crushed home onto a boulder, which crash-

108

ed against the Bansmier house; and she landed on a heap of hay miraculously whirled there from the coal company's destroyed horse barns. There she was found, laughing and unscathed.

There was no laughter from Mrs. William Warrington and her seven children. They were all encased in a silent crypt of rock a hundred feet deep. Their only human memorial was the row of frozen diapers, still hanging untouched on the clothes-line and creaking sadly in the breeze.

Meanwhile, Joe Chapman and his gang of sixteen men were sealed a mile inside the belly of Turtle Mountain. The avalanche instantly bludgeoned to death four hapless miners working at the mouth of the tunnel, and plugged up the mine entrance with one hundred feet of solid limestone. To make matters even more grim, the slide had dammed up the Old Man River, and the backing waters threatened to drown the seventeen trapped miners. Working furiously in fifteen-minute shifts, rescue crews took turns at dynamiting away rock to release the river and to penetrate the walled-up tunnel. They kept working all day long for thirteen hours, more from stubbornness than hope.

Inside the coal mine, Joe Chapman and Halfpint Jones kept cool. "I felt the concussion of the explosion very severe," Chapman later testified. "The blast of hot air struck me, and picked me up, and threw me into the manway. But we didn't lose our heads."

Amid the buckling timbers and the choking coal dust, Chapman gathered his men together. When he found the front entrance hopelessly blocked, and water creeping up the lower level, he led his men in a "shouting and pounding party" beside the upper air shaft. The gang pounded on rails and sang "Onward Christian Soldiers"; and Halfpint Jones, "since he was the smallest man in the crowd", volunteered to be shoved upward through the rocks to holler for help. His call brought only an eerie echo.

"The air was beginning to get foul," Chapman later said. "And twenty-four hours would fetch the seeping water into our cutting. So we decided we must make haste to do something. Anything."

What he decided to do was to have the gang hack a fresh tunnel upward through thirty-six feet of soft coal. At 5 P.M. they finally dug their way through to the light.

109

First to be lifted out was William Warrington, strapped to a plank because he had fractured his leg in the heaving tunnel. He gazed in disbelief at the valley of destruction, and then gave a sob of anguish. All that was left of his wife and seven children was the graveyard of limestone, and the forlorn line of diapers flapping in the wind.

> The night shift was comin' out of the mine,
> They found their exit fouled.
> Should have known that something was very wrong
> For a dog that was with them howled.
> Set right up and howled and howled
> There in the shiverin' mornin'.
>
> The boys went down with many a tear
> For their wives and children amournin',
> And not a one who came out of the mine
> Had a bite of breakfast that mornin'.
> Had a bite of breakfast to eat, to eat
> There in the shiverin' mornin'.

Perhaps most poignant was the story of what happened to Old Charlie, the pit horse. Chapman and Halfpint Jones and the others had to leave him behind in the main shaft. It was twenty-nine days before they were able to clear the rubble in the original mine entrance. They found Old Charlie gaunt and spindly but still alive. He had survived by gnawing bark from the pit props and licking water from the seepage.

The rescuers jubilantly fed the weak creature a few drops of brandy and some oats. Then the party left in search of blankets to keep the horse warm, since he was too feeble to be lifted. As they walked away, Old Charlie lifted his head and neighed faintly, and then sank back. When the crew returned ten minutes later, he was dead.

Halfpint Jones always said, "I'll never forget the pitiful look of entreaty in that horse's eyes. I tell you, Old Charlie died of a broken heart. He thought we were forsaking him, and leaving him all alone in the mine once again."

Not so touching was the immediate reaction of many Frank townspeople the night after the avalanche had passed.

110

Some, to be sure, behaved admirably. The town's two doctors patched up the wounded in the Mountie detachment's office, which was converted into a hospital. In the school-house, which served as a morgue, the town's three ministers preached that the disaster was a lesson to remind people of earthly futility. The resident missionary, Dr. David A. Stewart, gave comfort by quoting Shakespeare's *Macbeth* to prove the victims weren't alone in having suffered distress:

> The night had been unruly. Where we lay,
> Our chimneys were blown down, and, as they say,
> Lamentings heard i' the air, strange screams of death,
> And prophesying with accents terrible
> Of dire combustion and confused events
> New-hatched to the woeful time. . . .
>   Some say the earth
> Was feverous and did shake.

Most of the miners, though, went on a gigantic binge. As one saloon merry-maker rationalized, "Let's have a good time while we're on earth, since this earthquake shows we won't be here much longer." Their "obscene revelry" was condemned in searing editorials that appeared in the next issue of Mark Drumm's *Sentinel*. Grotesquely, the same newspaper ran a grocery ad on the front page, and the store owner's name in the list of the dead.

An attempt to gloss over the miners' spree was made by the town's Presbyterian minister, Rev. Donald G. McPhail. In a dispatch to the Toronto *Globe*, he merely said, "The foreign element, more superstitious, have nearly all packed their belongings and gone to Blairmore. But dozens of finer spirits have been at work all day, rescuing all who could possibly be reached, and lamenting over their fellow citizens who sleep 'the sleep that knows no waking'."

The Prime Minister, Sir Wilfrid Laurier, heard about the miners' boozy hijinks in delayed fashion. He first read aloud to a hushed House of Commons a personal wire sent to him by S. W. Chambers, president of the Frank board of trade: "Terrible catastrophe here. One hundred killed. Must have government aid. Reply quick."

The wire that Sir Wilfrid read aloud the next day was not received in so reverent a fashion. It was from William Pearce, Inspector of Surveys for the Northwest Territories, who had been rushed to Frank on behalf of the Ministry of the Interior. "Place very orderly this morning," his wire read. "Men that were drunk and disorderly yesterday in lockup. Twelve Mounted Police and two officers here. Plenty to maintain peace and order. Pack trail is being built around slide-covered railway tracks. Stage-coach wagon road is needed."

Indeed, a stage-coach road was needed for the reporters, extra doctors, and mine inspectors, as well as for the battalions of Mounties hurried to the scene by Mountie Superintendent Col. P. C. H. Primrose. A rather plaintive note was sounded by the Calgary *Herald's* impeccably attired correspondent:

> To traverse two miles of boulders, some bigger than a railway coach, tossed into piles and ravines, is a task that tries a strong man well shod. For people with thin shoes, unaccustomed to mountains, the trip is almost suicide. I had a suit of clothes ruined by the white lime. My boots were cut to pieces, and my physical system is a wreck that calls for at least a week's recuperation. Editor, please note.

The first man to cross the jagged gauntlet of the landslide to Frank was a mail clerk on the Crow's Nest Pass Railway, David Bayne. Now eighty-six and living in Medicine Hat, Bayne recalls: "I scrambled across the rocks with the train brakeman, Ernie Charboneau. I thought to myself then, 'Even a mountain goat would have a tough time making *this* crossing!' I noticed an immense boulder, lying right on the main street, when I got to Frank. I asked a responsible-looking man, the postmaster, 'What do you estimate would be that rock's weight?' He sized it and drawled, 'Oh, about five hundred tons.'"

Other survivors today recall the good deeds done by the townsfolk. Adelaide Weese, now of Lumsden, Saskatchewan, whose uncle died in the avalanche, remembers the surgical skill of the Frank physician, Dr. George Malcomson. Without a hospital, the good doctor curtained off the four rooms of his cabin, and worked night and day, assisted by his wife and a medical student named McKenzie, performing miracles of surgery. After Dr. Malcomson saved the life of the pincushioned orphan, Lester Johnsen, recalls Adelaide Weese, "the lad was adopted by a couple in Fernie, British Columbia".

George Bolduc, now of Wanham, Alberta, was then a six-year-old boy. His father, David Bolduc, was moving the family from Fernie to Lille, and they were spending the night in the Frank Hotel. "I can remember our bedroom window was open," George Bolduc recalls, "and it was chilly, and at the roar of the avalanche I was crying. But the hotel was saved, and the kind local folks helped us to move."

One of the kindest local citizens was a French-Canadian pioneer from Peterborough, Ontario, named Henri Villan. He is singled out by Mrs. Inez Hosie, now of Regina, Saskatchewan, whose parents, Mr. and Mrs. William Connors, were then pioneers in Blairmore. That morning, her mother was awakened by "what she thought was a heavy clap of thunder. She felt the house shake, and got up, and looked out the window, but everything was calm. She was astonished when the foreman of the McLarens Mill called at seven o'clock that morning and said, 'Frank is buried.' She never forgot Henri Villan, who went around to take up a collection for those saved, headed the list himself with a big donation, and divided the money among the stricken. Through his good deed, he earned the title of 'Big-Hearted Villan'."

On his arrival on the scene, the Premier of the Territories, Sir Frederick Haultain, ordered geologists to crawl up the side of Turtle Mountain. They found enormous, newly formed cracks, and warned that the mountain would erupt into death once more.

Whereupon, Sir Frederick immediately ordered compulsory evacuation of the whole town of Frank to neighbouring Blairmore. Storekeepers simply locked their doors and left.

"Other families made short work of packing their belongings into wagons and on to the back of mules," reported a Toronto *Star* correspondent of the mass exodus. "One man was seen vainly trying to navigate the street under a burden of many lengths of stove-pipe. In another quarter, a family in a hurry to place danger behind them, carried a hot kitchen stove from which the smoke sputtered in little gusts. By Saturday, Frank was a deserted village, its inhabitants fled as though from Mount Pompeii."

For nine days, a careful watch was kept. The CPR's Chief Engineer, A. McHenry, kept peering at Old Turtle through his binoculars.

113

The Turtle showed no signs of moving, and so Premier Haultain allowed the citizens of Frank to return.

But it was the beginning of the end for Frank. Work was resumed in the coal mine, but minor slides kept hurtling down, and in 1905 two fires broke out in the mine pits. The mine was closed down permanently in 1908 with the death of its founder, H. L. Frank. The destruction wreaked by the avalanche kept preying on his imagination. The Montana visionary passed his last days in a mental hospital, with ghostly memories haunting the ruined corridors of his mind.

What was left of the old town was moved up the valley to the present site of Frank, a huddle of two hundred hard-core citizens clinging to the eastern edge of Blairmore. The ugly scar on the top of Turtle Mountain still stays, and so does the fantastic chaos of rock littered in the valley below.

It took four thousand Japanese labourers a month, working twenty-four hours a day, to rebuild the shattered railroad, cutting through rock piled to three times train height. A steam-shovel mounted on a railroad car was placed permanently on a side track — first to pull additional boulders off the rails as they kept tumbling down; later, to load trains with ballast from the fallen mountain. Rock-fills from Moose Jaw to the Kicking Horse Pass now are heaped with Frank limestone; but more than half a century of digging has left no visible hole in the seemingly bottomless pile.

Indeed, the rock pile still grips the imagination of local Albertans in curious ways. Ken. E. Liddell, the Calgary *Herald* historian, smiles over the story recited to him by the veteran CPR agent at Hillcrest, H. Harrison. A woman passenger, who had lived at Blairmore at the time of the Frank Slide, was on her way back for a visit. As the train whistled its way over the ocean of rocks, she glanced out the window, and turned to the conductor in amazement. "My goodness," she said. "Haven't they got that mess cleaned up yet?"

The hoary folk-lore grown up around the avalanche is perpetuated by the Turtle Mountain Hotel and Playgrounds Motel, built on rock a half mile west of the Frank Slide on No. 3 Highway, complete with a "glamorous heated swimming pool". In the interests of the tourist trade, it issues to its guests powder-blue pamphlets that spin out the legends about the disaster.

114

One sentimental yarn that the motel nurtures is about Sid Choquette, the CPR brakeman who flagged down the Flyer. In gratitude, the pamphlet claims, "the passengers presented the hero with a solid gold watch, suitably engraved, and the railway company promised him a position for life."

This Dick Whittington myth was spoiled by the Lethbridge *Herald*, which put together a half-century anniversary issue commemorating the Frank Slide survivors. The newspaper printed a letter from Mrs. Choquette, then in Chicago, who said the gold watch and lifetime job were pure moonshine. All that her husband received from the CPR was a twenty-five-dollar cheque and a letter of recommendation, and Sid was still labouring mighty hard with the Illinois Central Railroad.

Another pretty fable persists about the Frank Slide's "buried treasure" of $500,000 in cash. In vain, bank manager Farmer tried to convince people that the branch of the Union Bank — like all the other places of business in Frank — escaped destruction. The so-called buried bank was a frame shack where the mine manager, Sam Gebo, sometimes paid his men. But the fact was, Gebo reported, not a silver dollar was in the till when the mountain tumbled.

The hardiest of all the tall tales paints a pathetic picture of a baby being the sole survivor of the avalanche. This hoax was nationally circulated by the CBC in a radio play broadcast in 1949, "The Ballad of the Frank Slide". It was written by Robert E. Gard, a teacher conducting research on Alberta folk-lore at the University of Alberta on a Rockefeller grant. Gard knew he was embellishing a myth when he christened this shivering orphan baby "Frankie Slide"; but it was all so dramatically charming. To consolidate the charm, he wrote the lyrics for a ballad about the baby, with music by CBC conductor Lucio Agostini; and the plaintive lay was sung during the performance of the radio play by the Canadian folk singer, Ed McCurdy.

This fable, with its awakening of old memories, is not cherished by the real survivors after whom it is patterned. The baby who was cradled sleeping between her mother and father, Gladys Ennis, is now Mrs. Emil Verquin of Bellevue, Washington, and refuses even to talk about the disaster. Her mother, Mrs. Sam Ennis, is since remarried as Mrs. Enoch Williams of Duncan, British Columbia; she is a spectacled, grey-haired woman, and is voluble about debunking the Frank Slide legends.

"I wouldn't give you a penny for the life of anyone now living at the foot of Old Turtle," says the former Mrs. Sam Ennis. "But sometimes I wish nobody would mention it again. I hear all these stories — and the people telling them either were three years old then or twenty miles away. Why, I've even had to sit and listen while somebody talked about the 'only survivor' — a baby found on a bale of hay. I sit there and wonder, 'Only survivor? Well, then, where in the world was I?'"

But her pique does not compare with the indignation of the baby, Marion Leitch, who was discovered lying on that bale of hay amid the slide. She is today a pleasant, red-haired matron, Mrs. Lawrence Mc-Phail, living with her husband and teen-aged daughter in Nelson, British Columbia. Recently a magazine reporter knocked on her door and asked her about the Frank Slide.

"That thing again!" exclaimed the former baby. "Won't it ever stop? All my life, people have been looking at me as if I belonged in a zoo, just because of what happened to our family. Have you heard the song? It's a mountain ballad of the worst sort. About 'Frankie Slide', the poor little baby who never knew her own name. Leitch is a good Scottish name, and I've known it was mine all my life.

"Of course, I don't remember anything about the slide. I was a baby then — and I'm not a hundred years old now, though most people seem to expect me to be. Whenever they put that horrid song on the radio, people start ringing my phone. Come inside now. I want to put on my shoes. I can't get mad properly with my shoes off!"

Yet for all her wrath, people today will undoubtedly continue to stare at the awesome stretch of rocks in the valley of Turtle Mountain, and remember the charming "Ballad of the Frank Slide":

> On a grim and tragic mornin'
> In nineteen-hundred three
> A little babe lay weepin'
> A pitiful sight to see.
> A pitiful sight was she, was she
> As she lay in the shiverin' mornin'.

116

Around the babe was a sea o' stones
A million ton or more.
They'd slid right off the mountain top
With a horrifyin' roar.
With a horrifyin' roar they tore
Into the shiverin' mornin'.

The baby girl that lay on the rock
'Twas a wonder she never died.
There was only one thing the folks could do.
They named her Frankie Slide.
They named her Frankie Slide, they did
There in the shiverin' mornin'.

And when she grew to a maiden fair
She knew that she'd someday abide
Along somewhere in the Crow's Nest Pass
Where they tell of the Great Frank Slide.
They tell of the great Frank Slide, they do
There in the shiverin' mornin'.

_6_

Trapped in the Springhill Coal Mine

A RAW, CHILL DRIZZLE WAS SPITTING MOURN-
fully on the pit head of North America's deepest coal mine
at Springhill, Nova Scotia, on the evening of November 6,
1958. It was then the draegermen carried up into the wash
of yellow light the last body. Fidele Allen was the last of the 174
miners who had been trapped two weeks ago more than two miles
down in the guts of the convulsive earth.

Fidele Allen was not one of the lucky ninety-nine who survived.
These had been entombed in blackness for as long as nine days. Many
of them ate bark, sucked coal, and drank their own urine; they ex-
changed wisecracks and they prayed, until they were brought up, like
Lazarus, alive from the grave.

Fidele Allen was one of the unlucky seventy-five who died. Some
of these were killed immediately, when the air-pressure-triggered earthquake that miners call a bump rumbled through Cumberland's No. 2
shaft; it ripped the roof, crumbled timbers, and crushed men like ants.
Others died slowly, gripped between rocks, choking on blue methane
gas; wearing their fingers to stumps as they futilely tried to claw
through their stone coffin.

However he died, Fidele Allen was the last coal miner brought
up during Springhill's fourteen days of death. His widow Sadie, a good-
looking brunette of forty, had sat all that time on a hard kitchen chair
in the lamp tent beside the pit head, a red kerchief wrapped about

118

her black hair. Like the other widows, she didn't cry, barely ate, just waited.

Now Sadie's vigil was over. They showed her the body of Fidele Allen to identify, and she readily did so, though his bony French-Canadian face was crusted with coal dust and his lips were puffed. Dry-eyed, still not displaying her grief, Sadie and her four children had him buried that week in the cemetery of Springhill. She buried him in a jinxed town of seven thousand souls, amid the red Cobequid Hills of north-western Nova Scotia, which might be described as a main street with a cemetery at one end and a mine at the other.

Midway between these two points, Fidele Allen's funeral cortège passed the Coal Miners' Memorial. It is a twenty-foot granite shaft that supports the white marble figure of a miner. A cap on his head and holding a pick, he bears a safety lamp at his belt. The inscription on the base commemorates the 125 Springhill miners who died during the first explosion in Cumberland's No. 1 shaft, on February 21, 1891.

Since then, Cumberland has suffered 453 bumps. They took more than six hundred lives, an average death toll of at least six men a year. That does not include the gas explosion that blasted Cumberland's No. 4 colliery at supper-time on November 1, 1956, which killed thirty-nine miners, and allowed eighty-eight to be rescued after being buried alive for three and a half days.

The rescues that occurred during Springhill's fourteen days of death after its 1958 bump, however, were far more spectacular. And the full story of this epic is yet to be told. It is a story of international repercussions, which besides gripping Canada for two weeks, held in its embrace such disparate personalities as Prince Philip of England and the newly elected Pope John XXIII; Ed Sullivan of American TV, and a blonde singer of Canadian TV named Juliette; a clownish segregationist, Governor Marvin Griffin of Georgia, and a highly unclownish Canadian wrestler named Whipper Billy Watson.

The most grotesque thing about this most grotesque of Cnadian mine disasters was that everybody had expected it to happen. After the 1956 explosion — when the Cumberland Railway and Coal Company had sealed No. 4 colliery, with its twenty-six corpses still entombed at the 4,400-foot level — the company said it was going to close up the entire mine. It was too risky on lives; besides, the company was losing $400,000 a year on the operation.

But the remaining nine hundred miners of Springhill actually petitioned the company to keep the mine going. In the winter of 1957, the town council, too, implored the company not to shut down, for a $1.5 million fire had swept through the heart of the town that Christmas, ravaging practically all its Main Street shops and smaller industries.

"You can't ring the death knell on this mining town," pleaded Mayor Ralph Gilroy. "It may be a hard-luck town, but it's ours, and we don't want it another Nova Scotia ghost town."

Reluctantly, the company renewed operations in the deepest colliery of all — No. 2 shaft. With the curious fatalism of all Springhill miners, the men continued to descend the pit. They rode the "rake cars" at a forty-five-degree slope down into the bowels of the earth. They rode until they reached the labyrinth of gassy tunnels below — to a pick-and-shovel working level of 13,000 feet . . . 13,400 feet . . . and the very bottom level of 13,800 feet.

Their defiance of exploding gas and bumps was understood even by the fifty-eight widows (left with 169 orphans) as a result of Springhill's 1956 calamity. One of these was Norah Ferguson. She is a widow with pale, resigned eyes and a laughterless face. When her husband, Bill Ferguson, was asphyxiated at the one-thousand-foot level in 1956, he left her with two step-children. Bill was the second husband she had lost in the Springhill mine in twelve years. Yet she understood.

"You come to expect it," Norah Ferguson explained. "It's the only life we know. It's an awful price to pay for coal. But risk is in the book for us. Why do our men stick to mining? Suppose you had been raised in the mining business, and you lived mining, and ate mining, and slept mining, from the time you were a child. You'd still keep going back to it, no matter what the danger."

This attitude toward danger is common to the miners and their families who have lived for years in their small, dingy town huddled on Monument Hill. They are a clannish people, prone to intermarry (the tiny section of the telephone directory devoted to Springhill lists no fewer than eighteen McLeods and twenty-four MacDonalds and McDonalds); and they regard other trades as far more hazardous. Seven months after their own last disaster, in June, 1959, a raging storm off New Brunswick's Northumberland Strait battered thirty-five fishermen to death. The Springhill Canadian Legion immediately pitched in and collected two tons of canned goods and flour, which the miners sent to the fisherman's widows in Escuminac, New Brunswick. *"I'd never be a fisherman,"* said one Springhill miner. "It's too blooming dangerous, trusting yourself to the sea."

Indeed, the miners have for their vocation a kind of amused affection, blatantly displayed in the face of skeptics. They tell the story of the Springhiller who'd lost his father and his grandfather in mine catastrophes. A city slicker from Toronto found it incredible that the miner continued to risk his own life, in view of this family record. So the Springhiller finally challenged the city man, "What happened to *your* grandfather?"

"Well, he took sick one day," replied the nonplussed Torontonian, "and died several months later in bed."

"And is your father still alive?" asked the miner.

"No," answered the city slicker. "He went sick, too, one day, and died in bed a couple of weeks after."

"And you mean to say," exclaimed the Springhiller in mock horror, "that you still sleep in a *bed* after all that danger?"

This compulsion to laugh off peril while plumbing the womb of the earth for bituminous coal has sustained Springhillers ever since their sprawling hill town in Cumberland County was first settled in 1790. The Springhill miners — mostly of French, Scottish, Irish and English descent — organized Nova Scotia's first mine union in 1874. They began to improve their lot after the big bump of February 21, 1891. They refused to accept the gratuitous advice offered them in a book written about that catastrophe, *Story of the Great Disaster at Springhill Mines.* The author, R. A. H. Morrow, suggested that the bereaved "submit to the Divine Will". He cited the lament of Jacob in the Bible, "Me have ye bereaved of my children: Joseph is not, and Simeon is not, and ye will take Benjamin away: all these things are against me"; and he offered this recipe for resignation to death: "God lives — bless'd be my Rock."

Instead, the miners campaigned for more cash. Ultimately, by 1958, they were receiving a basic rate of thirteen dollars a day. The pay for one year's work fluctuated from $2,500 to $3,500; and their company pension (non-contributory) was as low as eighteen dollars and as high as seventy-five dollars a month. Seven out of ten of them owned their own home, and had a car at the front door. Their little town had a movie house, and the young people enjoyed country dancing and singing of cowboy songs in the local social halls. And the men who had managed to survive the bumps sat in the small lobby of the Carleton Hotel, and smoked their pipes, and talked quietly of the mysterious spell that drew them, and had drawn their forefathers, into the oyster-coloured clay catacombs.

"On top," explained Gorley Kempt, a small, sinewy miner with big hands, "I miss the *camaraderie* that we have in the pits — no jealousies, no rank down there. We are dependent on each other. In a crisis, a man's first impulse is to help a buddy — even if it means a fifty-fifty chance of getting hurt himself."

An official of the Cumberland Railway and Coal Company didn't try to negate the hazards of the trade that were so common to all Nova Scotia mines. "At Pictou, they have gassy coal that keeps breaking into flame," he said. "At Sydney, they take extra precautions because they go under the ocean. Coal mining is never easy. The men know it. We all know it. There is constant risk that a coal mine may be a graveyard for the young men who die to keep it going."

The smell of danger did not seem to hover in the crisp air on Thursday, October 23, 1958, when the coal miners of Springhill prepared for their 3-11 P.M. shift. In contrast to the cold, pelting rain that was to follow almost unabated for the next fourteen days, it was a cloudless Indian-summer afternoon.

Some of the men grumbled about having to go down into the pits on such a nice sunny day, as they changed into their mining clothes at the wash-house (nicknamed the "pest house"). They slipped into their mining shirts, overalls, plastic helmets and steel-toed safety boots; and since it would be hot below, they wore no underwear. Then they went to the lamp cabin, where each miner received a locked safety lamp containing a freshly charged battery that would supply light for ten hours. After filling their water cans to their quart-and-a-half capacity, all the men found a seat in the eight cable-operated rake trolleys. These would carry them down the long slope to the continent's deepest coal mine.

It was so summery out that Gorley Kempt went on the job licking a vanilla ice-cream cone. Earlier, at eight o'clock, his wife Marguerite, a tiny, sparrow-like woman of thirty-three, had aroused him from bed. She worked as a receptionist at All Saints' Hospital. Afraid of being late, she asked, "Will you drive me to work this morning, Gorley?"

Gorley, who had arrived home from his late shift after midnight, drowsily muttered, "I'm too tired."

"He was deep in the bedclothes," Marguerite later recalled. "All you could see was his little bald patch."

Gorley had finally got up at nearly eleven o'clock, and prepared lunch for his two teen-age children, Betty and Billy, who were at Springhill High School. They enjoyed his succulent dish — macaroni, ground steak, onions, canned tomato soup, and seasoning — and Gorley did the dishes and tidied up the house before he left for his shift. When his wife returned home that evening, and mopped up his spilled tea and sticky footprints, she muttered fondly to herself, "That man makes more work than a kid!"

As for Gorley, he bought his vanilla ice-cream cone at Joey Tabor's grocery store; and at the wash-house, before descending into the earth, he said to his miner buddy, Wesley Reynolds, "See you later, Wes."

"Yeah, see you," said Reynolds, as he descended to his level, with his compressed-air-driven chipper pick. He felt no shadow from his fate, which would leave him dead in five hours.

Just a few of the descending men brooded over the report that a miner had been injured from a minor bump the day before.

"I got up at nine today, and I felt shaky all morning," observed Henry Dykens, a grizzled, toothless miner of fifty, as he descended the slope down to the 13,800 foot level. "I don't know why, but I'm still shaky now."

He later remembered that Stanley Henwood, beside him in the tunnel, shook his head morosely and predicted, "All I can say is this place is due for a real good bump."

123

Most of the other men were thinking of more prosaic things, like the prospect of going deer-hunting that week-end in the Cobequid Hills, or their wives, or their children.

Before going on their shift, many of the miners had been watching television. Some were waiting to see the results of the music festival telecast on Moncton, New Brunswick's CKCW-TV, in which singing high-school children from Springhill participated. Others were watching an old Bowery Boys movie on TV.

The movie had still about fifteen minutes to go when Tom Marshall, a gray-haired chap, with three small children, left for the mine. "Watch it," he instructed his wife, "so's you can tell me how it turns out." He never did discover what happened to the Bowery Boys.

Maurice Ruddick, a black-moustached mulatto of forty-six, who loved to strum the guitar, slipped down to the thirteen-thousand-foot level while singing in a lusty baritone, "The Shiek of Araby". Maurice was cheerfully thinking of his newest baby daughter. She was just seven days old, Katreena May. He nicknamed her Ktinka, and kissed her good-bye as he left the diaper-hung kitchen of his nine-roomed frame house on Herrett Road, with his twelve children inside and his shiny 1955 Meteor outside. His wife Norma had returned from the maternity ward of All Saints' Hospital last Sunday, and was lying weak in bed. While packing his lunch can with bread, honey and cake, Maurice had tried to cheer her up.

"I know you, sweetie," he had joked. "You want another baby because you're after an extra six-dollar-a-month government baby bonus, to add to my sixty-buck-a-week pay cheque."

An equally merry miner, Bowman ("Bowsie") Maddison, forty-two, father of a three-month-old baby boy named Constantinos, sank down to the thirteen-thousand-foot level with a love song on his lips. On his way to the three-to-eleven shift, Bowsie had dropped over to the Main Street post-box to mail Juliette, the TV singer in Toronto, a song he'd written. It was entitled, "Dearest, My Heart Is Calling". He kissed the letter for good luck before slipping it into the mail-box, since he had begged her to sing it on her Saturday-night TV show. As Bowsie hacked away at the greasy seam of coal that long afternoon, he kept softly singing over and over the lyrics of his ballad, dreaming of the fortune it might make him:

Think of the years since we parted,
Feeling so lonely and blue!
Why should I be broken-hearted,
When I love only you. . . .

At 8:06 P.M., all thoughts of the morning shakes, or the Bowery Boys, or a seven-day-old baby named Ktinka, or a romance so lonely and blue, were shattered in the most devastating subterranean earthquake ever to rock the town of Springhill. It was, in fact so recorded on the Dalhousie University seismograph in Halifax, over one hundred miles away.

It was as though the earth itself had suffered a hotfoot and shrugged its shoulders in pain. A surge of hot air squeezed hard on all the seven-foot-high tunnels miles below. With a thunderous roar, the blast heaved up the earth, buckled timbers, caved in roofs like accordions. Miners were catapulted up in the air, some of them decapitating themselves with their own picks, to fall back headless in a black sea of coal dust.

The shock of the earth's inner turmoil spread for miles across the Cobequid Hills. A woman in Joggins, a colliery town thirty miles away, felt her house tremble. The impact split Springhill's water tower, two miles from the mine. Its force knocked a cigarette out of the mouth of nineteen-year-old Gary Embree, who was waiting for his dad, Buck Embree, to come home from the mine's late shift.

A miner lucky to be at the surface of No. 2 shaft, Jack Harrison, vividly described the concussion. "I was so shocked, my mouth went dry, and I was frozen stiff. There was a big swoosh of air from the shaft entrance. Then I could hear a series of belches down inside the mine. Like some big dragon was crawling up through the earth. Like a freight train in trouble."

The townspeople of Springhill, some of them jolted out of their chairs by the impact, poured out onto the streets and ran up the hill to the mine. Mayor Ralph Gilroy, in the midst of a town-council meeting, banged his gavel as soon as he felt the jolt, and cried out, "Council adjourned!"

Women, wearing kerchiefs and wrapped in grey blankets, took up a fearful vigil by the pit head. Electricians strung lines of emergency

125

lights that cast a misty yellow glow on the crowd. Two thousand watchers soon gathered there, held back from the shaft by ropes, and shivering in the twenty-degree cold, the pelting rain, and the slashing wind.

Even before the earth had stopped shaking, the company's own crew of twenty rescue draegermen were racing toward the pit head. Within fifteen minutes, company officials were phoning to have extra draegermen flown to the scene from mines in Pictou County and Cape Breton Island. The voice of the company's general manager, Harold Gordon, a grey-haired, fifty-nine-year-old mining expert, shook with emotion as he watched the draegermen go into action: "The energy they're putting in is amazing."

The draegermen — so named because of the German-made, forty-five-pound oxygen equipment, the invention of Alexander Bernhard Draeger, that was fastened on their backs — worked with a kind of steady fury. Down the slope they went, steel-helmeted, like a row of grey mushrooms. The tunnels were so packed with tons of debris that the units of five draegermen, linked together by a rope, had to crawl along on their bellies like burrowing moles, inch by agonizing inch. They barely had room enough to dig with small spades. They'd pull out the rubble, drag in timbers, then painstakingly shore up the area they'd just dug out.

The draegermen could only blink in distress as they would ferret out the corpse of an old friend, buried up to his neck. More alarming to them was the possibility of choking on the poisonous methane gas, for their oxygen respirators would last just two hours at a time. After the gas had escaped from a cavern through the passage cleared by the draegermen, the latter were followed by the barefaced rescuers, pluckily groping in the choking coal dust without oxygen masks.

"I saw one body without its head," gasped one barefaced rescuer, Joe Tabor, as he crawled out flat on his stomach. "Another was without arms. I saw a leg cut off and lying in the fallen rocks, like a doll's. But I'm going back in, as soon as I get rid of these clothes with the terrible stink of death clinging to 'em. I'm going back, because I got two brothers trapped in there somewhere."

126

Among the first survivors rescued was Henry Dykens, the miner at the 13,400-foot level, who'd had a queasy premonition of disaster that morning. He'd been working on the coal face with his old friend, husky, forty-four-year-old Tommy McManaman, when the roof and the floor slammed together.

"All of a sudden there was a roar like a cannon going off," Henry said. "The next thing I knew, I was buried up to my nose, smothering in coal."

Tommy was similarly exhumed from a mound of debris. "I started wriggling and pushing the coal, until I clawed myself free with my bare hands," Tommy said. "Then I spotted Hank buried just as deep as I'd been. So I dug him out of his grave, too."

Both men staggered along the tunnel, until they stumbled on another miner, Keith Cummings, buried up to his waist.

"We had no time to waste," Tommy later said. "We were forced to yank Cummings' broken leg out in a hurry. Then we carried him along fast, because the gas was starting to seep in awful fast."

After rescuers carried them up to the makeshift hospital set up by the Red Cross in the Springhill Armories, Tommy, with a fractured knee-cap, looked up from his bed to his old friend. "Well," he sighed, "we made it, Hank."

Henry Dykens turned his head. Weakly he managed a toothless grin through a gashed and coal blackened face.

"All I can say is I told you so," Henry said. "I had that old shaky feeling, as soon as I got out of bed this morning."

Other early survivors in the emergency hospital were able to recite unusual stories.

"I was sitting down eating my lunch," said Archie Legere, rescued from the 13,800-foot level. "I had just taken a bite out of a cheese sandwich. Then I found myself flying up to the roof like a birdie. Next thing, I was crawling on my hands and knees."

"Rocks the size of my head were hurtling by me. But what I really got mad about was losing my teeth," lamented Bill Totten. "I'd saved and saved and just got the new set three months ago. But the shock of the bump knocked them clean out of my mouth. And I ain't seen them since."

When dawn broke on Friday, the throng at the pit head was swollen by more than two hundred reporters, photographers, and TV cameramen. The Salvation Army had set up tents in the bleak, swirling mist near the shaft, and the draegermen paused in their around-the-clock shift to gulp cups of hot cocoa. Prime Minister John Diefenbaker had declared it a "national disaster", and Queen Elizabeth in England had requested Governor-General Vincent Massey to "keep me informed" of the unfolding drama of the rescue.

The spotlight was chiefly focused on the mine's tag-board. It was the program of this grim stage play. As each miner was carried to the surface, his numbered brass tag was removed from the wooden board. The gesture showed he was alive.

By noon that Friday, eighty-one "live" tags had been removed from the board. Day passed into night, and the draegermen brought up into the melancholy rain only the bodies of the dead. After spending eight hours below ground himself, General Manager Harold Gordon offered only "the vaguest glimmer of hope" that any miner might yet be found alive. With tears in his eyes and his voice breaking, he announced to reporters in even stronger language: "I regret very much, but I consider there is no hope for any man."

The only ones who refused to give up hope were the wives and the draegermen. The wives took turns sitting on a hard bench in the lamp tent. One of them brought a baby carriage, filled with bottles of milk and doughnuts, so she would not have to move away from her waiting-post. As Saturday, Sunday, Monday and Tuesday passed, they talked in low voices to each other, bolstering their dimming courage.

Mrs. Gorley Kempt said, "Everybody's saying Gorley is dead. I know differently. I keep the light burning all night in the house, and the fire going, and a pot of coffee on the stove. I keep thinking of the things we'll do when he comes home. Don't seem right to turn off the lights when you're expecting your man to come home."

Mrs. Hugh Guthro said, "I'd just finished my wash when the bump hit. It just felt like it lifted the house. I screamed and ran to the mine. I knew the worst had happened — my Hugh was trapped. But I know he'll come back. And when he does, I'd rather starve than see him go back down there."

Mrs. Levi Milley said, "I know I'll never make Levi's lunch pail again for him to go back to that mine — except to leave his lamp. He's worked there nearly thirty years, and that's long enough. I don't care what he does. Clean the streets maybe. But I'll even hold him back with a team of horses, if he tries to go back, after he's come home."

Mrs. Clyde Corkum said, "Clyde, he always honked his car horn at about a quarter to twelve when he drove into the yard. I would be sleeping lightly, and I'd jump up and welcome him. And we'd have tea and chat a while about our three kiddies."

But Mrs. Corkum was one whose vigil was in vain. They finally had to tell her that her husband's body had been located, and someone drove his car back to his cottage, and handed his widow his street clothes and personal effects. Cradling her six-year-old Cherry in her arms, she said, "I sit and pray. I can't give in — if I break down and cry now, my kiddies will cry, too."

Even the miners' children took it stoically. On Tuesday, a toddler of four was found by the mine's security officials ambling about the St. John Ambulance tent by the Armories, where doctors, with thick gauze masks and rubber gloves, were trying to piece together the dismembered corpses.

"Where are you going?" a policeman asked the child.

"I'm looking for my father. He's in the mine, and he hasn't been found for a long time."

The policeman found some candy for the child, and told him he'd take him back home.

"No, I don't want to go home," the child said solemnly. "They're all crying there at home."

On the sixth day, Wednesday, newspapermen had given up hope for the sixty-nine men still entombed. They began to leave for other stories, reporting how the single funeral director in town had worked through the week-end to make caskets, and seventy-two grave markers had been rushed in from New Glasgow for temporary use, until tombstones could be made.

But the draegermen, working around the clock in crews of seventy, had far from given up hope. They were led by Mine Supervisor George Calder, himself a mine worker for years. Chewing tobacco to keep the hot coal dust out of their throats, wearily kneeling, wiggling on their bellies down a yard-high, shoulder-wide passage-way, they hacked through rubble at a painful one foot per hour. They used hacksaws, chipper picks and their bare hands, and sent rock shale back through the tunnel in buckets passed from man to man.

Then, at 2 P.M., the first miracle happened. Blair Phillips, the mine's chief surveyor, was testing for gas at the thirteen-thousand-foot level. He heard a faint, muffled call sounding from the broken end of a pipe sticking from the rubble. "Men alive?" yelled Phillips through the pipe, and heard an answering croak from Gorley Kempt.

"Get us some water, you guys!" hollered Kempt. "There are twelve of us here."

There were, indeed, twelve of them there, separated from their rescuers by a sixty-foot block of solid rock. They had spent six days locked in a four-foot-high and fifty-foot-wide *cul de sac*. And it was a harrowing ordeal they had to describe, after the draegermen worked feverishly for the next twelve hours to blast out a parallel tunnel and deliver them from their sealed tomb.

Bowsie Maddison, the singing miner, who had sent his romantic ballad to Juliette, was among the entombed twelve. The blast bounced him up in the air, and landed him in the crushed tunnel. The first thing he did, when he found himself seated with the groans of dying men around him, was to pour some water on his face. He mistakenly thought that this would protect him from breathing any seepage of gas.

However, three of the present twelve had survived the 1956 disaster — Hugh Guthro, Joe Holloway, and Joe McDonald. They advised Maddison not to waste water that way. Anyhow, fresh air seemed to be entering from crevices in the wall. "Better save our lamp power, too," said Eldred Lowther. "They'll only last ten hours."

Maddison, gingerly groping in the darkness, his head bumping the jagged rocky roof, kept feeling for the man next to him — "to make sure I wasn't alone," he said later. "When I would feel he was there, I would know a human being was still with me. And it was comforting to know that both of us were still alive."

At least six corpses were strewn amid the rocks, and when Wilfred Hunter reached up, he was aghast to find a leg and entrails embedded

130

in the roof. "I looked close, and I swore it was the body of my twin brother, Frank," he said. "I withdrew my hand mighty quickly."

Gorley Kempt, acknowledged leader of the twelve, a handsome bushy-haired miner of thirty-seven, advised his buddies to form a chain of hands as they cautiously explored the cavern. He crawled over to a dead miner and took his lamp. "I felt bad to take it off him, but we used to eat together, so I knew he wouldn't mind."

Larry Leadbetter, at twenty-two the youngest of the captives, later recalled, "Gorley Kempt says, 'You'll have to go back where you was and get your water can.' I didn't want any part of where I was. But he says, 'You got to get her.' So I dusted in and got her, and dusted back."

Harold Brine, twenty-six, found a couple of stale cheese sandwiches on one body and a partly filled can of water on another. "I just figured my time wasn't up," he said. "We had a pick, an axe, and a maul, and we tore into the wall. But is was no go. It was eighty-five degrees, simmering hot, and after a while the smell of the dead was awful. We hollered — God, how we hollered! — but all we got back was our own weak, spooky echo. So then we decided we'd have to wait and stay with her."

Crouched in their low-ceiled catacomb, which wouldn't allow them to sit up straight, the men took stock. Eldred Lowther, a sober fellow of forty-six, with five children, estimated they had less than two cups of water collected from the canteens of the dead. He found a tiny aspirin bottle that held two ounces of water, and doled it around.

"That has to do us for six hours," he warned. "Just one sip apiece."

Caleb Rushton, thirty-five, a religious man who sang in the Methodist choir, later recalled, "I told my buddies I'd keep track of the time with my luminous watch. Since we had no moon or sun down in our hell, we'd scratch marks on the wall to show the days. She's pretty good, that watch of mine. Nothing stopped her. I guessed she was blessed by the same Higher Power I was sure would save us."

Hugh Guthro, thirty-one, father of two children, recalled, "That first day, we told every corny joke we'd ever heard. Nobody laughed much at the cracks, like, 'Hey, Billy boy, you won't get paid for sitting out this shift.' But the idea was to keep the conversation kind of light, and not talk about what we were really thinking — possible death."

131

They particularly tried to avoid talk about their families, since all were fathers. But Levi Milley, forty-seven, remembered, "When Caleb Rushton said it was nine in the morning, I thought, 'Well, my sixteen-year-old Judy is off to high school.' Then I remembered there probably wouldn't be any school, because of us."

Lowther recalled, "We especially didn't want to upset the two young fellows. I couldn't mention anything to young Larry Leadbetter that would remind him of his two-year-old Shirley, or he'd break out in tears. I kept thinking of my own wife, Goldie, all the time, despite myself. I kept calling the other fellows by my wife's name. When I called Caleb Rushton Goldie, he grinned and joked, 'Want to put your arms around me, dearie?'"

Milley, who raised poultry on the side, contributed a humorous note. "I've got fifty Rhode Island Reds and Barred Rocks, and you know, the thought that plagued me all the time I was down there was, 'Somebody else — the blankety blank! — has got my chickens now!'"

On the second day Bowsie Maddison, a Baptist Church choir-singer as well as a song-writer, encouraged the others to join in hymn-singing. "I got Caleb Rushton to sing a duet with me on "Stranger of Galilee" and "Abide with Me". If that didn't cheer them up, I'd sing them some of my own love ballads. It was kind of eerie, hearing them sweet tunes in that dungeon."

On Sunday, all the men began to pray aloud. "I prayed real hard," said Kempt, "and I'm not usually a praying man."

His praying caused Hugh Guthro to remember something. "It suddenly flashed on me that one of the guys had hung a carrot on the tunnel wall. It was a joke, you see, because one of the miners had the nickname of 'Bunny'. I stumbled along the wall until I found it. The others all blessed that joke as I shared the precious carrot with them."

By Tuesday, all their water was gone and their lamp batteries were exhausted, plunging them in darkness; and they finished nibbling all the stale sandwiches collected from dead miners' lunchboxes. "We always said grace after our crumbs," said the devout Bowman.

Their eyes smarted in the stale air, and they groggily scrambled around in offshoots of the cavern. They smelled gas, which was like

132

the burning of rubber, and sour sweat, and they thought they saw darting, elusive flashes of yellow light like the phosphorescent creatures that inhabit the deep sea.

"Look at that glow," said Joey Holloway. "It's almost bright in here."

"Once in a while, you stumbled into a real doozy of a pocket of gas," said Levi Milley. "You could tell, because it turned your bones clammy in the pitch blackness."

Levi Milley was no longer making jokes. When he first discovered himself trapped, he'd taken off his boots and drawled, "Well, I guess I'll stick around for a while." Now, he attempted to sing weakly to himself "O Canada" and "A Long, Long Trail A-winding".

Maddison kept brooding over whether or not he'd paid his last insurance premium and whether his wife Solange, in case of his death, would be able to get by. To ward off the agony of his thirst-swollen tongue, he started talking about odd things that came into his mind — dart-throwing, the Montreal Canadiens hockey team.

Lowther tried to talk about the magnificent baseball-playing of his ten-year-old son Bobby, and how the lad might be a champion pitcher some day. Beside him, Harold Brine hadn't moved in quite a while. Lowther reached over and touched him.

"I'm awake," said Brine. "I was thinking about a nice juicy steak."

"You shouldn't think of that," Lowther scolded. "Let's think instead about banging away at the pipes."

Lowther anxiously looked at his luminous wrist-watch, whose strap was broken but held together with a safety-pin. He murmured, "How long can we stand it?"

Teddy Michniak also had a wrist-watch, but it was not luminous. He broke the crystal and began to count the minutes by touch, and tried not to think of the flaring pain from his dislocated shoulder.

Young Leadbetter tried to stifle his sobs. "My grandfather was killed in this mine nearly thirty-five years ago," he said chokingly. "Now it's me. My two-year-old will never remember that she had a father."

Gorley Kempt kept licking his dry lips. He was sure his tongue had swollen to double its normal size, "thick and fuzzy like a wad of felt", and he kept thinking of the vanilla ice-cream cone he'd bought at Joey Tabor's grocery store on McGee Street just before the shift. Then he began wondering if it was cold above. He'd just bought anti-freeze for his car, as well as a length of rubber hose for its radiator. Incongruously, he now began to worry whether he'd ever be able to pay back the dollar and forty cents he owed to Art and Jack Hunter at Springhill Auto Supplies.

On Wednesday, hunger gnawed fiercely, and their thirst seemed unendurable. Joseph McDonald, prostrate with a broken leg and hip, recalled, "We chewed the bark which we stripped off the timbers used to shore up the roof. We moistened our throats with drops of our own urine. What else could we do? The pain from my leg was agonizing. When my leg was moved, I could hear my bones, sounding like a bag of broken glass. I kept praying, using my fingers for a rosary."

Then, at two o'clock, the indestructible Gorley Kempt crawled to a six-inch ventilator pipe jutting from the rock, and delivered his miraculously timed shout.

Incredibly, he heard the rescuer's faint, answering call coming from the other end of the pipe, sixty feet away.

"For God's sake, come and get us!" hollered Kempt.

Inside, the trapped twelve stared in dazed disbelief, and then slapped one another's backs exultantly. Outside, the shout went up, "There's life in the mine!" Mobs surged to the pit head, oblivious of the drenching rain, and the gloom was changed to a bedlam of honking horns and clanging church bells. The hard-bitten draegermen worked in a frenzy, and they wept unashamedly, tears cutting grooves through the coal dust that made odd masks of their faces.

The rescue team shoved a copper tube through the ventilator pipe, and poured down water, hot coffee, then soup. The mine physician, Dr. Arnold Burden, shouted instructions: "Take one swallow, count to five hundred, then take another."

An exchange of happy obscenities flowed through the pipe. A rescuer with a burr-tongued accent, George Scott, yelled instructions.

Harold Brine hollered back: "Take the marbles out of your mouth and talk English."

Gorley Kempt's old buddy, Gunner Reese, shouted down the pipe, "How you getting on, Gorley?"

"Pretty good," replied Kempt amiably. "How's your love life, Gunner?"

"We've got some soup," said Reese. "You guys want soup?"

Kempt, who hadn't eaten a meal since Friday, answered dryly, "It all depends. What flavour of soup is it?"

Levi Milley wisecracked, "Hurry up, you guys. I've got to get home and feed my chickens. I'm thinking of getting out of the coal business and concentrating on fowl. In fact, from now on, I'm not even going to *burn* coal."

All Maddison wanted to know was, "Tell me, was my song a hit on Juliette's TV show?" He was delighted to learn that Juliette had, indeed, received his love ballad, and was planning to plug it.

Joseph McDonald kept urging the diggers on. "I know those fellows," he said. "They'll just keep digging like madmen. Them's the babies I give thanks to — the barefaced men."

By four-thirty Thursday morning, six days and eight hours after they had been entombed, the last of the twelve survivors made the long joy-ride to the surface. Dr. Arnold Burden, who had once worked in the mines himself to earn his way through medical school, stopped filling out death certificates to warn each man inside the pit head, "Protect your eyes from the surface light."

But the men needed no protection as they were dragged by wire-mesh stretchers, like supermarket shopping carts, toward the surface. They were in a jaunty mood. As they approached the surface, one of the suvivors asked, "What's the noise up there outside?"

"Those are people cheering you," he was told.

"Oh, that's dandy," he said. "I thought it was bill collectors waiting for us."

Gaunt from having lost ten pounds each, the men were declared amazingly fit when the ambulance took them to Springhill Hospital. When a stretcher-bearer hesitated in moving him from the ambulance,

Eldred Lowther jested, "Come on, come on! Pick me up. They didn't break my bones, and never will. Get me out of this rig. I got to go home soon!"

Milley quipped to the doctor, "Better fix me up fast. I've got to get home and feed my chickens. You wouldn't be interested in buying a couple, would you, Doc?"

And when Caleb Rushton's wife Patsy thrust her tear-stained face forward to kiss her sooty husband, Rushton said, with tender jocularity, "Get that dirt off your pan, honey, before you take a peck at me."

The only major calamity was Wilfred Hunter. He was flown by Navy helicopter to Halifax, where surgeons amputated his left leg between the hip and the knee.

His agony, though, was relieved by the electrifying news of Springhill's second miracle, that was flashed across Canada Saturday morning. Wilfred's twin brother, Frank Hunter, was not actually embedded in the roof as a corpse, as Wilfred thought he'd seen him. Instead, Frank was very much alive; he was one of seven miners entombed for nine days in another pocket at the thirteen-thousand-foot level. All of them had survived by sucking on coal for water and gnawing on the bark from the spruce pit props.

Their rescue came at 4:45 A.M. Saturday, when barefaced rescuer Vernon Barry heard "a faint scratching, like a mouse, then a moan". It was from Barney Martin, who had been pinned, face downward in a praying position, in a stone grave six feet long and three feet deep. His nostrils almost plugged with coal dust, his lips swollen like a Ubangi's, he had spent two hundred hours without any food and all alone in his stone tomb, trying to scratch his way to freedom.

When they finally rescued the forty-two-year-old involuntary recluse, his fingernails were worn down past the flesh of his fingertips, which were rubbed to a bloody pulp. He had just strength to whisper, "God must have saved this little hole for me."

The rescuers thrust through the rock-jammed tunnel seventy-five feet away from him and found six others still alive. The man responsible for keeping their spirits high was Maurice Ruddick, the jocular Negro guitar-strummer. Putting aside his own longing for his family, and especially for baby Ktinka, he had sung to his trapped comrades all those nine days.

136

It was Maurice who had thought of celebrating the twenty-ninth birthday of Garnet Clarke with an underground birthday party the previous Monday. He'd broken their last stale meat-loaf sandwich into squares, and poured their last water into equal sips in a wine-bottle cap, and led them in crooning, "Happy birthday, dear Garnet Clarke, happy birthday to you."

When the draegermen broke through to their grotto, Ruddick greeted his rescuers cheerfully: "Give me a drink of water and I'll sing you a song."

One of the men in the pocket didn't make it. Percy Rector, a fifty-five-year-old, bespectacled man, died in the depths of the earth in agony because his mates didn't have a knife. Two heavy timbers had snapped shut like a giant trap on his arm. For five days, his comrades listened in numb horror to his cries.

"Please cut my arm off, boys," he pleaded. "O, God — O, merciful heavens — take my arm and let me go!"

"Even if we thought the shock wouldn't kill you, Percy, we couldn't help you," one of them comforted him. "We have no knife."

"Fellows, forgive me for causing you this trouble," Percy would apologize. Then he would moan imploringly again, "O Lord, have mercy! Rip my arm off."

God had mercy on Tuesday when Percy Rector finally died.

The other entombed men spent the nine days dreaming. "All the time," recalled Douglas Jewkes, a wiry little man of thirty-seven, "I dreamed of drinking 7 Up. I could imagine myself falling into a whole well of 7 Up. I thought, if I ever get out of here alive, I'll buy ten cases of 7 Up, and lap it up."

Herbert Pepperdine recalled, "I kept dreaming of a quart of whisky and a big popsicle. I thought, dying of thirst would be a horrible way to go. I had a terrible despair for water. If someone had come up to me with a gallon of water and said, 'Drink this and die in ten minutes,' I'd have drained it down and wouldn't have cared."

Currie Smith said, "We crawled into holes, touching each other. I'm glad we recorded our names with chalk on the broken timbers, and that we kept calling out our names after our lamps went dead. Just to remind us we were still alive and breathing."

Even Maurice Ruddick had his moments of nagging pessimism. "I often thought four of my twelve children were so young, they'd never remember me if I went — Leah, Jesse, Iris and Ktinka. Twice I broke down and cried quietly in the darkness. Still, I made sure nobody knew. It might have broken the dam and started the others leaking and moping with the eyes."

When the men emerged from the pit head, their red-rimmed eyes shielded against the glare of the TV klieg lights, the most touching response came from Currie Smith's wife, Mabel. "I just leaned over my refrigerator at the news," she said, "and cried until I couldn't stop."

"Those lights!" muttered one survivor, blinking and staring. "They look like angels coming from heaven!"

Herbert Pepperdine's wife fainted when she saw that he was safe, and his ill, seventy-four-year-old mother said, "This is the best medicine I've ever had. He's a beautiful boy — so good to us."

When Doug Jewkes was carried out on a stretcher, his brothers, Roy and Bobby, patted him on the shoulder. Doug Jewkes said to Bobby, "My pit boots are awful heavy, boy. Would you take them off for me?"

Bobby Jewkes took off his brother's boots and flung them as far down into the mine slope as he could. "You'll never be needing those again," he vowed. (As a fitting ending to his dream of drinking 7 Up, Doug Jewkes was offered — and took — a job in the warehouse of the Toronto branch of the 7 Up Company.)

Amid the universal joy, Mayor Gilroy said, "It was as if those six men belonged to every family." And Prime Minister John Diefenbaker exclaimed, "Courage paid off!"

As the survivors recuperated at All Saints' Hospital, finally allowed to gobble turkey and heavenly 7 Up, and as the draegermen dug indefatigably for more entombed bodies, the rest of the world responded to the valiant rescue. Some were genuinely moved by the heroism, and some just wanted to jump onto the ballyhoo band wagon.

To the nearly four hundred men who risked their lives to free the seemingly doomed miners went the medal of the Royal Canadian Humane Association — the first time the award was given to a group. To the same men went a special gold medal from the Carnegie Hero Fund

Commission. It was the second instance of a group award by the Hero Commission; the other went to the heroes at the sinking of the *Titanic* in 1912.

In Rome, the first action taken by the new Pope, John XXIII, was to send five thousand dollars to stricken Springhill. From Moscow, the USSR Coal Mining Workers' Union cabled, not cash, but a message. It said the Central Committee was "deeply shaken" by the plight of the proletariat workers of Springhill, and expressed "deep sympathy" for their families.

Prince Philip of England paid a special visit to Springhill, in perhaps the most informal royal visit ever made in Canada. He was offered a cup of "real English tea" in the humble parlour of Mrs. Harold Raper, whose husband had been killed in No. 2 colliery. At the Springhill hospital, the Prince went from bed to bed with words of encouragement, and broke protocol to autograph a bold "Philip" on the plaster cast of survivor George Hayden. 'He spoke to us at our level — at the thirteen-thousand-foot level, where all men are equal," said another survivor, Harold Brine. "He wasn't like a royal prince, but like a prince of a man."

In Montreal, the general manager of the Royal Bank of Canada, K. M. Sedgewick, took charge of a nation-wide Springhill Disaster Relief Fund. A goal of one million dollars was set; and within two weeks, pledges poured in for $900,000. "It's like Christmas all over again," exulted Springhill Postmaster Doug Johnson, as six thousand letters came in daily.

To provide Christmas toys for Springhill's orphans, the town's Mayor Ralph Gilroy spoke at a $100-a plate dinner in Toronto's Lord Simcoe Hotel, with survivor Harold Brine in tow. "It's not 'Hog Town', as my people have heard," said Mayor Gilroy, when the Torontonians present raised five thousand dollars. "It's 'Heart Town'. We had no idea the so-called cold town of Toronto had such a warm heart."

Some Torontonians helped corroborate this opinion. At Toronto's East York Arena, Canada's wrestling champion, Whipper Billy Watson, paid for the privilege of grappling with the 280-pound German gorilla, Hans Herman, and thus raised an additional five thousand dollars for Springhill's tots. And a Toronto promoter campaigned to stage a teen-age dance competition, to be called "Springhill Rock".

Regrettably, not all of Toronto lived up to its shiny new reputation. Police sought thieves who blew open the safe of Grace Church-on-the-Hill and escaped with $3,500 collected for the children of Springhill. They also threw out the net for two impostors who had assumed bogus Nova Scotia accents and conned eight hundred dollars by door-to-door canvassing along Tinder Crescent in suburban North York, on the pretence that they were *bona-fide* collectors for the Springhill Disaster Fund.

Springhill also had its jarring notes. Twenty lonely bachelors wrote in, wanting to marry women so recently widowed by the catastrophe. And a couple of smooth-talking salesmen from North Carolina called upon the widows with an offer to take snapshots of them and their husbands, enlarge them into "beautifully tinted" reproductions, and place them in elaborate frames — for fifty dollars.

One of their customers was Mrs. Angus Gillis. Like the other widows, she had immediately received two hundred dollars from the mining union, two hundred dollars from the Workmen's Compensation Board to meet funeral expenses, a monthly fifty-dollar pension from the Compensation Board, and an outright grant of $1,500 from the coal company.

"I suppose I was foolish," said Mrs. Gillis. "But I just couldn't resist it, the way the photo salesmen described them. The salesmen were so soft-spoken and seemed kind of religious, if you know what I mean. They showed me a picture of the Lord, and it looked so real, you could almost reach out and touch Him."

Ed Sullivan, the TV impresario, got into the act, too. On one Sunday, he sent a wire apologizing for the "unforgivable line" delivered on his show by comedian Shecky Greene. The indiscreet joke was that a trapped miner shouldn't worry because he was buried under "soft" coal. On the next Sunday, Sullivan made amends by flying in survivors Gorley Kempt and Caleb Rushton to take a bow on his show.

On their way to the Sullivan circus in New York, in their Sunday best, the two miners met Lord Beaverbrook, English press lord and native Maritimer. "A wonderful thing," Beaverbrook said, as he shook their hands and congratulated them on their escape. Then, with the shrewd assessment of a newspaper publisher, he added, "A wonderful story."

140

The Springhill miners were less titillated by the comment of another titled gentleman from England. Sir Roy Dobson, head of the British Hawker Siddeley Group Limited, which operated the Springhill coal mine through a subsidiary, told them flatly, "I don't think the mine will ever open again."

A protest meeting was called in Springhill by Munson Harrison, local United Mine Workers president, and three hundred miners were ready to go back to work in a "safe" mine. It looked as though Springhill was destined to be a jobless ghost town — despite the offer of a Toronto "business clinic" firm to go there, for a fee, and teach Springhillers how to build new industry.

"There's lumber around Springhill," said one of the advisers, J. D. Thomas. "Anyone who made matches there, and called them 'Springhill Matches', would get over $100,000 worth of free advertising from the name before he started."

Ultimately, in an ironic stroke of justice, Canada's Justice Minister Davie Fulton announced that the coal mine, which had imprisoned so many men, would have one of the new-style "open" prisons built on top of it. The Federal Government would buy the twenty-five-acre mine-head property of the coal company, along with three hundred acres of adjoining land. By 1961 there was to be in operation there a correctional penal institution, without walls or armed guards, where prisoners most likely to reform and re-enter society would roam freely.

Perhaps the strangest offer of all came from Governor Marvin Griffin of Georgia. He issued a blanket invitation to the nineteen rescued miners to recover from their harrowing experience by holidaying at his state's stylish Jekyll Island Park, a one-time vacation resort for millionaires. The Governor was somewhat taken aback on learning that the most popular leader of the group, Maurice Ruddick, was a Negro.

Nevertheless, he said Ruddick would be welcomed to Jekyll Island along with the other miner heroes, but on a segregated basis. "We have facilities available at Jekyll Island for coloured people," the Governor blandly said. And his executive secretary, Thomas Gregory, pointed out, "It is the law here, in fact, that the Negroes must be separate."

At first, the group of miners was reluctant to go. "There was no segregation down that hole, and there's none in this group," said Douglas Jewkes.

But Ruddick agreed to go along with the offer. "I knew that if I refused to go because of the segregation angle, my mates would refuse also."

Bowsie Maddison then spoke for the group: "I want to go, and if Mose says it's okay, we'll all go." Another of Ruddick's fellow-miners, speaking in all innocence, approved with a statement of unwitting and devastating irony.

"Maurice is being pretty darn white about this thing," he said.

_ 7 _

The Day Halifax Exploded

ON THE FROSTY, SUNSHINY MORNING OF THURSday, December 6, 1917, a telegraph operator named Vincent Coleman, idly sitting in his Richmond Terminal Office overlooking the piers, happened to glance out at Halifax Harbour. He was startled to see two tramp steamers, the *Mont Blanc* and the *Imo*, collide in midstream. The shock of their collision shook the whole world.

But Coleman was one of the few who seems to have realized the horrible portent as he saw tongues of ice blue flame snaking from the shattered hull of the *Mont Blanc*. He reached for his telegraph key and tapped out his last message on earth.

"Ammunition ship is on fire and is making for Pier Eight," he signalled. "Good bye."

Soon there was a sound like the crashing of a million chandeliers, and Coleman's head was blasted from his body. All they ever found of him were his brass watch and his telegraph key.

The dockside telegrapher was one of two thousand people killed in one of the greatest civilian disasters of this century. It was more spectacular than the San Francisco earthquake, and more devastating than the Chicago fire. It dwarfed the sinking of the *Titanic,* and was more dramatic that the Great Plague of London. For the havoc encompassed elements of all four of these catastrophes.

The explosion injured eight thousand people. Worst of all were flying daggers of jagged glass, which converted their victims into human pincushions and plucked out eyeballs from sockets. There are still hundreds of blind people in Halifax, their cheeks scarred blue by powder, their vision shattered on that terrible morning in their childhood. Edward M. Van Cleve, then managing director of the National Committee for Prevention of Blindness, estimated: "More than twice the number of Canadian soldiers blinded in battle during the entire Great War were blinded by the *Mont Blanc* explosion alone."

The explosion caused at least fifty million dollars' worth of property damage. Its suction ripped out nails from frame houses, its forty-foot-high tidal wave smashed walls as though they were cobwebs, and its upheaval of the earth snapped stone factories like turnip tops. Ten thousand people were left homeless in its wake, cowering as the sky rained red-hot meteors of steel.

Their cup of misery overflowed that night when Halifax was battered by its worst blizzard in twenty years. Slashing sleet and snow, driven by a forty-mile-an-hour gale, blew down the white tents set up by the crowds shivering in the Halifax Commons and Paradise Baseball Park. Then the air was filled with the moans of mothers, giving birth to babies in the open fields.

It was a day of macabre sights, of human courage and human folly, and Haligonians never tire of talking about them.

There was Chief Petty Officer William King, gym instructor at Halifax Naval College. He lay on a slab in an improvised morgue for forty-eight hours, apparently dead, wrapped in a white sheet. He was conscious during the entire nightmare. But he couldn't move a muscle or speak, until he finally clutched the ankle of a terrified soldier passing by, crying, "Don't leave me. I know I'm not dead."

There was the imperious schoolmaster at Chebucto Road School. He was known only by the nickname of "Old Gander" to one of his grade-nine students, Thomas Raddall, now a Halifax author. As the explosion interrupted the singing of morning hymns — hurling the blackboard off the wall and whizzing the clock over his head — the schoolmaster thought only in terms of juvenile pranks. Sternly he scolded, "Some naughty little boys have been playing with dynamite again!"

There was G. A. Holmes, operator of a ferry service between Halifax and Tufts Cove in Dartmouth. He was fifty yards distant when the

144

Mont Blanc exploded. He landed in a heap of ashes two miles away, stark naked except for his rubber boots. Still alive today, he remembers awakening delirious on New Year's Day, "wrapped in bandages like an Egyptian mummy, all my fingernails off, and my left arm swollen like Popeye the Sailor's."

Private S. Henneberry had just returned from overseas with the 63rd Battalion. He dug feverishly through the rubble of his Campbell Road home to find his wife and five of his children dead. Then he heard a faint moan. Under the protective ash-pan of the pot-bellied stove, he scooped up his eighteen-month-old daughter, Olive, miraculously alive. Thereafter, she grew up known as the "Halifax ash-pan baby".

Mrs. Florence Chisholm, in bed with sciatica at Victoria General Hospital, dreamed that morning of meeting the devil: he told her to hurry on, because he was expecting a lot of souls. She awoke to find herself the only patient left alive in the ward, the floor buckled upward, the dead buried under twisted beds.

Vince Gully, now a Dartmouth motel-keeper, was then a child of five on his way to Victoria School. He remembers pulling his brother John out from under the stove, and helping his mother Ada from under the sink. The minister's son next door, he recalls, gathered up chocolate bars outside the shattered window of the general store, and sold them to explosion refugees.

Sergeant E. Matthews was an invalid at Camp Hill Military Hospital. He had served in France with the Nova Scotia 25th Battalion. According to the story he told his son-in-law, Arthur Hambleton, he was playing a game of poker in the hospital recreation room. As the other players ducked and ran for shelter from the blast, the sergeant had the presence of mind to first scoop up the money from the table and pocket it.

Mrs. Alf Lafferty, now of Trenton, Nova Scotia, had a grandfather who was a contractor. When the explosion struck, he was working inside a steel pipe on a Halifax city job. The pipe sailed him out unscathed in front of a bank, where dollar bills were fluttering on the ground. "But as the place was full of other people," she says, a mite regretfully, "he was unable to help himself to the free mint."

Mrs. Mary Logan remembers the corner butcher on Cork Street, who lived over his shop. His ceiling toppled, and he was pinned by his

145

foot, hanging head-down over his burning store, screaming. He roasted to death like a capon on a spit.

Eight-year-old Lola Burns was saying her prayers in her Granville Street bedroom, a rosary clasped in her fingers, when the explosion came. Her father, John Burns, found her in the middle of the devastated room. Spears of glass were strewn all about her, but she was still offering prayers and quite uninjured, her puppy snuggled up close to her.

Captain Alfred Seaman had a lucky haircut that morning. About to sail on his ship, the *Chomedy,* he paid his customary visit to the waterfront barber shop. For years he had sat in the chair just inside the front door, beside the plate-glass window. "For some inexplicable reason," recalls his wife, Mrs. A. E. Seaman, now of Peterborough, Ontario, "this time he decided to sit in the third chair — something he had never done before. After the explosion, my stunned husband found that a large piece of the window-glass had sliced off the head-rest of the chair in which he'd always sat before."

J. Frank Willis, the celebrated CBC radio announcer and host of the TV show "Close Up", was then a youngster of nine. "Tempted by the lovely bright morning," he remembers, "I was dawdling on my way to Tower Road School, standing entranced before a candy-store window. Suddenly the window disintegrated before my eyes. This was followed by a roar which I can still sometimes hear. Hugh MacLennan, one of my schoolmates, got a novel out of the explosion, *Barometer Rising.* All I got out of it was a ringing in the ear."

Young Lillian Burbridge was in the school yard at Chebucto Road School with a playmate, May Murphy. They were waiting for the bell to ring. Suddenly slivers of glass flew around their heads. Untouched, Lillian ran all the way to her home at 366 West Young Street, and wept to her mother and sister amid the ruins, "What happened?" Her sister exclaimed, "The bloody Germans have got us!" When Lillian — now a Halifax matron, Mrs. W. E. Kidd — tells the story today, she says, "I hope you will pardon the 'bloody' expression."

A happy coo saved the life of Mrs. Doris M. Shaw, then a baby six months old, now a Toronto housewife. "Mother had my bath water ready when the explosion occurred, and I was lying in my crib," she says. "Mother was shaking her head over me to make me smile and coo. Then it struck. If it hadn't been for Mother taking the time out to play

146

with me for a minute then, I would have been killed. They found my bathtub filled with debris. Mother received twenty-two superficial cuts on her face. I got a cut on my head. Curiously, my baby carriage, kept in the shed at the back of the house, was one of the few items not damaged."

A strange case was that of Mrs. Jean Fry Finigan. She was then a twenty-two-year-old invalid, with a paralyzed spine, lying in her bedroom at 44 Le Marchant Street. "The nerves of my back were so bad, I couldn't tell a hot-water bottle from a cube of ice on my spine," she says. "Doctors said only a shock could cure me." That morning, both windows in her room shattered into a thousand pieces, but she was unharmed. The man she was to marry, Dr. Lindsay M. Finigan, carried her in a stretcher to the Dalhousie University campus nearby, and she is now the healthy mother of two, "spreading sunshine whenever I can. The explosion was the shock that cured me completely."

Rear Admiral T. Bidwell, R.C.N. — now retired — was then a cadet seated in a class room of the Halifax Naval Academy. He was concentrating on trying to write his final examinations. News of the two ships afire in the harbour induced him to make a quick exit from the building to watch the excitement. He had taken only a few steps down the street when the blast occurred and a flying splinter gashed his arm. He was treated at a drug store, and joined the rescuers, but never finished his examinations. Instead, he got an automatic commission, and embarked on his long, honourable and adventurous service with the Canadian Navy.

Mary K. Watson tells of a minister who was standing in his living-room door when the explosion hit. He was watching his wife play the piano, while his son practised singing for a concert. Later, they placed in one coffin all that was left of his musical family — the backbone of his wife, the collarbone of his son. The minister muttered bitterly at the church service, "Rot to all this praying business!" Another minister nearby nodded and said, "Those are the first natural words I've heard since the disaster."

Another pianist, Edward Davis, a blind boy from Saint John, New Brunswick, was practising at his piano in the Halifax School for the Blind. The lurching piano dealt him a mighty blow and sent him hurtling across the room. He simply got up, and with the sensitive hands of the sightless, calmly attended to a dozen other hysterical children, who retained their vision but not their wits.

The explosion brought heart-break to Rosie, the prettiest waitress in the Green Lantern restaurant. "Rosie was engaged, and came through the explosion little injured," recalls Hugh Laborde. "One side of her face, however, was scarred. Still perfection on one profile, she was mottled on the other. That was too much for her gallant boy friend. He broke off their forthcoming marriage."

An odd view, akin to the parting of the Red Sea for the Children of Israel, was seen by Inspector John A. Kinsmen, now of the Halifax Police Force. He was then a seventeen-year-old member of the searchlight unit of the Canadian Engineers, stationed on McNab's Island. "It was fine enough that morning that we were in our shirt-sleeves, throwing a softball on the parade grounds," Kinsmen says. "When I heard the explosion and looked, I saw a huge cloud of black smoke rising in the north. Sergeant Ernie Cox ran out of the barracks crying, 'It looks as though George's Island has exploded.' I looked at the harbour again — and it was as though a huge knife had parted the water."

J. D. Monaghan was also stationed then at McNab's Island, as quartermaster of the Halifax Rifles. It was part of his routine to come into Halifax each Wednesday to visit Moirs Limited on military business. "I was standing in the office, leaning over the counter to give instructions to one of the girls," Colonel Monaghan recalls. "Then the blast came. If I'd been standing erect, I wouldn't be here to tell the tale. For the glass in a huge window shattered and a large chunk of it sheared off. It passed over my head and imbedded itself in the time-clock on the other side of the room."

Curiosity saved Mrs. Gertrude A. C. Pettipas of Dartmouth. She was at the window her newly built bungalow, which commanded a view of eastern Halifax Harbour. Suddenly she saw a great black ball of smoke rising out of lurid flames. "It was a magnificent, though terrifying, sight," she remembers. "Just then, I raised the window to call to two women, who were talking in an excited manner on the corner of the street. This probably saved my life, and certainly my eyes. As I leaned to call, I saw a blinding sheet of fire shoot a mile high in the sky. Immediately, the concussion struck me in the face and threw me across the room. I lay half under the bed, while the floor sank down in the shape of a hammock. I could count a full forty seconds, while the horrible, grinding, deafening noise continued, and I thought of my husband, who was in the city, and my mother. Then came a dead calm. I could not believe it was all over, and that I had been spared."

George Yates, then secretary to Prime Minister Sir Robert Borden, recalled a bit of grim humour. An aged man, working for a Morris Street family, was chopping wood in the yard when the explosion came. He looked up for a moment, then bent down to his work again. After the family had recovered, with minor injuries, from the shock, they called out to the wood-chopper to know if he was harmed. "No, I'm all right," he sang out. "But I told you that you'd have trouble with that darned old oil stove."

The itchy back of her Aunt Bridget is remembered today by Dorothy Lynch Mulcahy. Her Aunt Bridget was relaxing after the tragedy, discussing the good fortune of their family. She interspersed her remarks by scratching her back against a door. In desperation, she asked her husband to scratch the inaccessible spot. He found a large piece of glass firmly lodged in her back. "My Aunt Bridget," she says, "soon found herself in hospital with the other survivors, not feeling so lucky."

Mrs. Louise Girvan, now a Toronto travel agent, but then an emergency nurse, vividly recollects her horror when a surgeon carried through the hospital wards a whole bucket full of removed eyeballs. One doctor at Victoria General Hospital alone removed sixty sightless eyes from their sockets. And during the first frantic hours at Camp Hill emergency hospital, overworked physicians performed operations with bare hands, instruments unsterilized; and they sutured long wounds with a needle and ordinary cotton thread.

Doris McCoy tells of two men in a row-boat in the harbour who were caught by the suction of the explosion. They swooped up into the air, boat, oars, and all. They were suspended up there for a split second, an absurd tableau, then returned to the water, speechless but intact.

A bizarre spectacle, like the last day of Pompeii, was provided by the thousands fleeing up Chebucto Road, Kempt Road, and Quinpool Road to escape to the safety of the woods beyond Armdale. In their panic, some of the refugees behaved in a strange manner.

A woman was seen trudging up a corpse-littered street, naked except for an apron tied around her waist and brandishing a broom. A

149

crazed mother in silk pajamas clutched her baby to her breast, trying to croon it asleep, quite oblivious of the fact that the child's head was blown off. A cook named Mrs. Maud Foley, rushing to find her two children left in care of a neighbour on Gerrish Street, remembers passing a parrot that kept squawking on the shoulder of its dead master, "A devil of a mess! A devil of a mess!"

Mrs. H. St. George Woodill recalls that when her father spotted what appeared to be a hugh ball of fire in the sky, he ducked under the verandah and exclaimed, "The end of the world has come!"

When Mrs. James Mulcahy first felt the blast, she snatched up her toddling sons, and spied a vacated bread-wagon. Quickly she tossed her children on top of the still-warm loaves in the back. She had never driven a horse; but now she drove the team for ten breath-taking miles. When she reached the small fishing village of Herring Cove, she let her children out and then dazedly handed out the bread to the villagers.

Thomas Raddall saw two horses lying dead on the street between the shafts of their unharmed Imperial Oil wagon. The teamster was squatting beside their heads, caressing their ears. He gazed at Raddall and said forlornly, "Would you think a man could stand a thing that killed a horse?"

The thing that killed so many humans and beasts that terrible morning began as no more than a traffic accident in the Narrows — the thin strip of water linking outer Halifax Harbour with inner Bedford Basin. At 8:40 A.M., in the brilliant sunshine, at fifteen degrees above zero, the sea was calm. Canada had been at war for three years and four months, and Halifax, its sovereign Atlantic seaport, was bustling. The normal fifty-seven thousand population of the conservative "Garrison City" was swollen with servicemen, as was the small town of Dartmouth across the channel. All manner of black-out precautions were taken, in fear of the German U-boats prowling off the coast.

But full precautions were not taken by the inward-bound French munitions freighter, *Mont Blanc,* entering the Narrows to join an Allied convoy being assembled in Bedford Basin. The 330-foot, 3,000-ton steamer, painted a sombre war-time grey, was flying the French tricolour. But her skipper, Captain Aimé Lemedic, neglected to hoist a

150

red flag — the international emblem meaning "explosives aboard". And yet her cargo, recently loaded in New York, was a lethal devil's brew. She was loaded to the scuppers with 2,300 tons of picric acid, 500,000 pounds of deadly TNT — a perfect detonator for the rest — 61 tons of other explosive acid, and, as ideal lighter fluid, 35 tons of benzine in tins sitting on the deck.

Nonchalantly heading for this floating atom bomb was the outward-bound tramp steamer, *Imo*. It was skippered by a Captain Fram, so obscure that his first name has eluded the record of all historians. His ship was a 5,041-ton iron vessel of ancient vintage, belonging to the South Pacific Whaling Company of Oslo, Norway. Giant letters on her gaunt flank spelled out the words, "Belgian Relief", signifying that she carried a cargo of grain and clothing for war victims in Belgium.

The two vessels steamed directly in each other's path. Aboard the *Mont Blanc*, Captain Lemedic swore angrily in French. His harbour pilot, Francis Mackay, who later testified he'd never touched a drop of whisky in twenty-four years of Halifax piloting, ordered two blasts on the whistle. It meant the *Mont Blanc* intended to pass starboard to starboard.

But aboard the *Imo*, Captain Fram's harbour pilot, William Hayes, stubbornly gave a conflicting signal. He ordered a single blast of the whistle. It meant the *Imo* intended to pass port to port.

"*Arrêtez!*" Captain Lemedic, in the pilot house of the *Mont Blanc*, shouted through the engine-room intercom. "*Coupez! Coupez les machines!*"

But his command was too late. Amid clanging bells, the manoeu-vering ships lunged in the same direction, then lunged back again, in an awkward minuet. Then, with a violent shock, the bow of the *Imo* ploughed through the plates amidship of the *Mont Blanc*. It went grinding a third of the way through the deck and the forward hold, splashing a shower of sparks. Both vessels shuddered to a halt.

A spectator on a steamer lying nearby, Third Engineer Alfred Kingsford, later testified, "The colliding ships were so noiseless, I did not think they had broken an egg when they smashed together."

In fact, it would have been no worse than two bumping eggshells, if the *Mont Blanc* had not carried her satanic cargo. The crash punctured the tins of benzine on her deck, and the liquid immediately caught fire. Tendrils of blue, chemical-fed flames soon shot up through billows of tarry smoke.

Captain Lemedic, his hands fearfully clutching the rail of the bridge, ordered the *Mont Blanc* to pull away. Then, what was later claimed to be an act of sheer, irresponsible cowardice, he commanded the crew into the life-boats on the double. He was aware of the ominous powder keg that lay under the glowing, red-hot deck-plates; and yet he did not communicate his knowledge to anyone in Halifax. Intent on saving only their own lives, he and his men rowed like maniacs across the channel to Dartmouth. They leaped out, sprinted up the beach toward a nearby clump of spruce trees, and flung their heads into the sheltering snow.

Meanwhile, knots of people idly gathered on the sunny slopes of Fort Needham Hill in north Halifax to watch the spectacle of the *Mont Blanc* blaze up in purple flames. So far as they were concerned, it was a simple matter of two cargo ships that had locked hulls in collision. Captain Fram nosed the *Imo*, relatively undamaged, toward Dartmouth — though he never got there under his own steam. The burning *Mont Blanc*, with not a soul aboard to guide her except the ship's cat, bobbed haphazardly toward Pier Eight on the Halifax shore — a sizzling bomb adrift in a vagrant current.

As the city-hall clock chimed nine, a Barrington Street grocer, Constant Upham, thought to turn in the fire alarm. The horse-drawn fire wagon, pulling the city's first new motor pumper, the *Patricia*, clanged noisily toward the water-front. Two British cruisers in the harbour, the *Niobe* and the *Highflyer*, dispatched launches to put out the fire on the *Mont Blanc*. They surrounded her like midges, the water from their hoses arching up with infinite delicacy and hissing into the oily smoke.

At five minutes after nine, bluejackets aboard the small ship *Stella Maris* successfully grabbed the Jacob's ladder dangling alongside the *Mont Blanc*. Their flesh shrinking from the intense heat, they scrambled half-way up, determined to open the sea-cocks and flood the ship. They never made it. A needle of flaming gas knifed across the deck of the munitions ship, and with an ear-piercing, screeching blast, the *Mont Blanc* exploded. A skyscraper of smoke, shot through

152

with cardinal-red flames, towered five miles up in the sky; and twenty-eight years later the survivors were to remember that it assumed the shape of a fantastic mushroom, precisely like the one that spelled doom for the people of Hiroshima.

The force of the explosion unleashed three hellish furies: a tidal wave, an earthquake, and a tornado-like air concussion.

The water underneath the keel of the *Mont Blanc* opened up, so that the very bottom of Halifax Harbour, sixty feet deep, was exposed. Then the displaced water curled up forty feet high, spouting fish, and gathered speed like an express train run amok. The monstrous circular wave snatched the steamer *Stella Maris* and flung her bodily over Pier Eight as though she were a toy. It boiled forty feet over the tracks of the Intercolonial Railway, lifting and carrying off three hundred loaded freight cars. Tons of hissing brine swept as far as Campbell Road, catching two hundred stevedores and engulfing them in a watery grave. The *Imo* was hurled to the shore near Tufts Cove, where forty of her crew (including Captain Fram, with his head blown off) were immediately killed; where forty Micmac Indians on their reservation were slain; and where a smashed brewery was left forlornly pouring a river of beer into the harbour.

When the violence of the explosion struck the earth, the whole granite bed of Halifax Peninsula rocked and swayed as if with St. Vitus's dance. Sixty-two miles away, in the town of Truro, the clock was hurled from the wall of the Learmonth Hotel. At Sydney, two hundred miles away, the tremor set houses shivering. In downtown Halifax, telephone poles snapped like toothpicks, and the city's entire lighting system crumpled into darkness. Stores telescoped, tumbling their displays of bacon, fruit and jewellery, amid showers of plate glass, onto the cracked pavements.

Householders were caught stoking their coal-burning stoves against the morning cold, and the earthquake tossed the blazing coals against the tinder of shattered walls. Entire buildings — such as the Protestant Orphanage, the King Edward Hotel, and the Home for the Deaf — tottered into rubbish heaps. The glass-and-iron roof of the North Street Depot, the city's solitary railway station, crumpled like paper.

The tall brick bulk of the Arcadian Sugar Refinery snapped off as though if were a carrot, and its syrup-soaked timbers gave off a sweet smell as they burned fiercely. Thirty girls were killed instantly in the demolished Richmond Printing Company, and the lives of a hundred children were crushed under collapsing beams of the Richmond Public School. Only three of forty workmen escaped alive from the razed Hillis Foundry. In its smoking wreckage a blacksmith was found dead, still holding his hammer raised.

Even more grisly was the ruination wreaked by the air concussion. Like a giant fist, this tornado blast flattened two square miles of the entire Richmond district of north Halifax. The vacuum-pocketed air smote every flimsy frame house in it path, sucked doors from hinges, twisted iron rails into writhing metal snakes. Every window split into driving daggers of glass, which sent people screaming through the streets with torn faces and slashed eyeballs.

The wave of air hammered the new motor-pumper, *Patricia,* to flinders; all that was ever found of her crew of firemen and her team was a charred horse collar, stamped "H.F.D.". The official motor car containing Fire Chief Condon and Deputy Chief Edward Brunt was blown clean off the road by the blast, and they were found dead beneath it. Reporter Jack Ronayne of the Halifax *Echo,* who was following the speeding fire car to Pier Eight, was also smashed to death.

Though the shield-like bastion of Citadel Hill deflected it and fanned it, the air blast continued to slash through the white-hot atmosphere like a cheese-cutter. As far away as Ingramport, thirty miles south-west of Halifax, a young lumberyard supervisor named Phillip Geoffrey Morrow saw the effects of a "sword of wind". Now retired at seventy-one, Morrow remembers he was half-way down the six steps of his bungalow, on a high hill overlooking St. Margaret's Bay, when it happened.

"Suddenly, the sparrows in the birch trees at the side of my bungalow were shot out of their nests as if by a cannon," he says. "The birds under the eaves were whizzed off, not under their own power, in the same way. Yet at the level of my own head, my soft felt hat didn't even flap a brim. My sealyham terrier, Thisbe, ran as though pursued by the devil."

The forces of unleashed havoc played odd tricks. Though Africville was only three hundred yards away from the explosion, only one person was killed in this Negro slum ghetto. Yet the red-hot steel that filled the sky — splintered fragments of the *Mont Blanc* — rained molten death for miles.

The ship's anchor plummeted through a roof on the other side of the Northwest Arm, three miles away. Its cannon, the barrel bent like soft wax, swooped into Albro's Lake, about three miles in the opposite direction. A half-ton plate of the *Mont Blanc* descended through the roof of the Royal Naval College class-room, and crushed like a match-box the platform where an instructor stood.

In St. Paul's Anglican Church, they still preserve a piece of stained glass with a hole allegedly caused by a man's head being blown through the window on that morning of fury.

After the explosion, when the city hall clock stopped at precisely five minutes after nine, all the people in the city seemed to stop, too, in stunned shock. It was as though they were suddenly afflicted with mass blindness and paralysis. Then they reacted with panic. The mob psychology that prevailed has been described graphically by Dr. Samuel Henry Prince, a University of Toronto sociologist, who made a study at the time for Columbia University.

"People thought immediately the Germans had come," he wrote. "A man on the outskirts of Dartmouth 'heard' a German shell pass shrieking above him. A moment after, a citizen 'saw' clearly a German fleet manoeuvring in the distance. The head of one firm advised his employees not to run elsewhere 'because two shots never fall in the same place'. Many, witnessing their whole family wiped out 'in one red burial blent', fell to their knees in prayer, thinking it was the end of the world. One woman was found in the open yard by her broken home, repeating the general confession of the Church. A distracted father looked into his little girl's face four times, but did not recognize her as his own. Not a few saw in the death cloud a hallucination — the clear outlines of a face."

Yet not all the victims responded with hysteria. An intimate portrait of spunk in the face of catastrophe is reflected in the story of Mrs. Mary Logan and her family. Now seventy-one and a widow, Mrs. Logan is a tiny Scottish woman, round-cheeked, with amused green eyes

155

and a halo of white hair. She has a superb memory; and among her recollections of that grim time she finds a few flashes of humour.

Mrs. Logan was then a housewife of twenty-eight. She lived in a six-room, two-storey frame house, newly painted white, on Cork Street; it was in the north-west end of Halifax, and commanded a fine view of the harbour. She sublet rooms upstairs to a Mrs. Gentle, a tall, wiry widow in her late twenties, whose husband had recently been killed at Vimy Ridge, and who looked after two daughters, of three and four years of age, and a baby son six weeks old.

Mrs. Logan had her own brood of three children to handle. There was Johnny, eight, Earl, six, and baby Jean, just four months old. Her husband, David Logan, was a corporal with the Pictou Highlanders stationed at the nearby Halifax Wellington Barracks; he was a cheerful, red-haired Haligonian, who occasionally bedevilled her with his pre-dilection for the odd drink of whisky and his Irish wit.

Her husband woke up late that morning; he had been out on the town the night before "with the boys". He was supposed to be at the Wellington Barracks at eight o'clock to serve as corporal of the guard.

"Phone up, honey, and tell them I'm ill," he groaned to his wife.

"I will not," Mrs. Logan said firmly. "You deserve to be punished for drinking all that booze last night."

Her husband pulled on his uniform and hurried off without eating breakfast. "I'll be punished, all right," he said ruefully at the door. "Don't expect me home for dinner. I'll probably land up in the clink for being late."

Mrs. Logan smiled to herself. In her plaid dressing-gown tossed lightly over her silk nightie, she busied herself in the kitchen. She wanted to prepare a breakfast of hot porridge for her two sons before they went off to school. John and Earl squatted in their short pants on the kitchen couch near the pot-bellied Quebec stove, wrapped up in a gray blanket to keep themselves warm.

In the bedroom adjoining the kitchen, baby Jean gave a faint whimper. Mrs. Logan hurried in, bent over the crib to fondle her head, and covered her against the morning chill.

At five minutes after nine, just as she was leaning her face over her baby, Mrs. Logan heard what appeared to be a tremendous clap of

156

thunder. "At first," she later said, "I thought it was my husband back. I thought he was tramping his heavy army boots up the three front steps."

Then the whole house trembled and swayed as it was smitten by the concussion. Doors and windows blew in, a huge corner of the roof was ripped off, and a beam tottered to a rakish angle, like the hat of a drunkard. Plaster from the walls tumbled everywhere. There were two double windows over the crib in Mrs. Logan's bedroom, and they flew across the room, crashing against the opposite wall. Since Mrs. Logan was leaning over the crib, she escaped with just a few needles of jagged glass that slashed the right side of her neck. She had just covered Jean, so the baby was protected from the shower of plaster.

"The destruction happened in seconds," Mrs. Logan recalls. "The rumbling noise lasted for two minutes. I thought it was an air raid from a Hun zeppelin. We'd been warned a month before we might be bombed. That's why I dimmed the lights and closed the window curtains at night. Now, I felt curiously calm."

Fearful about the safety of her sons, Mrs. Logan rushed slipperless from the bedroom into the kitchen, hardly aware of the door hanging crazily from one hinge. She found Johnny and Earl sprawled on the kitchen floor. The couch was poised half over them, and they were screaming. A large can of red paint had tumbled from a cupboard and struck Johnny sharply on the forehead. Red paint flowed and mixed with his blood, and Johnny yelled because he thought the scarlet gush was all blood.

Johnny scrambled to his feet and rushed to his mother. The younger boy, Earl, considering it all an adventure, began to laugh. Mrs. Logan saw instantly that neither was seriously hurt, and she embraced them and kissed away their tears.

Just then the widow, Mrs. Gentle, came rushing downstairs. She hopped over mounds of glass and plaster, and seemed unaware that the balustrade had been pulled away completely. Her left eyeball was hanging bloody on her cheek. She appeared to have gone completely berserk.

She clawed Mrs. Logan around the neck. "My three children are killed!" she shrieked. "Phone my mother in England. I must talk to my Mommy immediately. I must tell her that her grandchildren are killed."

157

"Your children can't be killed, dear," Mrs. Logan said gently. "I can hear them crying upstairs."

She struggled to release the widow's grip from her neck. Then she ran barefooted up the stairs, oblivious to the daggers of glass that ripped into the soles of her feet. She gasped with relief as she spotted Mrs. Gentle's two little daughters in their white nighties. They were lying in a heap of rubble, with surprisingly few cuts.

Mrs. Logan hoisted one child under each arm, and carried them down the stairway. Their distraught mother seemed utterly unconcerned about her daughters and her still missing baby boy. She wildly grabbed at Mrs. Logan and wailed, "I want my Mommy in England! Let's go down in the cellar and hide until this air raid is over."

Mrs. Logan was getting annoyed. She sat Mrs. Gentle firmly down on a chair. "You'll just *have* to stay here, until I rescue your baby."

Her feet gushing blood, Mrs. Logan ran up the jagged gauntlet of the stairs again. "Thank God," she whispered, as she saw the widow's six-week-old son lying in his crib. Glass and plaster were heaped on his blanket, but he was alive. She brought the child downstairs, and snuggled him into the crib beside her own baby, Jean.

A moment later, Mrs. Logan had reason to thank God again. Her husband burst in where the front door had been. In his arms he carried a small boy, who had been blown right out of his house and onto the pavement.

"David!" exclaimed Mrs. Logan. "I thought the bomb had killed you."

"No," her husband said. "I was walking along Cogs Street, when I saw a street-car coming toward me, and I felt a blast of air. I thought, 'My, that's an awful lot of air from that trolley.' Then I was knocked flat on my face. People poured out of the trolley, and I turned around and ran back home. I stopped just to pick up this poor wounded little lad. Tuck him in bed, will you, honey?"

Mrs. Logan was vastly relieved to let her husband take over. He took a basin of water and washed the faces of the children, and tried to bathe Mrs. Gentle's eye. The mother-in-law of the blinded widow arrived, terribly upset; but she took Mrs. Gentle and her three children to her house, wrapped in blankets.

158

Suddenly Mrs. Logan began to tremble violently in the cold. Her feet bled painfully from the slivers of glass. Her husband pulled a pair of socks and a pair of galoshes over her feet. "Crawl into bed with the kids," he implored her. "I'll cover you all with my army overcoat, until I can fix the blasted stove."

No sooner was she lying down than three soldiers carrying bayonets rushed into the house. They were from the Royal Canadian Garrison Artillery, stationed at Citadel Hill; and they exclaimed, "You'll have to hurry to the south end of the city. A fire's raging at the main garrison magazine of Wellington Barracks. Enough powder's there to blow northern Halifax to kingdom-come!"

Mrs. Logan swiftly wrapped blankets around her children. One of the soldiers carried the wounded boy rescued by her husband. Before sounding the alarm down the rest of Cork Street, the other two soldiers helped wrap Mrs. Logan's black lamb fur coat around her trembling shoulders.

"I was frozen stiff," she remembers, as they joined the crowds rushing frantically for the icy fields of Bedford Basin. "I had no underwear. Though I wore socks and galoshes, I had no time to hunt for my shoes. I walked spraddle-legged, looking like Donald Duck."

The night before, Mrs. Logan had been to see the movie, *The Rape of Belgium;* and the exodus of blood-smudged humans through the streets of Halifax reminded her of the war refugees in that film. A cotton factory nearby was shooting up tongues of cherry-red flames two hundred feet high. Great lumps of ice coated with black soot were falling. From the gaping shells of their homes, the wounded and the dying moaned softly; but they were ignored by the terrified thousands who clogged the streets.

Sleigh cutters raced by at breakneck speed, containing torsos loaded like sacks of flours. Little children toddled along dangerously near the hoofs of plunging horses, and it was pathetic to see them hugging their pet dogs and cats in their arms. Numbed by shock, the people talked as little as possible; directions were given with an index finger. "Your family has gone to Paradise!" was the laconic message shouted to a father, horrified until he realized that Paradise Park was meant. Most of them hurried along wordlessly, glancing back over their shoulders in anticipation of the catastrophe they had been led to expect, like the Biblical Lot's wife before Sodom and Gomorrah were engulfed in flame.

A dazed boy of about eight began to walk beside Mrs. Logan. His face was pockmarked blue with powder scars. He carried the top of a schoolbag by a strap, but the entire bottom of the bag was blasted away.

"Where are your parents, sonny?" Mrs. Logan asked.

"I don't know," he said.

"Then you stick with us," she said kindly.

At length, Mrs. Logan and her family huddled in an ice-crusted field along the shore of Bedford Basin. Her husband discovered a small store, not too badly damaged, and he bought cake, candy and soda pop for the children.

Through the cruel afternoon, they stood shuddering in the wind. Anxiously, they watched the smoke pall over the burning north end of Halifax, waiting for a blast that never came. Lieutenant A. Olmstead, of the 72nd Battalion of Ottawa, asked for volunteers to flood the Wellington Barracks magazine, which was threatened with raging fires on three sides. As a supreme act of valour, every man in his battery volunteered. They pumped water into the arsenal, standing in the middle of the explosives until the icy water rose to their chins. And not until all peril of explosion in the magazine was over did these heroic men leave their posts.

Ultimately, Mrs. Logan remembers, an army truck made the rounds to the crowds at Halifax Commons and Bedford Basin with the news. A soldier hollered through a trumpet, "All clear! You can go back to your homes, folks — if you have a home left."

Back to her shattered home went Mrs. Logan with her family, holding the hand of the scarred waif with the schoolbag. Her husband scrounged some tarpaper at the Halifax Exhibition, whose great grandstand, just constructed for fifty thousand dollars, was a shambles. Vainly he tried to hammer tarpaper and carpets over the gaping windows and door frames of their house.

Mrs. Logan continued to shiver. Luckily her landlady, who lived nearby, a plump, jovial woman of fifty named Mrs. Emma Deer, came around with an oil stove. She also brought some candles, since the

160

city's electricity was snuffed out, and some canned tomato soup and baked beans, since a doctor had come around to warn against eating food that might be laced with glass.

"Let me have that little boy," said Mrs. Deer, pointing to the stray waif with the scarred cheeks. "I'll give him some supper at my place."

"Only if you promise to bring him back tomorrow morning," said Mrs. Logan. "The poor lad doesn't know his own name, or if he has a mother or father."

Soon Mrs. Logan had tucked her three children into bed, fully clothed, and was herself in bed, completely dressed and covered by her black lamb fur coat. But at midnight she was aroused by Halifax's worst blizzard, which was to rage unabated for fifteen hours. It was a gale of wet, clinging snow that howled over a city with scarcely a pane of glass intact, and carried its chill over a thousand beds of pain.

As the storm swept gusts of snow through the hole in the roof and into the bedrooms, Mrs. Logan's pent-up tensions broke through, too. She burst into tears.

Her husband tried to cheer her up. "Ah, honey," he said. "If you'd let me have whisky in the house, a nip would do your Presbyterian backbone a lot of good."

Mrs. Logan sobbed on, "This blizzard's too much. It's as though everything were conspiring against us."

"Ah, honey, it ain't that bad," her husband persevered. "You know that plant you had hanging by a chain in front of the kitchen windows — your favourite creeper? Well, all the windows and doors may be blown away. But I just looked, and darned if that creeper of yours ain't still hanging there, a blooming miracle."

Mrs. Logan's crying jag turned to laughter, and she fell asleep with a smile on her lips.

Next morning, after she tried to sweep the snow and glass debris out of the bedrooms, she went to her landlady's to claim her waif. She was profoundly disturbed when Mrs. Deer told her, "He's gone. The boy walked out of my kitchen last night into the snowstorm. I'd just gone upstairs for a minute to attend my daughter, who was blinded by glass. When I came down, he'd wandered away."

161

Mrs. Logan set out to look for him, and to have her stabbed neck and feet bandaged at one of the emergency hospitals. She was appalled by the aftermath. Soldiers, including her husband, were delegated to shovel charred human remains into wash-tubs, and carry them to the emergency morgue at Chebucto School. After relatives identified victims by dentures and wedding rings, the bodies were coffined and piled out onto the sidewalk, this gruesome array extending almost down to the city hall.

The Salvation Army had set up free food and clothes depots at the Academy of Music and Alexander McKaye School, and the scenes here were equally poignant. A little boy, given a pair of mittens at a relief station, commented, "They fit me pretty well, don't they, Mama?" A moment later, his face saddened as he murmured, "Oh, I forgot. I haven't any Mama any more."

It was two days before anyone was able to buy a newspaper. Failure of the gas plant forced the Halifax press to publish sheets done entirely by hand, consisting mostly of columns and columns of casualties, and details of the unclaimed dead. "YET MORE APPALLING," ran the headline in the Halifax *Herald-Mail*. "THE DEATH ROLL STILL GROWS."

Messages of sympathy were cabled in from all over the world — from King George in London, from President Woodrow Wilson in Washington. The Canadian Prime Minister, Sir Robert Borden, called for a nation-wide mobilization of relief facilities, and dispatched nineteen million dollars in funds. Most blessed was Massachusetts, which raced to the scene a train-load of medical supplies and a corp of skilled glaziers to protect survivors against the cruel winter winds.

As Halifax licked it wounds, the newspapers were most distressed by what they called "thieves holding high carnival". Looters rifled pockets of the dead, snatched rings from icy fingers, ripped fur coats off unconscious women. A shopkeeper asked a starving child an exorbitant thirty cents for a load of bread, and was punched in the nose by an outraged soldier, who handed the child some free canned goods besides.

Halifax Deputy Mayor H. S. Colwell had to issue an order barring merchants from overcharging for glass, nails and coffins. Plumbers refused to hold their union rules in abeyance and work one minute beyond their regular eight hours, unless paid overtime. Bricklayers assumed a dog-in-the-manger attitude, and refused to allow plasterers to help repair chimneys. To charges against the unions, the Halifax Trades and Labour Council retorted by condemning rent-raising landlords for "squeezing the uttermost farthing out of the anguished necessities of the homeless".

Mrs. Logan regretfully admits that her own husband was a party to the general freebooting. On Saturday, he brought home on his shoulder a keg of beer foraged from a brewery near Cork Street, where the soldiers had broken in. He set it up in the snow in the upstairs room, where the blinded boarder, Mrs. Gentle, had lived. He plugged a tap in its bottom, and drank a quart in a jam jar.

When Mrs. Logan questioned him about it, he hemmed and hawed and finally said, "Ah, honey, it's just for the poor homeless boys at the barracks. They haven't a dime left in the world."

When her husband went out, Mrs. Logan poured all the contents of the keg into a pail, and spilled it foaming down the toilet. Then she refilled the keg with her own mysterious concoction.

That night, her husband carried the keg down to the barracks for an evening of revelry. He returned, spluttering, "Why, the boys said the foul stuff tasted like nothing at all. What did you do with my beer, honey?"

She smiled righteously. "I just fancied it up with my own Presbyterian brew, honey — a recipe of scrub snow and dirty water."

Mrs. Logan can now smile also at the attempts of her neighbours to pin the blame for the catastrophe on secret enemy agents. Two days after the explosion, amid hysterical rumours, Halifax Police Chief Hanrahan rounded up fourteen Haligonians of German descent; he arrested them as "Hun spy suspects". They were all released as guiltless by Police Commissioner Sir Percy Sherwood.

In Dartmouth across the channel, Police Chief McKenzie investigated the charge that a saboteur's carrier pigeon had flown through the broken window of a Mrs. A. McCool, bearing a message "written either in German or Austrian". It turned out that Mrs. McCool was the wife of a loyal quartermaster-sergeant, that the wounded pigeon had lit on the shoulder of one of her children, and she refused to give the innocent pet up. "The celluloid band around the poor thing's leg bore no Kaiser's spy message," she doughtily insisted. "Just the number 2,929, that's all."

163

Another German-spy charge was laid against John Johansen, helmsman aboard the ill-fated *Imo*. At the Massachusetts Relief hospital, where he lay wounded, an American nurse alleged that he "acted queerly" and was "shamming illness". She swore he offered her fifty dollars to "go out and get me a newspaper"; it was clearly a ruse to escape in her absence, with a secret German code hidden in the lining of his pajamas. An affidavit was further presented by a Mr. and Mrs. Andrew Ward of Denver, Colorado, claiming they recognized his picture, and that he was a German who had worked for them and left a year ago to return to the "Fatherland". An armed guard was immediately posted at the poor chap's bedside. But he was freed from suspicion and tendered an apology, when it turned out that he was a true-blue Norwegian.

The seeming culprits, Captain Lemedic and harbour pilot Francis Mackay of the *Mont Blanc,* were both arrested on a charge of manslaughter. A week after the disaster, they were tried in the official probe conducted in Halifax by Justice Drysdale, Judge in Admiralty.

Captain Lemedic blithely insisted he had carried no red flag warning of explosives aboard, because it would have lured every hostile U-boat off Halifax. A grimly humorous exchange arose when it was established that Captain Lemedic and Pilot Mackay had no way of conducting a conversation aboard the floating bomb of a ship. The captain admitted he spoke no English; and Mackay's claim that he knew "a little French" was soon shattered by the court.

"How would you instruct a Frenchman to reduce to half speed?" Mackay was asked.

He replied, "I would shout, *'Demitasse!'* "

Second Officer John Levêque of the *Mont Blanc* was then asked by the court through an interpreter, "What would you, as a French officer, do if a pilot cried *'Demitasse'*?"

"Naturally," the Frenchman replied, "I would go down below immediately for a cup of coffee."

Justice Drysdale found both the captain and the pilot guilty of "violating the rules of the road", recommended that their licenses be cancelled, and censured them both for being "guilty of neglect of public safety in not taking proper steps to warn inhabitants of the city of a probable explosion."

The manslaughter charges against both, however, were later dropped because of "insufficient evidence". Their alleged private guilt, after all, could not be equated with the two thousand newly dead being buried in the frosty, tortured ground of Halifax.

Mrs. Logan recalls attending the mass funeral service on December 17 for two hundred of the still unclaimed dead. Rows of coffins were gathered outside Chebucto Road School, and under wintry skies the crowds stood in the snow to weep and sing "O God, Our Help in Ages Past" and "Abide with Me", while the 66th Regiment band played the melancholy dirge, "The Dead March" in *Saul*. The unknown dead were buried in a common grave, 6 feet deep, 8 feet wide, and 120 feet long, dug in Fairview and Mount Olivet Cemetery by sailors. And the cold earth was heaped on the coffins in sight of the granite gravestones that marked the resting-place of the victims of another disaster — the sinking of the *Titanic*.

Mrs. Logan never did find her stray waif. "For years after," she says, "I kept looking through the streets of Halifax for that lost boy, with the blue powder scars eroded on his cheeks. I feel that the reason I never found him was that Halifax was left with too many lost and maimed strays just like him."

_ 8 _

The Flood That Drowned Winnipeg

A GENTLE, MISTY SPRINGTIME RAIN WAS FALLING outside his kitchen window that "Black Friday" of May 5, 1950. Lawson Alfred Ogg, an accountant, turned to stare at the yellowish-brown waters of the Red River lazily nibbling at the steps of his Kingston Crescent home in the St. Vital area of Winnipeg.

At twenty-four, Ogg was a good suburban citizen, a volunteer of the Winnipeg Optimist Club. He was one of the hundred thousand volunteers who had spent the last nine days sandbagging the thirty long miles of dikes that protected Greater Winnipeg against its worst flood in a century.

The swollen Red River, snaking northward from Minnesota, had converted the six hundred square miles of Manitoba farm land between the United States border and Winnipeg into one swirling inland sea. Canada's fourth-largest city itself now looked like a prairie Venice.

Suddenly, that sleety night, the temperature dipped down to freezing. A fifty-mile-an-hour wind spanked the flood waters against the city's great new Chinese walls, and dike after dike burst like paper bags.

In his kitchen, Lawson Alfred Ogg was stunned as his barricaded back door collapsed under the sheer volume of the water. The Red River was not ferocious in its death clutch. Like a giant, fumbling-tentacled squid, it groped for him under the armpits, and pulled him down to the basement, and slowly and inexorably drowned him there.

166

Lawson Alfred Ogg was the only Winnipegger killed by what was called the "Great Red River Rampage of 1950". This was perhaps the most remarkable aspect of Canada's most remarkable flood. It was not a disaster of death; it was a disaster of real estate. One hundred million dollars' damage was wreaked on five thousand homes, factories, and farms.

It was not a disaster of panic; it was a disaster of mass dislocation. In a Dunkirk-like evacuation, 107,000 out of Winnipeg's total population of 330,000 were forced to flee in the most orderly "war exercise" ever conducted in peace-time Canada. Above all, it was not a disaster of sudden violence; it was a disaster of slow, insidious, gnawing menace.

Behind their façade of cheerfulness, the hundred thousand men, women and teen-agers manning the dikes were gripped by dread. They had to watch the hungry waters inch up day by day, until on the night of May 18, the crest reached an incredible height of 30.3 feet above normal. The tension was such that, for six months after the onslaught, Manitoba was stricken with a record number of emotional disorders. Housewives who had always prided themselves on being good housekeepers collapsed into nervous wrecks as they tried to scrape the muck off homes that were now slimy ruins.

The headline-writers euphoniously referred to the river as the "rampaging Red". They were wrong. The Red has always been a waddling, somnolent clown of a river, rarely addicted to flashy violence. At the height of the flood, when it was most truculent, its speed never exceeded four miles an hour. It was more like a lazy serpent, its coils growing fatter and fatter from the run-off waters of the spring thaw. Then the bloated serpent rolled over the top of its cage, and placidly swallowed houses and bridges in its greedy maw.

The river's sinister buffoonery was glimpsed by Ralph Allen, author of the prairie novel, *Peace River Country*. He remembers a man piling up sand-bags against the encroaching Red at Fort Garry. The river was leaning against the dike with the seedy, aimless air of a drunk hanging onto a lamp-post, and smelled more of disinfectant than of danger.

Before the man's very eyes, a strangely gentle finger of water poked through the twenty-five-foot base of the dike, then plucked a pathway to the streets behind. The man dropped his sandbag, raised his fist to the sky, and uttered a heart-broken curse: "How can you lick a river like that when the dirty damned thing won't stand up and fight?"

The Red River has never fought back, just enveloped its prey, ever since its first recorded flood in 1826. Then, as now, it looped and twisted out of North Dakota, meandering northward for 730 miles across the flat carpet of the Red River Valley that was once the bed of glacial Lake Agassiz, and finally flowing into the lips of Lake Winnipeg. Then, as now, the Red's evil trio of flood conditions — unusually deep snows, a late thaw, heavy spring rains — combined to unlock its tributaries from their icy sheaths and make them overflow. First to spill over the countryside were the Red's early-melting tentacles in North Dakota — the Pipestem River, the Wild River, the Cheyenne. Then came the later-melting Manitoba rivers, the Pembina, the Rat, the Assiniboine. Clogged with their run-off and jammed with ice, the Red itself burst out at the seams, like flabby flesh that could no longer be contained by a corset.

In 1826, as in 1950, the Red flood drowned but one victim living in Winnipeg — the colony that was pointedly named from the Indian word *ouinipeg,* meaning dirty water. The other pioneers escaped to the higher ground of Stony Mountain and Bird's Hill; and an eyewitness, Alexander Ross, of the Hudson's Bay Company, described their frenzy:

"The people had to fly from their homes for the dear life, some of them saving only the clothes they had on their backs. . . . The shrieks of the children, the lowing of cattle, and the howling of dogs added terror to the scene. . . . The frightened inhabitants collected in groups on any dry spot that remained visible above the waste of water. . . . Hardly a house or building of any kind was left standing in the colony."

One hundred and twenty-four years later, the Red's havoc was infinitely greater. But the panic was kept bottled. Red River Valley people, inured to drought and grasshopper invasions, had since learned to laugh rather than whistle when passing a graveyard. Like those living in the shadow of Mount Vesuvius, they had grown accustomed to the seasonal tantrums of the elements. As late as April 3, 1950, the Winnipeg *Free Press* reported that the surging Red River was forcing evacuees to flee from Moorhead, Minnesota, and from Fargo in North Dakota. On the same day, it quoted D. B. Gow, the Federal Government's district engineer in Winnipeg, as making soothing, non-Cassandra-like sounds: "We expect nothing this year to approach the 1948 flood. We will have high water. But we always have high water."

168

Within two weeks, the six hundred square miles of farm land south of Winnipeg was a spreading, turgid lake, moving sluggishly and inevitably at the rate of six miles a day toward the city.

People woke in the morning to find the chill brown waters lapping over their beds in the rural French-Canadian towns of Ste. Agathe, St. Adolphe, St. Norbert. Morris and Emerson become completely engulfed ghost towns, their houses floating like play blocks thrown into puddles by a capricious child. The seventy-five Indians at the submerged Netley Creek Reservation had to pitch their wigwams on higher ground, while the RCMP sleigh dogs at Horndean perched precariously on top of their kennels.

Rats floated by Starbuck and Gretna, their sharp green eyes glistening like beacons in the night on their plank sampans. Near Letellier, where the Hespeler dam crumbled like a sugar wafer, cows floundered dejectedly toward islet patches of frosty ground, and a flood evacuee named Mrs. Ed Lesperance moaned, "It was enough to make a body cry. The cattle were neck-deep in water, poor things, and bawling fit to break your heart."

A bedraggled woman on a raft went spinning by Altona, singing at the top of her lungs:

> Jesus, lover of my soul,
> Let me to Thy bosom fly,
> While the waters nearer roll,
> While the tempest still is high.

Mounties paddled canoes to rescue families stranded in the top storeys of their isolated farm homes. Some of the refugees refused to budge ("My tank of goldfish need a change of water every day"), and others clutched precious possessions. A preacher wouldn't move without his family Bible, and an old-age pensioner without his canary in a cage. And a wife left all her jewellery to the mercy of the flood, as long as she could salvage her coveted curling trophy.

"Gentlemen," said a spry old gaffer, as he clambered from his McTavish roof-top and jumped into a boat, "can any of you redcoats give me a plug of baccy for my pipe? I don't smoke tailor-mades."

Another man, poling a raft made of old planks and oil drums, waved aside a proferred mug of coffee at Rosenfeld. "Please," he said cheerfully. "Let me have cream and tea in my coffee — absolutely no water."

When the RCMP paddled into the French-speaking village of Aubigny, one of the Mounties said, "I guess we'll have to shoot all the women and children out of here tomorrow." The men-folk exploded, *"Mon Dieu!* What do you mean, shooting our families?"

A farmer at St. Norbert, sleeping atop the piano in his attic — amid twenty thousand dollars' worth of scurrying mink, and bleating goats, and cackling roosters — stubbornly refused to evacuate his Noah's ark. "I have everything here that I own," the prairie curmudgeon said. "It is all under water, and the river makes it look like a ship. If my ship goes down, gentlemen, I am going down with it."

Two new-born babies were named Flood. And a Ukrainian mother, who gave birth to a son while being carried on a drenched mattress, promptly christened him Moses. She cited the Biblical verse, "And she called his name Moses . . . 'Because I drew him out of the water'."

"My baby's name is subject to change," said Mrs. John Corneilson of the town of Rosenort, after she gave birth to a dimpled girl with brown eyes named Loraine Joyce. "Maybe we could call her something more appropriate. Like Aqua — Latin for water."

There was plenty of aqua when the child was born at 5 A.M. It happened after an Odyssey that took the expectant mother on a ten-mile trek in three cars and two boats along the washed-out highway from Rosenort to the Morris General Hospital.

"Of all the babies I have delivered this was the trickiest," said Dr. J. W. Holowin. "We rode like mad. And all the time it was kind of half-snowing, half-sleeting. It was so cold, we had to break through the ice on the water. The mother was a real trouper. She lay in the cold, damp bottom of that boat without a sound, and her expecting her baby any second."

Loraine ("Aqua") Joyce emerged safely, weighing eight and a half pounds. She seemed quite unconcerned that the hospital in Morris was in the middle of its own fourteen-mile rice-paddy lake, ringed by a faltering dike that the citizens were futilely sandbagging.

Indeed, Morris was one of the two most deluged towns in the clinging Red River Valley. The other was the town of Emerson. Wind-

170

whipped snow and rain hammered at both, and merchants boarded up store windows ready to flee. Cars were left abandoned on flooded main streets; and as the rising water hid their bodies, the tops took on the appearance of water bugs.

In Morris, six CNR sleepers and a diner at the railway platform fed and housed the evacuees, and were affectionately nicknamed the "Express to Nowhere". In Emerson, where CPR bunk cars did equally valiant duty, a railroad bridgeman called Jim Boyd was nicknamed "Barnacle Bill". He patrolled thirty-five miles of the breakwater along the inundated railroad line in a doughty little boat nicknamed the "Empress of Emerson". When asked how he kept his bearings on the expanse of water, the CPR adventurer said, "I steered by the names on the tops of submerged elevators."

In both towns, the Manitoba Telephone Company girls worked around the clock at their switchboards. With their knees tucked practically under their chins, they squatted on a platform sandbagged against the rising waters. They wore orange "butcher boy" pajamas inside hip-waders, lived on canned beans, and snatched sleep in a trailer.

"We were always forgetting about the drop into four feet of icy water beside our platform," said one girl at the Morris exchange, Doris Walter. "I forgot one day. I stepped off the darn thing while carrying a batch of cookies. Down I went. But I managed to keep the cookies dry over my head."

"If you can believe it," said another Morris switchboard operator, Shirley Coates, "we got so tired of sharing one mirror and just looking at men, we waded uptown just to get a look at another woman. There weren't any. We were the last women in town to evacuate."

In Emerson, the telephone-exchange superintendent, Jim McGregor, had to argue the remaining three girls into leaving. They wanted to stay at their posts, even after the protective wall of sandbags collapsed and two feet of rushing water swirled around their legs. "That was some week we put in," McGregor said, after finally being forced to cut the service. "We did all our own cooking, and slept on collapsible camp cots. Thank Heaven we had a staff with a sense of humour."

The humour of the last straggling refugees from both towns was high-spirited. Fred Edge, a reporter from the Winnipeg *Free Press*, was marooned with these die-hards on the highest point in Morris — the CNR railway platform.

"An RCMP officer and I spent the whole night trying to figure how to dive into the cellar of a submerged hotel," Edge remembers. "We wanted to come up with a couple of cases of whisky for the men refugees. We decided against it, on grounds of contamination. Instead, I bought a case of oranges from a local warehouse — all the fruit, luckily, was stacked on the top floor. I split the case open for the hungry refugee kids on the railway platform. Then I hand-lettered a sign: 'Help yourselves as guests of the Winnipeg *Free Press*.' This went over mighty big.

"Then I telegraphed the CBC in Winnipeg. I suggested they broadcast for a motorcade of volunteers to come to a high point of land twenty miles away. The army would meet them there with the loads of remaining Morris refugees in the amphibious trucks called DUKW's or 'ducks'. Well, when the army started shuttling back and forth with the people, there were more volunteer cars waiting there than we could use. That shows you the all-out-help spirit of prairie people in a time of crisis."

Ultimately, the only people left in deserted Morris were two Mounties in Inspector K. B. Lockwood's office. They presented a wry spectacle. The officer in charge would sit at a desk on a chair mounted on stilts, and another RCMP officer would paddle a canoe right into the room, and salute him with a wan smile.

One of the last people to leave Morris was a merry, Lancashire-born butcher, John Davies. The flood inundated his home on James Street East to a depth of seven feet, and left seven outhouses floating outside his back door. When he saw a log spinning by, with a rabbit on one end and a skunk on the other, Davies decided, "Well, the flood has come, and it's time for all Morris to go visiting." He evacuated, with his wife Kay, and their five children, to the farm-house of Harvey Stevenson, two miles north on higher ground. Then, as "Lake Morris" still billowed up, they all had to move to another farm-house. There twenty-five people, huddled together in what they good-naturedly nicknamed "The Covernton's Hotel", lived on a diet of milk and eggs for two weeks.

"Our neighbour had a pair of leaky hip-waders," Davies recalls with a grin. "When he'd step into the water, they'd soon be filled with

172

uncomfortable, icy slush. 'I'll fix that,' he said. So he heated up a kettle of water and poured it into his rubbers. 'I'll at least *start out* with warm toes!' he said."

Davies was perplexed at the dilemma posed by his four horses. When the water crept into the barn, he swam out to the manure pile. He paddled out to feed them every day with hay from the top twelve bales still dry in the barn. He was trying to loosen the last tier of hay, when he was suddenly confronted with two barn skunks.

"Lo and behold," he says, "in my excitement, I leaped off the bale. I caught my toe in the bale wire, and plunged head-first into three feet of water. I could have shot the pesky sprayers. But I wanted them to hold fire, so their perfume wouldn't spoil our hay."

As the river kept rising, he recalls, the four horses kept crowding each other for space on the manure pile, "like kids playing 'I'm the King of the Castle'." Finally, he built them a raft by wiring together forty floating telephone poles. Each day an RCAF helicopter would hover overhead and bomb them with fresh bales of hay.

"The first day or so, when the helicopter dropped hay from the sky," Davies says, "the horses would get awfully wild, and threaten to break loose and plunge into the river. But they soon got used to the hay plane, and would look up as good as to say, 'Thanks, pal.'"

One day a nearby neighbour named Bruce MacKenzie was squatting atop his machine-shed and waved a friendly hand at the "Operation Haylift" helicopter. "But the pilot thought Bruce wanted a load of hay," Davies remembers."So he swung around and dropped a big bale on the machine-shed, almost smacking Bruce in the kisser, and causing him almost to take a swan-dive into the murky waters. But being a non-swimmer, Bruce sadly decided it would be better to take a chance on being whacked with a bomb of hay, than on sinking into a grave of mucky gumbo."

In Emerson, a wheat farmer named Nicholas Constantine sat at the coach door of the last train to leave town. A western meadowlark perched on the top rail of a nearby telephone pole sticking out of the flood, and called the six clear, crisp notes peculiar to that bird. Nicholas Constantine whistled the same sweet notes back to the bird. The meadowlark answered, and Constantine replied again, and he shook his head and cursed.

"Do you know what that bird is calling?" he asked. "When I was a little squirt going to school, we were told that when the meadowlark whistled like that, he was saying, 'Please-God-give-me-some-wheat.'"

Constantine spat toward some plows and harrows jutting from the Red's yellow-brown water, which under the obscenely bright sun seemed somehow to assume the colour of blood. "I don't think," said the wheat farmer, "that the little meadowlark is going to get his wish this harvest season."

The train pulled away. Half a mile north, the railway tracks vanished under two feet of rushing water. Two bridge experts stood on the cow-catcher, gingerly probing ahead of the slowly moving train to make sure the ribbons of steel were still there. Constantine was still whistling the sweet meadowlark notes as the train chuffed across a bridge and its floor bellied against the blood-coloured waters.

They never made it to Winnipeg. The "D.P. Special", as it was nicknamed, crammed with 525 refugees and a dozen cars of livestock, gave up in a track wash-out close to Winnipeg. The people were shunted to a siding in Winnipeg's suburban Fort Garry, and the cows moved bellowing by barge to Ste. Agathe.

Winnipeg by now was a dike-encircled fort bracing itself for the full shock of attack. Sandbag ramparts were thrown up at each of the ten loops where the Red coils like a snake through the heart of the city. By the beginning of May, the jogs in the Red's serpentine path were spilling over, and the water rose a foot in a day.

Most direly menaced were the suburbs, linked to Winnipeg proper by bridges. A small volunteer citizen army sloshed through knee-deep mud to strengthen the dikes at the adjoining cathedral city of St. Boniface, at St. Vital, Fort Garry, East and West Kildonan, and Point Douglas; on Lyndale Drive and Riverview, and on Elm Park and Norwood and Wildwood. But despite their herculean delaying action, new rains swelled the tide of flood to twenty-three feet above normal, and the Red River bubbled and swirled relentlessly higher.

Zero hour came on the night of "Black Friday", May 5. Rain, sleet and snow, lashed by a fifty-mile-an-hour gale, stung the placid river into a fury. White-tipped waves gouged deep bites out of eight dikes, and the sandbag bastions crumpled and spread like chocolate-cake batter in

174

a pan. Four of the city's eleven bridges snapped like clay pipes, and houses were washed out as though a child were wiping a pictured village off a blackboard.

The wall of water that pulverized the Wildwood dike drove three hundred families trembling from their homes into the bitterly cold night with only the clothes on their backs. The people of St. Vital were caught like a nut in a nutcracker between the Red and the angrily swollen Seine River, normally a creek to spit across. Two hundred patients were hurriedly carried out on stretchers from swamped King Edward and King George Hospitals, students were evacuated from Ravenscourt Boys School, and the Playhouse Theatre on Market Avenue had to shut down after a hasty performance of *The Wise Virgins*.

In the early pre-dawn hours of Saturday, May 6, the siren atop the Winnipeg *Free Press* Building (mute since air-raid exercises during the war) wailed its urgent warning. The river had approached disaster stage — twenty-seven feet above normal, and still implacably rising. The city itself seemed to have settled tipsily on one side, plunging one-third of Winnipeg into water. Premier Douglas Campbell of Manitoba declared a state of emergency. Vice Admiral H. T. V. Grant, chief of Canada's naval staff, declared the situation "the most catastrophic flood ever seen in Canada." And Prime Minister Louis St. Laurent told the House of Commons in Ottawa that flood assistance would be rushed to the disaster area.

In beleagured Winnipeg, Flood Control Headquarters were set up under the command of Brigadier Ronald E. A. Morton, D-Day Commander of the Fort Garry Horse in the Normandy Invasion. From a makeshift command post in the Manitoba Legislature Building, this composed, black-moustached soldier of forty-nine, in red-tabbed battle dress, fought a battle of containment against the flood.

His orders flowed by field phone and the city's three radio stations to nearly five thousand army, navy and air-force men, working in three shifts around the clock. Occasionally he hopped into a helicopter for a hurried look at new danger points. His main concern was the city's vital power stations, entrenched behind straining dikes more than six feet high; if they collapsed, the whole city would be plunged into a chaos of darkness.

175

Some of the hundred thousand volunteers, sweating on the dikes, grumbled at the authoritarianism of "army brass". Most Winnipeggers gave a waterlogged cheer for the discipline imposed by the boss of "Operation Red Ramp". As in a war, food was stockpiled; emergency passes and ration cards were printed. Schools, movies, taverns and many restaurants were closed. The radio stations went on twenty-four-hour flood duty, and the *Free Press* and *Tribune* were urged to print Sunday editions. Ten thousand people daily were inoculated against typhoid. And emergency flood centres feeding cocoa and sandwiches to evacuees and dike workers were set up in the YMCA's, Canadian Legion Posts, and the University of Manitoba buildings. The city auditorium itself was converted into a vast Red Cross dormitory.

Most of all, besieged Winnipeggers were reassured by the help from all over Canada speeded to their battle front. An RCAF and TCA armada airlifted 1.5 million sandbags. Highballing freights of the CNR and CPR rushed in a million pounds of flood-fighting equipment. The men and supplies ranged from navy frogmen and divers from Halifax to precious rubber boots and pumps from as far away as San Francisco.

Now the throbbing of the pumps began to take over the whole city, like the pocketa-pocketa-pocketa of the machines in Walter Mitty's daydreams. It added to the eerie atmosphere. In downtown Winnipeg, two hundred-pound manhole covers popped like corks under the pressure from overloaded storm sewers; and the streets were laced with fire hoses as the pumps laboured to force back the stale-smelling sewage. In the suburbs, bulldozers ripped through lawns, gardens and golf courses like giant moles, chewing the earth and spitting it out against the rim of the ravenous river.

By day, gulls wheeled and screeched over puddle-pitted Portage and Main, as though downtown Winnipeg were a seaport. By night, army searchlights stabbed through sleet and rain. They illuminated the dike workers heaving sandbags under the stark branches of Manitoba maple and scabrous elm. Winnipeg's residential streets assumed the aspect of trenches in a no man's land.

There were scenes of freakish humour and ironic contrasts everywhere.

At the approach to the Norwood Bridge — open only to the army's lumbering, thirty-foot-long amphibious ducks — a police officer directs

176

the stream of traffic by standing hip-deep in the centre of a lake. A baby's highchair and a park bandstand come dancing by a traffic sign; the sign is nailed to a post that has tipped into the street, and it reads, "Go Slow".

Yet the Royal Alexander Hotel still stands high and dry downtown, still providing impeccable service — except in the opinion of a dowager who grumbles, "Your Turkish bath is not operating."

While a swarm of dike workers passes by, grimy in hip-waders, a chic lady shopper pauses at the corner of Portage and Main. She dips the toe of her new galosh in the swirling gutter and watches the mud wash off, her foot arching to meet the water as though a cat were daintily washing its paws.

At an impassable spot not too far away, a newsboy ponders how to cross to a customer's house on the other side of the Seine River. He is twelve, and he is tired, and he is crying. His problem is a large one, for he and his kind can't find half their customers any more. "They have all run away," he says.

Atop the firehall in St. Vital, a garish red, white and blue poster screams, "Welcome!" There is no welcome. The firehall is the only dry spot left in this seven-mile-long and four-mile-wide municipality, whose eighteen thousand people have been forced to flee the river. The only sound left in this hushed desolation is the incongruously cheerful twittering of robins. They swing north with the spring, and flood cannot stop them. They perch above the water in the top branches of the scrub-oak trees; they fly from roof to roof of once smart stucco homes that now are silent shells.

"My husband and I have a hundred dollars' worth of groceries stocked away," says Mrs. John Angel. Her husband must police the abandoned homes, and so she stays in St. Vital — the only housewife left there. Wading in hip-boots, she hangs out the washing above her backyard lake. "The only things I miss," she says, "are the daily papers and fresh milk. I'm kept busy watering everybody's plants around here, and feeding nine deserted dogs. It's pitiful, the way they keep swimming back to their homes every day, searching for their masters."

There is a touch of comedy in suburban East Kildonan, when a housewife in hip-boots sloshes across her kitchen, knee-deep in water, to

177

answer her door. It is the postman, also in hip-boots, who delivers one letter — her monthly water bill.

There is a touch of pathos at the Elmwood Cemetery, where the grave-diggers have abandoned their jobs to man the dikes. Her sister having died, Mrs. Lillian Kirkley sighs, "Dozens of caskets have been left untouched for days. There's no one to bury them. Some are in cold storage. I don't know what to do with my poor sister's body."

There is a touch of jubilation in St. Boniface as the cathedral bells ring out to celebrate a wedding. Two refugees from soaked St. Norbert — Deloraine Martel, twenty, and Camille Dorge, twenty-four — are determined to get married behind the protection of the Norwood dike. Red Cross volunteers serve as a guard of honour, and the groom carries his bride across a water-covered sidewalk, using sandbags as stepping-stones.

There is a touch of the macabre as an impresario, William Bernard, wonders what happened to his wandering troupe called the World Series Freak Show. They cleared customs last at Port Huron, Michigan, and were supposed to have opened on May 9, in St. Vital. He rhymes off the cast, including a snake girl, a fish boy, an ossified man, a two-headed baby, a leopard-boy; he mentions a trunk full of human heads. "I don't like to think of those freaks of mine roving about helpless in a flood," he says dolorously.

There is a touch of ingenuity in North Kildonan by a sixty-three-year-old market gardener named Jacob Vanderhorst. His home and greenhouses are washed out, but he thoughtfully salvages his automobile by hoisting it with block and tackle high and dry in a shade tree.

There is a touch of heroism in Fort Garry, as a forty-eight-year-old construction worker named Lloyd Vezey gives army engineers permission to dynamite his life's dreams sky-high. They want to blow up the four-thousand-dollar cottage that Vezey has newly built himself on Crescent Drive. Torn loose from its foundations by the Red, it perches hazardously on the edge of a coulee; it threatens to drop into twenty feet of water, float down-stream, and knock asunder the Elm Park bridge. "Guess I'm wiped out," Vezey says quietly. He continues to shovel sand into bags for the McGillivray dike. "Guess I'll just have to live in my brother's trailer."

And there are touches of religion in all its manifestations.

178

In the small frame Gordon United Church, on a flood-washed hill in East Kildonan, dike workers take time off on Sunday to hear the choir, consisting of four women and one man, sing "Lead On, O King Eternal", and to listen to Rev. E. A. MacLean intone "Rock of Ages, Cleft for Me" and the consoling verses of the Forty-sixth Psalm:

God is our refuge and strength, a very present help in trouble. Therefore will not we fear, though the earth be removed, and though the mountains be carried into the midst of the sea; though the waters thereof roar and be troubled, though the mountains shake with the swelling thereof.

Yet on Woodrow Place, a CNR expressman named Fred Gallagher, troubled by the flood in his basement and his electricity snuffed off, is not comforted by the spiritual guidance issued from Toronto. A religious commentator there, Jane Scott, announced that the flood was caused by the sins of the people; and she urged Winnipeggers to "pray, lest ye enter into temptation, for Satan and his hosts are just like the Red River." Irked no end, Gallagher wrote to the press that sin had nothing to do with it, and that all the praying in the world would be no substitute for sandbagging.

"I was flooded with telephone calls," Gallagher chortles. "A great many congratulating me, and a great many condemning me."

And in St. Boniface, at the dike protecting the Sanitarium of the Grey Nuns, there is a gentle fusion of prayer and sandbagging. With their robes pinned an inch above the mud, thirteen old nuns smile their sad-sweet smiles at the restrained curses of the soldiers working beside them, and they pray softly while they fill bags with mud.

The Grey Nuns are joined at their job by the Most Reverend George Cabana, Coadjutor Archbishop of St. Boniface Diocese, his clerical collar concealed by overalls. Industriously, the Archbishop begins shoveling six shovelsful of sand per bag, instead of the customary three or four. An army private, who has been toting bags steadily for twenty-four hours, protests.

"Look, you big lug," the soldier growls, "either shovel four to the bag, or I'll plug you into the dike."

"Okay, Bud," the Archbishop replies mildly.

The cheerfulness of the voluntary workers in the face of the Red's creeping menace was extraordinary. The Salvation Army, which sent out trucks loaded with refreshments, "deserve a special clap on the back," recalls Mrs. Lillian Tucnik, whose home was located near the Salter Bridge. "The people who worked on those trucks usually had daytime jobs, too," she says, "and the prospect of going out on damp, cold evenings was not very pleasant."

J. Ayotte was one of the volunteer rescuers who worked night and day to help evacuate inundated St. Jean Baptiste. He still recalls with sorrow one man who got tangled up in a live Hydro line that was hanging close to the water. "He escaped with burnt hands — which were later amputated."

Others prefer to recall the comic relief. Mrs. S. J. Morency, whose husband was one of the reserve navy men who helped fight the flood, recalls a certain boastful gentleman. "He was bragging about how his home was the only dry one on the block," she remembers. "So he invited several of the rescue boys in to see how cleverly he had plugged his drain pipe with a large four-by-six. He demonstrated its security by shaking it. To his chagrin, it came loose. In seconds, he too had a wet house. The rescue boys had to break windows so the embarrassed fellow could swim out of his supposedly safe haven."

Mrs. Ruth Drysdale, on the nursing staff of the Winnipeg Health Department, believes the flood even exercised a beneficial effect. "If brought to light unsatisfactory conditions in some of the city nursing homes," she says. "Had the Red River not routed them out, the drab and dreary existence of their inmates probably would have gone unnoticed for years longer."

Mrs. Drysdale helped transport many of these chronically ill patients to Regina. "I can never forget one elderly man, propped on an elbow by the train window," she says. "His face glowed with the fascination of watching the countryside. He remarked wistfully, 'I hope there's a flood every year! Behind four walls, I haven't seen grass in five years.'"

The flood was a great social leveller, linking in sandbag chains old codgers in their seventies, Boy Scouts, and zoot-suited members of the Winnipeg gang known as the Dewdroppers. Every twenty-four hours, about five thousand of these volunteers would be shuttled from the

Winnipeg *Free Press* Building to the city's various dikes, in free cabs offered by Moore's Taxi.

They coined their own "dike ese" lingo. To "chain up for tailor-mades" meant to pass from hand to hand bags already filled with sand and tied at the top. A "stockpile of sausages" was the scornful epithet for potato sacks too large for the needed three or four shovelsful of sand in them. Looping rough binder twine about the neck of a sandbag was "tying blisters". And many fortyish volunteers forgot their middle-age spread as they developed instead "sandbag shoulders" and "flood fatigue" at the bag-filling "salt mines".

The volunteers cheered themselves at the dikes with their own popular songs. They sang, "If I'd-a Known You was Comin' I'd-a Built a Dike", and "If You Dike Like Me and I Dike Like You", and "Evacuate, It's Later Than You Think". Top on their hit parade was a parody of "Music, Music, Music", composed by Eddie Paleshnuik and Eddie Werrun, and played endlessly by the Winnipeg radio stations:

> Chuck another sandbag on,
> On the dike that's wide and long,
> All we need is volunteers
> And sandbags, sandbags, sandbags!

Scott Young, the Winnipeg writer, can vouch for the gutty endurance and humour of the dike volunteers. He spent fifteen days helping to sandbag the massive seven-mile Norwood dike along the curving stretch of Lyndale Crescent, and he wrote a novel based on it, *The Flood.*

"I never hope to see anything again like that fight for the Norwood dike," he remembers. "Three human beings, one on a shovel, one on a bag, and one with twine, can fill and tie five sandbags a minute at a pace they can keep up for hour after hour. You get into an impassioned state of mind. You work groggily until 3 A.M. and you're up at 7 A.M., back for more. Sleep gets to mean nothing. Yet there was no over-all direction, no foreman, no time-clock but the river."

As a greenhorn on the sandbag chain, Young could only converse in a series of exhausted grunts as he caught and tossed these flying

181

medicine balls. Yet he recalls one sandbag-filling station where two dozen boys and girls from high school interspersed their labours with jitterbugging to tunes from a battery radio.

"When each load of sand came, they worked like rockets until the supply was all sandbagged," he says, with amazement. "Then they turned the music higher, and danced on the sandy pavement under the yellow street light in the soft, damp spring night. The menacing river, a hundred feet away, was six feet above the street level that they danced on. And yet they danced, until the next load of sand came."

Young remembers fondly the ribaldry that the volunteers directed at the windy rah-rah speeches of officialdom. The night that Defense Minister Brooke Claxton and Winnipeg's Mayor Garnet Coulter delivered a radio broadcast, Young was helping two men fill sandbags at the "salt mines".

"I heard Claxton and Coulter and those other big shots speak on the radio," one worker said.

"Yeah?" asked the other. "What did the guys say?"

The first man filled a couple of bags and paused. Then he observed dryly, "They said we sure got a big flood on here."

Another Winnipeg author, Laura Goodman Salverson, remembers how the battle against the flood prevented her from finishing the writing of her novel, *Immortal Rock*. Everyday her husband George would measure how far the river had crept up the trunk of a poplar tree in an escarpment in front of their six-room stucco bungalow on Churchill Drive in Fort Rouge. After three weeks, when the tree was totally immersed, she knew it was time to flee to Toronto.

A spunky, hazel-eyed grandmother of sixty-nine, Mrs. Salverson recalls with amusement one stormy night when she was all alone in the house, and sheets of rain were gusting through the window of the top storey. Her husband rushed home from his job as CNR dispatcher at Winnipeg's Union Station, to find her in an odd stance.

"The electricity was cut off," she says. "And I was standing there, with my nightgown tucked between my knees, and holding a candle in one hand and a pail in the other, and trying to scoop up the dirty brown water. Just as George entered, I caught a glimpse of myself in the

182

mirror, and I couldn't help bursting into laughter. 'Oh, my God!' I gasped, 'Lady Macbeth!'"

She also recalls with delight how Winnipeg suburbanites dealt with the few snobbish neighbours who preferred to stay in the living-room and play cards, instead of pitching into the communal dike-building. "In typical western revenge," she says, "the volunteer workers would stand outside the picture window of the snobs, fold their arms, and just glare into the parlour malevolently. We called it the 'prairie evil-eye hex'."

Another Fort Rouge housewife, Mrs. Alice L. Squires, felt in a trance-like state; she was marooned in her one-storey house on Rosedale Avenue, while her husband Maurice was out sandbagging. "As I gazed at the black expanse in our flooded basement each day, and saw lovely old homes floating down the river, I seemed to be living in a dream," she recalls. "You can achieve the same peculiar sensation by staring into a lake until almost mesmerized. The whole world seemed to be made of water, and many a man would have sold his wife for a pump."

Like other home owners in her residential area, Mrs. Squires wondered what to do when the sewers began to back up through toilets. It brought only happiness to her seven-year-old son Bob; he rushed into the kitchen exultant with the news: "Mom, the sewers are coming back up, instead of down! Oh, boy!" Some of her neighbours tried to plug up the sewer traps with linseed, rags and newspapers; others purposely flooded the basements of their homes to equalize the pressure exerted by the river.

"It was an eerie sensation," she says, "seeing the water rise out of the saturated ground of your own back yard. My husband and I were busy trying to pump our basement. Then I looked out of the basement window, and I saw the water starting to bubble right out of the ground, like an artesian well. We then realized the absurdity of what we were doing."

A dike worker on Jubilee Avenue nearby, Don Mole, prefers to recall the light banter of his fellow-volunteers. One night an army officer sonorously informed the sandbaggers, "Men, do you know that as much water has evaporated during the last twenty-four hours as has run downstream?"

Next morning, as the eight o'clock shift shivered on the soggy dike, a drizzle began to pour down. Someone, Mole recalls, sang out, "Well, here comes that damn evaporation!"

This same spirit of *bonhomie* on the dikes is recalled by a CBC Winnipeg newsman, C. E. L'Ami. After the local radio station, CBW, had broadcast an appeal for dike workers and sandwich makers, this conversation occurred when a call was put through to emergency headquarters at the East Kildonan dike:

"How are you getting along down there?"

"Oh, fine."

"Lots of dike men?"

"Mister, we got enough men here to *drink* the flood."

"Oh? And how about sandwiches?"

"We been fillin' sandbags with 'em for two hours — and we *still* got three tons left."

More than two hundred newspapermen from throughout Canada, the United States and England descended on Winnipeg and contributed their share of hijinks.

Some slept on camp cots in the Winnipeg *Free Press* news-room; after being aroused in the morning by their "dormitory house mother", Orton Grain, the news editor, they would drink a slug of rye or rum for breakfast in the men's wash-room. The Toronto *Star* dispatched its usual battalion of some twenty reporters; and one reporter kept continuous watch with a telescope from his window in the Fort Garry Hotel, in order to signal when the Norwood dike might collapse. One enterprising reporter from the Toronto *Telegram,* John MacLean, initiated a beauty contest to find "Miss Dike Builder of 1950" — and, naturally, won a scoop with his photo of the winner.

The prose churned out by some of the out-of-town newspapermen was lush. "A Pelion of calamity," wrote one word-painter, with a flair for the classics, "is piled with each passing hour here upon the Ossa of calamity already showered upon this stricken city."

"This city is sick of working against the flood," began the Toronto *Telegram's* Ron Poulton in a forthright dispatch. "You're fed up reading about the flood. I'm tired of writing about the flood."

184

The legend arose that a green correspondent cabled his London editor: GOD LOOKED DOWN FROM THE PEMBINA HILLS NEAR WINNIPEG TODAY ON AN AWESOME SCENE OF DESTRUCTION . . .

The editor wired back: FORGET FLOOD. INTERVIEW GOD.

According to the records kept by the Canadian Red Cross, a Los Angeles newspaper reported that the flood had washed away the entire city; and a New York correspondent announced that every inhabitant had fled Winnipeg.

This was scare-mongering; but Winnipeg's plight was in fact growing more grim. On May 10, the city's steam heat was cut off, and the Red continued rising insatiably to nearly thirty feet above normal. It threatened to devour the reeling bridge that linked Winnipeg with its twin city of St. Boniface. In a futile effort to save the Leighton Avenue dike, men of the Queen's Own Cameron Highlanders were lying on their bellies, flinging sandbags into the rushing torrent just before they ran, while a piper staunchly stayed to play The Road to the Isles.

In an effort to "thin out the population", Brigadier Morton advised immediate evacuation of all Winnipeg's "non-combatants" — its women and children. So began an exodus of more than a hundred thousand persons. Roads out of the city were black by day and brilliant by night with traffic. Hundreds of the aged and sick were stretcher-borne to planes or sleeping-cars, which were called "dawn to dark evacuee specials" The last patients to leave the unheated King George Isolation Hospital were nine polio-stricken Eskimo children, trembling and able only to mutter through chattering teeth, "Too much water. Too much cold." And at Grace Hospital, Nurse Laura Mickler bid farewell to a flood-exposed woman diker whom she fondly called "Miss Seepage".

From throughout Canada poured thousands of telegrams, offering the evacuees shelter. A Toronto woman extended the use of her Eaton's charge account up to a hundred dollars to buy clothing for the children. And owners of summer cottages in resort towns outside Winnipeg mailed keys to the Red Cross, asking that their places be used for the homeless.

The city's block-square civic auditorium, which had been taken over by the Red Cross as an evacuation centre, looked like a war-time barracks. The place smelled steamily of mud and wet wool, and overlooking it from a glass case was a huge stuffed buffalo. The floor of the assembly hall sprouted double-decker wooden bunks, each humped with sleeping figures under dun-gray army blankets. The platform was piled with baby bottles and cat food and canary seed, and the walls were lined with second-hand clothing, with men's long underwear strung unchastely beside pale blue panties; and free for the asking were dry stockings nicknamed "Red River nylons". The loud-speaker — its acoustics so splendid that an evacuated pet tomcat yowling in his crated box sounded like a caged lion — blared its melancholy refrain over the evacuees seated on benches: "Two places still empty in the car leaving for Brandon. Two places empty in the car leaving for Brandon. . . ."

Charles B. Ayres, a salty Irish gym instructor of seventy, handled the overflow of refugees at the six-storey Central YMCA on Vaughn, off Portage Avenue. "Mostly, it was a matter of bunk a bunch of them, fill their bellies with hot stew, give them warm socks and underwear, and get them out," he recalls. "But things happened to tug at your heart-strings and tickle your funny-bone.

"We strung up a blanket affair for the women-folk to get behind while changing; and once it fell down, and that started them laughing. There was a little woman, about as big as a pound of tea, and her little husband, who looked like a peanut, and they overwhelmed us with their — imagine it! — nine big children. There was one poor old lady about sixty-five, moaning all night about losing her Annie — she saw her go down in the river; and in the morning you could have knocked me over with a feather when we found Annie was her cow. And there was one good sport who came in at lunch-time, and said she was the Queen of Sheba, and demanded regal-like that someone wait on her — and, well, you just can't down a proud spirit like that. I had to laugh after it was all over when my wife remarked, 'Well, we sure got rid of a lot of our old clothes.' But we both agreed a calamity like this shows that most people are swell guys."

On the night of May 18, the Red soared to a fantastic crest of 30.3 feet above normal. At Flood Headquarters, two alternate plans were readied. One was "Operation If" or "Blackboy" — a disaster plan for evacuation of the *entire* city, if the Red rose another two feet. The other plan was "Operation Rainbow" — a plan to get back to work and rehabilitate Winnipeg, if all went rosy.

For long days the fate of Winnipeg hung in balance. Finally, on May 25, with the river creeping down to 28.5 feet under a blazing

186

western sun, a dry, light breeze actually lifted dust on Portage Avenue. Brigadier Morton relaxed his evacuation order

Thus ended twenty days and nights of constant siege, of effort to conquer a river and save a city. Winnipeggers trudged back into "Operation Rainbow", scraping the slime from their homes.

The inevitable name-calling began. Winnipeg Alderman C. E. Simonite complained that Premier Douglas Campbell's indecisiveness had been "pretty close to criminal neglect". Some home owners, surveying their buckled pianos, their sewage-fouled cellars and their back-yard quagmires, derisively began calling the flood scene "Campbell's Soup". A sign appeared in a Winnipeg suburb: "I paid $17,000 for this magnificent house overlooking the river. Will sell for $17."

Generally, though, in the western tradition, Winnipeggers were buoyantly optimistic. On the city hall, the flood slogan, "We're Weary and Wet But We'll Win", was replaced by "Let's Look Nifty in Fifty". The city's biggest hardware store advertised: "We have no elevator service; no heat; practically no light on upper floors; three feet of water in our basement. But we are open, and will do our utmost to serve you."

A Royal Commission investigation was initiated. It resulted nine years later in a scheme for a $57 million, thirty-two-mile canal system, designed to loop the Red's overflow around the city. A Manitoba Flood Relief Fund was launched, and it drew $8.7 million in money and goods from contributors around the world — cutlery from Sheffield, England, Royal Highland livestock from Scotland, a thousand dollars from Pakistan. Indeed, after insurance appraisers settled 8,800 claims, the Fund had some three million dollars left in the kitty.

As a souvenir of the disaster, Winnipeg poolrooms today still display the sign over spitoons: "Don't spit on the floor. Remember the Red River Flood of '50!" But the mementoes most cherished by Winnipeggers are the flower gardens that today flourish so luxuriantly throughout the city, for they are built on the earth that was dug to sandbag the heroic dikes in the city's time of crisis.

"They say that Winnipeg was saved from complete disaster by a miracle," City Engineer William Hurst said later. "It was — a miracle of guts and hard work." He held up both hands. "The miracle of one hundred thousand multiplied by ten. A million fingers in the dikes."

_9_

Fire in the North

A FOREST FIRE IN THE NORTHERN ONTARIO BUSH has the sweep of an opera, the colours of a pageant, and the terror of a melodrama. Usually the stage is set weeks before by sultry heat. A copper sun burns a feverish red each day in a dirty saffron sky. The summer air hangs shimmering and oppressive. So tindery are the baked woods that forest rangers nervously joke, as they mop sweat off their brows, "It's so dry, the trees are running after the dogs."

Enter a chance spark. It may have escaped from a bonfire, lit by a lumberjack to dry his socks, or by a prospector brewing a pot of tea, or by a settler burning stumps on his scrub farm. The tiny spark falls in a bed of dry jackpine needles. It glows, dims, then glows alive again, like the winking of a malevolent eye.

Once it takes hold, men are powerless before its devastating advance, and it leaves in its wake a forest of black and leafless ghosts, hushed in awesome silence. The pools are aboil with the white bellies of dead trout, and the trails are corduroyed with pitiful balls of meat and fur that once were squirrels and partridges; and for hundreds of miles the stumps of jackpine, spruce and cedar stand like sable tombstones.

Forest fires eat up three million acres of Canadian forest each year, inflicting a total annual damage of nine million dollars. We pay attention, alas, only when the fires emerge from the forest like a tiger to ravage a town and murder the populace.

The two most spectacular forest fires that ever ran wild in northern Ontario were the Porcupine Fire of 1911 and the Haileybury Fire of 1922. Neither was Ontario's worst man-killing fire; that grisly distinction belongs to the one centring on the town of Matheson, which in one week in 1916 cremated 223 people. As against this, seventy-three lives were lost at Porcupine, and only forty-four at Haileybury.

These last two forest fires, however, were notorious for the wide-roaming chaos they caused in such a brief spell of time. The Porcupine Fire, roving over 864 square miles, destroyed gold-mining property worth three million dollars; it left three thousand pioneers homeless as it wiped out South Porcupine, Pottsville, Cochrane, and Goldlands, and ate into Porquis Junction and Golden City.

The Haileybury Fire, crackling over two thousand square miles, devastated silver mines and clay-belt farms worth six million dollars; it rendered six thousand settlers homeless as it flattened Haileybury, North Cobalt, Charlton, Thornloe, and Heaslip, and licked into Englehart and New Liskeard.

When fire razed it clean, Porcupine was just about to celebrate its second birthday as the "Klondike of New Ontario". It was almost five hundred miles north of Toronto, amid a wilderness of virgin jackpine, bottle-green spruce, and jungle muskeg. A fabulous gold strike had been made there on July 13, 1909, by two venturesome prospectors.

On a hunch, Tom Geddes of St. Thomas, Ontario, and his partner George Bannerman, had hopped aboard the leisurely Muskeg Special of the newly built Temiskaming & Northern Ontario railroad (fondly nicknamed "Time No Object"). They got off at the end of steel 220 miles above North Bay. Then by portage and birchbark canoe they struck out thirty miles westward. They paddled up the Porcupine River, past the porcupine-shaped island that gives it its name, and finally camped by the river's mouth. There, on the north shore of little Porcupine Lake, their picks uncovered a dazzling filigree of gold, as thick as the waxen drippings of a candle.

News of their bonanza spread like a fever and drew a stampede of greenhorn and sourdough prospectors. A twenty-four-year-old prospector named Benny Hollinger was grubstaked for forty-five dollars by a dealer named John McMahon of Haileybury, Ontario. When Benny

189

found three feet of gold jutting clear out of the moose moss, he "whooped like crazy and threw his hat up in the air." His claim, to the west of Porcupine Lake, was the beginning of the famed Hollinger Mine. A blacksmith named Gilbert Rhault and his buddy, Harry Preston, found a "golden stairway" of yellow-spattered quartz when the heels of their boots accidentally slipped on a nearby knoll. So vast was the crater left when their gold was dug out that their Dome Mine was nicknamed "The Glory Hole".

A sister star in the Porcupine constellation, West Dome Mine, was unearthed by a bushwacker from the British Columbia Kootenay country named F. Augustus Heinze. He was grubstaked for $250 by the eccentric Sir Henry Pellatt, who used the resulting gold fortune to erect his madman's Toronto castle, Casa Loma. A red-bearded Scot from the T. & N.O. construction gang, Alexander Oliphant, who had changed his name to Sandy McIntyre to escape paying alimony to his Glasgow wife, stumbled on the McIntyre Mine. Though his find ultimately produced a fantastic $230 million worth of gold, Sandy McIntyre sold one-eighth-ownership shares in his original claim for as little as twenty-five dollars to get quick booze money. He spent the rest of his days weeping into his beer at saloons in the Porcupine gold camps.

The boom towns that sprang up around the rim of Porcupine Lake — a coffin-shaped body of water two miles long and one mile wide — were really nothing more than wooden-shack gold camps, with adzed-log sidewalks. On the north tip of the lake stood Porcupine proper, better known as Golden City. It was a jumble of pool halls, blind pigs, stores selling prospectors' supplies, and packing-case hotels like the Murphy House. One of its quainter boarding-houses, the Stag Hotel, bore the sign: "We ain't the Waldorf-Astoria. If we were, you wouldn't be here. You ain't Pierpoint Morgan. If you were, you wouldn't be here. We know this hotel is on the bum. What about yourself?"

A half mile from Golden City, on the north shore of the lake, squatted the cluster of cabins and tents called Pottsville. It was named after the corpulent Maw and Paw Billy Potts, who used to manage the Haileybury Social Club; now they blind-pigged a shot of rye for fifty cents at their two-storey Shunia Hotel (*shunia* being the Indian word for gold).

The rowdiest of the towns, South Porcupine, flourished at the south end of the lake. The "soft-drink parlours" along its boggy gumbo main street, Golden Avenue, only slightly disguised the fact that they also sold hard liquor on the sly. The coyest sign was displayed by Charlie See, the druggist; he advertised over his store the sale of "Pills and Things". The stress, of course, was on "Things". Most of the sour-doughs knew they could buy a swig of "Things" at the White Rat Laundry, run by the immense ex-wrestler and vaudevillian, Mrs. John Dewar; at Billy Gohr's or Andy Leroux's Café; or at the King George Hotel, run by Cliff Moore, the "Cobalt Kid", who always had a cigar butt jutting from his jaws.

The reason the saloons only claimed to sell weak 2 per cent beer was that they had to outwit the law. The law said no strong liquor could be sold within six miles of any mining property. And the long arm of the law was extended by the beefy provincial police constable, Charlie Piercy. His clutch was enforced by the equally beefy police magistrate, Tommy Torrance, whose usual judgment, except in liquor cases, was "Not guilty — but don't do it again." As Cecil Adrian Culbert, who ran a combined general store, shoemaker's and barber shop in a one-storey shanty on Golden Avenue, has since observed, "Tommy Torrance was always easy to get along with. Except in liquor cases, when he had prosecuting provincials breathing hard down his neck. Unfortunately, Tommy got the proceeds of fines mixed up with his own bank account and was later relieved of office."

The miners often entertained themselves by staging eating contests. The most Falstaffian eater was Robert ("Little Eva") Weiss, supervisor or "captain" of the West Dome Mine. A former football star from Butte, Montana, he was a six-foot-seven mammoth, who weighed 440 pounds. He was so huge that he often got stuck in Mervin Strain's barber-shop chair and had to be pried out.

Big Bob Weiss had a rival eater in Sam ("Bear Steak") Shovell, a six-foot, 240-pound Torontonian, captain of the nearby Philadelphia Mine. Another zestful bear-steak eater was Patrick John Paterson ("Pat") Sinnott, secretary of the American Goldfields Mine near Pottsville. He was a jaunty, round-faced Scot, who used to love telling how, as a lawyer in Victoria, British Columbia, he had represented ex-Police Commissioner Joe North, who was ousted from Victoria's Athletic Park for the over-exuberant way he rooted for a baseball team. At the trial, Sinnott called his client to the witness stand, to demonstrate the rude Bronx cheer that had caused his expulsion.

"Sure, my client didn't win his suit to return to the ball park," Sinnott used to tell his cronies with glee. "But it was the first time in Canadian legal history that a delicious 'Br-rr-rr-a-ack' was ever heard by a judge as evidence."

Still another eater of heft was Jack ("The Nevada Kid") Munroe, former mayor of Ontario's Elk Lake and heavy-weight ex-boxer. He won knockout bouts with the mat king, Kid McCoy, and laid out the once unbeatable Jim Jeffries for a count of nine in 1902. Though he was still a big-shouldered giant with a trip-hammer punch, his fellow-prospectors in Golden City found Munroe amazingly gentle. He spent hours patiently training his collie sleigh dog to open a round-handled doorknob with its paws.

The sourdoughs were surprisingly devout. By the summer of 1911, they were erecting the camp's first log-cabin church in the Golden City. Cecil Adrian Culbert, the general storekeeper, recalls that Sunday services were held next door to him in Basil Wilson's Bar and Pool-room. The miners would turn the beer kegs upside down and use them as seats, and gravely listen to an itinerant minister fulminate against sin.

The need to escape the misery and the tedium of the wilderness through poker or whisky was well understood by Jimmy Forsyth. A South African who'd fought in the Boer War, he was a six-foot-one, barrel-chested 225-pounder, with red hair, green eyes, and a liking for rolling his own Bull Durhams. He and his twenty-four-year-old Kentish wife, Edith, came down to South Porcupine on a cutter in sixty-below winter flat broke; a fire in 1910 had wiped out their fourteen-thousand-dollar general store in Cochrane.

Working out of a tent off Golden Avenue, Forsyth soon had a mine- and claim-trading business going in partnership with Tom Geddes, the original co-discoverer of Porcupine gold. They also ran a "Snake Room" in the back of their Waweeatan Mining Exchange, where they entertained prospectors with duets on the banjo and generous gulps of whisky.

"You almost *had* to drink a quart of booze a day to ward off the blues," Forsyth recalls. "The sand-flies would sting you into madness. The miners were lousier than pet pigs. When you came home from the mines, you'd first have to use a hot iron on all your clothes to kill the bugs. When I woke up mornings, I'd reach down beside my bed for a hooker of whisky, and prepare myself for the day by drinking my all-liquid breakfast."

On the dire Tuesday morning of July 11, 1911, Jimmy Forsyth woke up with a hang-over. He heard his tiny brunette wife Edith fussing about one of the six rooms of the two-storey log cabin he had just built.

"Wake up, Jimmy," she said. "It's awful outside. Looks as if the whole bush is burning."

Forsyth buried his head in the pillow and groaned, "Let it burn!"

By 10 A.M., however, he too was up and worried. For weeks the Porcupine had been simmering in 106-degree heat. Dozens of muskeg fires were springing up in the bush. Only last Sunday, a wind had carried a blaze into Pottsville, and twenty shacks were consumed before the bucket brigade had doused it. Now the sky to the south-west displayed an ugly yellow pallor, with a red glow at its base. The separate brush fires were merging; they seemed to be heading toward the Porcupine on a united horseshoe-shaped front over twenty miles broad.

To ease their fear, Forsyth and his partner, Tom Geddes, dropped around to Andy Leroux's blind pig for a drink.

"Have a slug of whisky on me," said Leroux. "We may not see each other again. That's a pretty vicious wind whipping the fire toward these parts."

The men raised their glasses in salute, and took their farewell snort. "Better help the ladies pack and send them across on boats to Golden City," said Forsyth.

Andy Leroux's wife Blondy, who had won three beauty contests staged by the Montreal *La Presse*, took three suitcases. Forsyth's wife Edith took her small satchel and her cocker spaniel Peter, but was persuaded to leave behind her square alarm clock, which played "Yankee Doodle Went to Town".

The men got the ladies and children into the gasoline boats at the wooden docks, but only with difficulty. A gang of five Italian miners rushed Butch Burns's little boat and demanded space. Charlie Piercy and his fellow-constable, George Murray, knocked one of the ruffians out, and herded the others back at gun-point.

193

Forsyth, Geddes and Leroux returned to carry buckets of water from Jack Dalton's transport stables, in an attempt to douse the flying sparks already dancing along the wooden roofs of Golden Avenue. At 1:15 A.M. the Dome Mine whistle, a mile from town, blared its emergency *whoo-whoo-whoo*. Panic started to mount.

Cliff Moore picked up handfuls of cigars from their boxes on the counter of his King George Hotel, and began handing them out.

"We might as well smoke 'em as burn 'em," he said amiably.

They were still serving lunch in his dining-room when a raging south-west wind hurled whirling slabs of fire at the hotel. Cliff Moore waddled down to Lake Porcupine, and was last seen standing neck-deep in reddish slime, a soggy cigar butt still gripped between his teeth.

Hawley Clayton, the Pottsville bank manager, who had just opened a new branch of the Bank of Ottawa on Bruce Avenue in South Porcupine, calmly entered Henry Joy's Hardware Store.

"Lend me two long-handled shovels," he said. " I want to dig a hole in the earth and bury our bank ledgers."

"What will I do with my new shovels after you're through?" asked Joy.

"You won't need 'em after today," said Clayton. "Because the whole bloody Porky town is done for."

Joy laughed joylessly. "You're just a city tenderfoot. This wind will veer any minute."

"Tell you what I'm going to do," said Clayton. "If you want these shovels back at the end of today, I'll pay you *double* their price — if your hardware store is still standing."

"That's a bet," said Joy.

Clayton and his three bank clerks buried the ledgers in two feet of wet earth. They stuffed forty thousand dollars in the seven-and-a-half-ton safe. Then they ran for the docks and jumped into a canoe; and as they paddled toward Pottsville, Clayton could see yellow prongs of flame raking Henry Joy's Hardware Store.

They found all Pottsville razed, except for Clayton's log house, which stood on posts four feet off the ground, on Powell's Point south

194

of the town. Clayton was determined to save his house, because he had prepared it as a honeymoon cottage for his Ottawa fiancée, Beatrice, whom he intended to marry in a few weeks. He battled the barrage of sparks and flaming shreds of birch bark for two hours, dousing them with cans of water. At last successful, he passed a bottle of whisky around to his thirty-four burned-out Pottsville guests, had druggist Lorne Wright squirt eye drops into their begrimed eyes, and invited Maw and Paw Billy Potts to sleep for the night in his honeymoon bed.

Cecil Adrian Culbert carried six cases of goods from his shop to the lake one block away. He put them in two feet of water, but to no avail. The furious gusts of wind created by the fire swirled the water away, and flames devoured his stock. Even the woodwork of his iron shoe-patching machine was eaten.

On his last trip, to collect his suitcase, Culbert trembled in fright. A solid wall of orange fire, one hundred feet high, was roaring down Golden Avenue.

"For God's sake, Cap, run!" he yelled to Captain Thomas Dunbar, a sixty-five-year-old ex-captain of the Lake Temiskaming boats, who was manning a pump.

"Sorry, matey, I got to put out this fire," said Cap Dunbar. He was later found dead, with his charred fingers still grasping the pump handle.

"For God's sake, Rosie, run!" Culbert yelled to Rosie the laundress, who claimed she was a Hungarian aristocrat.

"If the men stay, I'll stay," she replied. Culbert last spotted her as she ducked into the lake, removing her skirt to cover her hair from flying embers. She revealed "the most beautiful embroidered white silk petticoats I ever saw, probably the last vestige of her halcyon aristocrat days. Rosie died later as a wealthy prospector in Kirkland Lake, surrounded by twenty faithful friends — all sleigh dogs."

By the time Culbert reached the wharf, his shirt and the seat of his khaki pants were aflame. He grabbed a loose guard rail from the wooden pier, rolled it into the lake, and dived after it, flinging away his suitcase. A French-Canadian prospector was sitting in the oozy slime, holding a gray blanket over his head. "Come join me, *mon ami*," the French Canadian said. Blazing green alders along the shore were

195

showering them with sparks and acrid smoke. The two men would duck their heads into the water to escape the sparks, come up to gulp a mouthful of hot smoke, and then bob their heads down again into the spring-fed icy lake.

Hundreds of others were similarly sucking for air in the savage heat around Culbert. Their anguish was later stated with poignancy by Lindsay Morton, an English mining agent, crouched on the lake shore with his wife and baby.

"The whole thing resolved itself into a question of dying decently," Morton said. "We lay in the mud, sometimes crawling into the water and then out again to gasp a breath of air. But it wasn't air we got to breathe. Just smoke, so bitter that it made the baby cry out, 'Mama, O Mama, give me air!' At last I became so exhausted, I buried the family books and papers close beside me, so as to make sure I would leave a trace of identity behind me."

To add to their woes, the survivors had to endure an explosion. At 1:40 p.m., a spark touched off 350 cases of dynamite and five hundred kegs of powder, heaped on a railway siding to the east of South Porcupine. With a horrendous *sss-boom,* the explosion tore a gaping hole in the ground twenty feet deep. A piece of jagged railway track sliced off the arm of a nearby miner like a cleaver. The concussion smashed every pane of glass in Golden City, two miles away. Worst of all, the explosion lashed up white-tipped waves in Porcupine Lake nine feet high, and capsized escaping boats as though they were egg-shells.

Culbert remembers ducking under the wharf as a hail of huge white-hot rocks plummeted from skies that were now "as black as Egypt's night". Others remember scrambling wildly for the swamped boats. "The explosion," recalls one survivor who just barely escaped, John T. Preston, "was like the end of the world."

Kellard Gamble, after seeing his dad's Arcade Ice Cream Parlour go up in a puff of smoke, dived off the pier, concerned only with saving the family's pregnant Russian boar-hound, Nellie; the brindle sleigh dog survived to give birth to eighteen puppies next morning in a Golden City tent. Pat Sinnott, of Bronx-cheer fame, saved a mother and her two children, then got into the last launch to leave on a scheduled run. In Golden City, he prudently rescued all the suits from the tailor shop of his friend Sam McChesney, by piling them in a trench.

196

One prospector, Charles Mickle — according to his sister, Grace Mickle of Waterloo, Ontario — escaped after seeing a mother protect her child by placing it in a ditch and covering it with her own body. (The child lived.) Another prospector, Harold Wessel, "survived by digging himself into a mud-hole and pulling his wet shirt-tail over his face," says his sister, Ona Burgess of Norland, Ontario.

A Pottsville prospector, René Hansen, now of Rawdon, Quebec, recalls, "In Pearl Lake, where the McIntyre Mine now stands, some moose took refuge, and came quite close to the men, as though they felt safer in their company. Some birds even rested on men's shoulders in the trenches."

A South Porcupine old-timer, A. S. Bellingham, now of Hamilton, Ontario, ultimately escaped by pumping a hand-car thirty miles to Porquis Junction. He remembers:

The fire raged in from the south, and some of the boys, including myself, did manage to contain the flames at this street line. The hardware man refused us pails, so we just helped ourselves to a crate of them and saved his store for him. As the water melted from the frozen muskeg into the ditch of the grading, we dipped it up in pailfuls and threw it back on the brush flames.

After many hours of this work, the flames died down. We were all tired, when suddenly down the street a man came running, leaping and jumping, and clapping his hands in glee. "It's all right now, boys," he exclaimed, "The priest is here! The priest is here!" Sure enough, along strolled a young priest with a bowl of water, which he sprinkled on the road from his fingertips. And that, after the hours we had laboured with pails of water! We just heaved our pails into the air and quit.

At the height of the fire, people had to keep moving into the lake up to their necks, and ducking their heads as the gushes of flame swept along the water surface. Dalton's transport horses in Porcupine Lake had their backs roasted — one of them broke away and headed for the stable and to its death. Had the car of dynamite blown sideways, instead of straight down, the people in the water would have been decapitated.

A young student then prospecting for the Jupiter Mines, J. E. Somerville, now of Victoria, British Columbia, says, "I will never forget how I sat on the north shore of Pearl Lake on the McIntyre property and watched the fire eating its way through the heavy spruce trees. I found forest fires have a curious habit of leaving green islands of trees and grass as they pass along. Some islands are quite small, and others quite large. One student was fleeing South Porcupine when he sprained his ankle and could go no further. He sat down, expecting the end. But when the exploding fire and smoke had passed him by, he found himself sitting on one such green island — an oasis of safety amid the fury."

John Novack, a Polish prospector from Mattawa, Ontario, was putting a timber collar on his gold-mine shaft, six miles south of South Porcupine, when he heard a deafening *whoo-oo-oo*. A solid jet of lemon-yellow flame lunged over the hill. Novack shouted to his brother Fred: "Holy Moses, come on out! The end of the world's here, by gosh!" Before they raced to the swamp, John threw his sweater on the ground.

"My little spaniel, Browny, thought I wanted him to watch over that sweater," recalls John Novack, now a Toronto stockbroker. "When we returned hours later, Browny had the pads of his feet burned off. But he was still lying on my sweater, guarding it. I wept at his loyalty, and praised the good Lord my dog continued to live."

Arthur H. Ward, a green immigrant from England, where a year before he had been an apprentice paint-brush-maker, was a fifty-five-dollar-a-month cook at the West Dome Mine. A bachelor had taught him how to bake bread, and he had picked up the other culinary arts by reading *Mrs. Beeton's Cook Book*. Ward became jittery when the flames began to roar through the tops of the spruce and balsam trees, and the overheated turpentine in the trunks started to explode like jungle drums. He left a group of miners who had taken refuge under an overturned out-house. ("They used it as a shield from the heat, turning it over constantly as it caught fire.") Ward raced along the road toward South Porcupine, leaving all his belongings behind. ("I don't know what the hurdle record is for that distance, but I have no doubt that I broke the record that day.")

When he saw that the flames were obviously going to doom South Porcupine too, Ward hurried to a motor boat leaving for Golden City. Now a retired prospector in Thornbury, Ontario, he clearly recalls:

198

The one thing that stands out was the sight of a man trying to get into the motor boat with two large suitcases. We promptly tossed them into the lake. There were about eight people in our boat, mostly brave women and children. I was startled when the propeller suddenly got tangled in the weeds. I waded out to push it clear, until I was up to my neck in the water. The occupants then helped me out of the water, and I didn't notice how freezing it was. I sat straddle-legged on the bow of the boat, until we finally paddled her over to Golden City, without aid of the motor. It was a rough ride, but because God had spared our lives, it was a pleasant one.

Others weren't so lucky. A canoe pulled out into Porcupine Lake, paddled with a board by Billy Moore, a popular prospector from Cobalt. It was loaded with Tommy Torrance, the magistrate, Jack McMurrich, a lawyer, and Sam the Chinaman, a gambler. A mob of crazed men rushed the canoe, clamouring to get in. Billy Moore patiently explained that the crowded canoe was already in danger of sinking. No sooner had the men slunk off when the Haileybury barber, Merv Strain, waded out into the water.

"My God, I can't swim!" pleaded Strain. "Please take me along. If you can't let me in, let me at least hang onto the back. But for God's sake, don't leave me behind, or I'm done for."

The men paused in silence. Then Billy Moore said, "Get in, Merv."

They paddled on again. But the waves, tortured into violence, upturned the crowded canoe, and the men tumbled into deep water. Billy Moore, clinging to the board paddle, saw Jack McMurrich floundering helplessly.

"Here, Jack, use this," said Moore, tossing the lawyer his paddle.

The lawyer, the judge and the gambler survived, but the heroic Billy Moore and the hapless barber both drowned.

Nor was Billy Gohr, operator of the blind-pig bar, in luck that day. He insisted on staying up on the blazing roof of his Golden Avenue bar to the very end, while his bartenders, Mack Smith and Rosaire Bourbean, handed him buckets of water. The climax was described to a reporter by Bourbean:

199

"Come down, come down, Billy Gohr," I says. "It's no use, it's no use, come down quick!" He told me to pass the water. I did not pass the water any more. Smith had taken all the money from the bar and run alongside me toward the street. He fell. I had my own life to save. I of instinct put my handkerchief over my mouth and run. I crawl out into the lake and go for deep water. . . . We find them the next day. Seven dollars and sixty cents of Billy Gohr's bar where Smith is dead. The dollar bills is all burned up.

Mrs. Billy Gohr stood for hours with her baby in her arms, first at the edge of the pier and then in the numbing water up to her breast, waiting for her husband to take her to Golden City.

"Please, won't you get into a boat, Mrs. Gohr," Charlie Piercy had begged her. "It's getting awful bad. He'll come later."

"I'll just wait for Billy," she said. Billy never came.

Neither was Robert ("Little Eva") Weiss, the Falstaffian eater of the West Dome Mine, more fortunate. To escape the hot licks of flame, he led a party of nineteen refugees down the 135-foot timbered mine shaft. Among them were his tiny wife Jennie and their three-year-old daughter Ariel.

"Jennie, you're not afraid, are you?" he asked, as he and his wife descended the ladder.

"Come on, Bob," she replied. "If we're going to die, we'll die together."

The mine manager, William ("Shotgun Bill") King, managed to climb out for a spell and sprinkled water down the shaft with an old coffee-pot. But the others all suffocated. Big Bob Weiss was found at the very bottom, his daughter tenderly cradled in his arms. It required a block and tackle to hoist his 440 pounds out, and fourteen men to carry his outsize coffin.

His rival eater and mine captain, Sam ("Bear Steak") Shovell, fared better. Shovell was just sitting down to a lunch of bean soup and pork at the Philadelphia Mine cook-house, when he glanced out the window. He saw flaring spouts of fire boiling down towards the cook-house with hurricane fury.

200

"Run for your lives!" Shovell bellowed. Then he grabbed his tiny wife Nellie by the hand and carried her through the undergrowth toward Lake Porcupine, a treacherous three miles away.

Stopping only to scoop dirty swamp water over their noses, they finally staggered onto the railway track skirting the lake. Four Italian miners came along in a hand-car, pumping for life. Without a word, they stopped to let the Shovells on. At a shallow beach, they all jumped off and plunged into the lake; and Sam held Nellie's head above water for three hours.

Nellie never forgot how, when they finally ventured out of the lake, singing "Praise God from Whom All Blessings Flow", she slipped off her stockings to dry, and out popped a ten-dollar bill. "Look, Sam, we're not broke," she said with a laugh. "I tucked this bonanza into my stocking at noon, just before our race to safety."

Later, her husband recalled: "I'll never forget the sight of an old prospector being led along the shore, with both his eyeballs burned out blind. Yet he was weeping in sorrow only because he had seen his partner die."

A similar experience befell Jimmy Forsyth, the South African mine trader, who was the last to escape stricken Golden Avenue. After carting buckets of water to save their newly built office, his partner, Tom Geddes, yelled above the thunder of wind and flames, "For God's sake, come on, Jimmy, or we're goners!"

Forsyth rushed into the office to release his three sleigh dogs and free a cageful of English canaries he'd recently bought for his wife Edith. He scooped up in his arms his pet wire-haired terrier Toddy. Then he and Geddes ran toward the lake. They hadn't gone twenty yards when Geddes stopped.

"Jimmy," he said, "I'm going back for my coat."

"Don't be a damn fool!" cried Forsyth.

"We'll have need of it before the day is out," Geddes said. "Go ahead. I'll catch up with you."

They were the last words spoken by Forsyth's partner. All that Forsyth later found of Tom Geddes was a cobalt ring bearing the initials T.G. on the charred trunk where his coat had been flung. His few bones fitted into a cardboard shirt-box.

Forsyth's run down to the lake, amid catapulted balls of fire, was a nightmare. The last three hundred yards he had to crawl on his stomach. His khaki shirt was burned off the back of his shoulders, and his shoelaces, his red hair, and the fine hairs in his nostrils were aflame. Around him were strewn the scorched bodies of his friends who had died on their hands and knees, roasted alive while trying to get their mouths near the ground to breathe. He clawed his way to the lake among wildly scurrying rabbits, plunging horses, and even a lumbering bear.

Since he couldn't swim, Forsyth grabbed a piece of adzed plank from Golden Avenue's sidewalk, and flung himself into the water. With one hand, he continued to hold his terrier Toddy. While choking for oxygen, he felt himself and his dog lifted high when the tons of dynamite blasted into explosion.

"The shock literally made the water fizz," he later wrote in a letter to South African relatives. "The whole sky seemed as if it was going to fall, and the bottom of the lake seemed to have dropped out. This was the demon that upset nearly all the canoes on the lake. It drowned Andy Leroux, in a boat with three wrestlers who were to have performed at his blind pig. My swollen eyes were practically blinded and I was suffering the agony of the damned. After this, one could almost travel through hell with a smile on his face."

Hours later, Forsyth groped half blind through Golden City, looking for his wife Edith. He found her and Andy Leroux's wife Blondy, and four other wives, wailing in anguish at reports that their husbands were all dead. He kissed Edith's tears away, and gently told Blondy Leroux about the death of her husband. He was so touched when she gave him Andy's gold-plated watch, that he swore he would never touch a drop of liquor again — a vow he has kept to this day.

The fire consumed one-third of Golden City, including its newly built church and the Stag Hotel. But the business section was saved, thanks to Jack ("The Nevada Kid") Munroe, the ex-pugilist. Brandishing two six-guns, he went around to all the saloons, exclaiming, "Are there no men left? If you still want to be called men, break open the stores, grab all pails and follow me." One hundred and fifty men formed a bucket brigade, and so the remaining two-thirds of town stood intact.

202

The fire died down after five hours, and that night the whisky flowed in Golden City, peddled at fifty dollars a bottle. It also flowed in the chaos of Cochrane, where two thousand homeless slept in boxcars and on the floor of Union Station, and where a constable killed a man in a vain attempt to close down a blind pig.

In crowded Golden City that night, the refugees slept on the sidewalks and on top of poolroom tables. Cecil Adrian Culbert, the burned out general storekeeper, recalls slipping into the Murphy House dining-room, stripping off two tablecloths, and bedding down exhaustedly on the floor. Next morning, when the waitress came to claim her table-cloths for the breakfast shift, he bowed and said, "I have your sheets well pressed for you, dear madam." Within three days, Culbert had a white-wall tent shipped up from Haileybury, and was back in business on his old, flattened site in South Porcupine.

Hawley Clayton, the Pottsville bank manager, rented a corner of Hughie Mullins' Bank Saloon and Pool Hall in Golden City. He had a carpenter erect a bank cage inside, so the teller could reach over from the cage and hoist a seidel of beer from the bar. When Clayton brought in his bride Beatrice from Ottawa, he was able to point out proudly the new black-and-white sign he had painted in front of the building: "The Bank of Ottawa". Below it was Hughie Mullins' old sign for his saloon and pool hall, reading starkly and emphatically: "The Bank".

Soon the blackened Porcupine flowered with a meadow of white tents, and the survivors cooked meals on stoves supplied free by the T. Eaton Company of Toronto, and ate a thousand loaves of bread sent by the Toronto Nasmith Baking Company, and cases of cereal from the Shredded Wheat Biscuit Company.

At sunset that Sunday, all the survivors paddled across Porcupine Lake in a silent funeral. They towed in scows seventeen rough pine boxes containing the dead. The coffins were buried in Edward's Point, a fire-swept finger of land midway between the ruins of Pottsville and the ruins of South Porcupine. The point was then renamed, to be known forever after as Deadman's Point.

On the day that fire demolished Porcupine, the Government weather man made a laconic entry in the record book at Haileybury, 120 miles to the south. The black pall of smoke could be seen clearly from his town, midway between Porcupine and North Bay. Yet the Haileybury meteorologist blithely wrote under the heading of *Miscellaneous Phenomena* just one word: "Gale". This reluctance to take warning was characteristic of the civilized Haileyburian.

On Wednesday, October 4, 1922 — eleven years after the Porcupine fire — Haileybury and the eighteen townships surrounding it were smitten by a gale and a forest fire of equal ferocity, and the people were equally helpless to cope with them.

The Haileybury fire was unique for two reasons: it vented its wrath in the autumn, followed that night by a snowstorm; and it conquered a populace that was relatively settled.

When fire struck, Haileybury was proud of being the county seat of the District of Temiskaming, the most urban settlement in the Ontario north country. It had grown to a population of five thousand since that day in 1887 when Charles Cobbold Farr, a Hudson's Bay Company chief agent, settled there. He had decided to transplant a little bit of his native England to Canada by naming it after his old school, Haileybury in Hertfordshire.

Now the mushrooming residential town hugged the spine of a hill that gently sloped east, down to the blue waters of Lake Temiskaming. Steamers brought to its wharf cargoes from Ville Marie on the Quebec side of the thirty-mile-long lake. Off its macadamized main street, Ferguson Avenue, loomed the stone armouries, three movie theatres, the office of the weekly *Haileyburian,* and the school of music and dancing. It boasted a stately three-storey stone court-house, where Supreme Court Justice J. F. Orde presided at the assizes; the only hospital in the north tall enough to possess an elevator; and handsome four-storeyed hotels like the Vendome and Arthur Ferland's Matabanic Hotel (Indian for "place where the trail comes out").

The prosperity of Haileybury derived from the silver mines of Cobalt, five miles to the south. Indeed, an electric trolley, owned by the T. & N.O. Railway, shuttled every half-hour through the no-man's-land bush between the two towns. A treasure cave of silver was first discovered under Cobalt's solid slab floor of rock on September 15, 1903. The prospector was a blacksmith named Fred LaRose, financed by the general storekeepers, Noah and Henry Timmins, of Mattawa, Ontario.

204

By the fall of 1922, Cobalt bristled with fifty-two silver mines, circled around "Poison Lake", where the gray cyanide slime was dumped. It contained a population of four thousand miners, who gambled and drank at the Silver and Lang Street blind pigs. But it also boasted three theatres and a Grand Opera House; two weekly newspapers, the *Nugget* and the *Northern News*; and a cocky attitude toward every other northern town, as witness the joyful ballad, "The Cobalt Song":

Old Porcupine is a muskeg, Elk Lake a fire trap,
New Liskeard's just a country town, and Haileybury's just come back;
You can buy the whole of Latchford for a nickel or a dime —
But it's hobnail boots and a flannel shirt in Cobalt town for mine! . . .

About a mile north of Colbalt stood its slag-heap slum suburb of one thousand workers, North Cobalt. It is described graphically by Madeline Johnson, one of the ten children of a French labourer on the T. & N.O. Railway, who lived there.

"Every house in the 'millionaire town' of Haileybury had its domestic servant," she recalls. "Just about every house in Cobalt had its domestic servant. But North Cobalt was their breeder of domestic servants. I was one of them. Even as a child, I worked in Haileybury and Cobalt homes after school."

She was appalled by the risks the North Cobalt mine workers had to take. "High-grade ore was conveyed by cable right over the town in buckets, often spilling down death," she says. "Tons of dynamite were moved over the bumpy corduroy road in an ordinary wagon pulled by a team of horses; one man walked in advance, holding a red flag to keep people away. And the only fire protection was a barrel of water set on each wooden bridge in the neighbouring bush. If a spark from the train set the bridge afire, you were supposed to splash it out with the solitary barrel."

Five miles north of Haileybury, nestled on the bay head of Lake Temiskaming and linked to Haileybury by electric trolley, was its rival sister town of New Liskeard. It had been so christened in 1893 by the Ontario crown-lands agent, John Armstrong, in honour of his Kentish home town of Liskeard. Now, with four thousand population, it was the agricultural heart of all the farms in the northern clay belt.

North of it, stitched together by the T. & N.O. railway, were threaded the patchwork of farm communities maligned in "The Cobalt Song", zigzagging up as far as Matheson.

The clay-belt settlers were incredibly hardy as they tore their 160-acre farms out of the jungle of jackpine, spruce and foot-thick muskeg. Joseph M. Beemans, a seventy-four-year-old Montreal surveyor of timber limits, who barely escaped with his life in the Matheson fire of 1916, is still astonished in his peppery fashion at their toughness.

"I remember one typically rugged farmer pushing back the wilderness," Beemans says. "He'd taken up land a mile and a half from the T. & N.O. Railway. In between was swampy muskeg. To get his team and first cattle to his farm, he bought a number of sixteen-foot planks — and have you ever tried lifting a sixteen-foot plank by yourself? — enough to build the floor of a little platform over the muskeg. He drove his animals onto the planks. Then he took up the rear planks, and laid them ahead, driving the herd a little further, until at last he'd leapfrogged them the mile and a half to firm land. Unbelievable, until you see it!

"And those early fire-fighting measures — I shudder to think of them! The Government divided the railway into roughly twenty-five-mile stretches. To each stretch it assigned a 'fire fighter', usually an old geezer too feeble for heavy labour. He was given a shovel, an axe, and a railway hand-car. If he saw a plume of smoke, he was supposed to pump his car to the area, take his shovel and axe, and put out the fire."

On the Wesdnesday morning of October 4, 1922, even the most rudimentary of fire fighters were taken off their patrols, by virtue of the fact that the calendar showed that the forest-fire season was over. The bush country north of Haileybury up to Matheson was all rusty gold, the colour of an old tapestry. The autumn air was like mulled wine; it hadn't rained for a month, and the temperature was an unseasonably hot eighty degrees. The settlers were doing their usual fall burning of rotting stumps and slash in their farm clearings.

Then a north-west wind stirred. It grew, and the small fires began blossoming into little bobbing flowers of yellow flame. The wind developed into a demoniacal eighty-mile-an-hour hurricane. The ground

206

fires kindled the tawny trees, from toe to crown, into roaring columns of flame.

Entire birch trees rose and tossed forward like chaff in front of a giant fan. In seven-league boots, these separate fires marched down toward Haileybury in freakish leaps and hurdles: flattening some homesteads, yet leaving others untouched; shearing just the edge of one hamlet, but wiping out another village entirely; skirting some families, yet wiping out others as one would singe mosquitoes with a candle.

On a farm near Swastika, a thirteen-year-old deaf mute, Johanna Schultz, tried to escape the flames in a well containing twelve feet of water. The marks of clawing on the wall bore mute testimony to her death struggle.

At Heaslip, the pioneer who gave the village its name, Amos Heaslip, as well as the eight children of farmer Edgar Bond, and a hired hand named Jack Marshall, sought cool refuge from the searing heat in a root-house. It proved a sepulchre of suffocation for all of them; and Marshall's charred fingers were found stretched forth as though reaching out to protect the Bond baby nearby.

At Charlton, a crazed French-Canadian farmer was seen escaping from his ruined home, wheeling a baby carriage with one hand and leading a lamb by the other, and crooning a lullaby as though his heart would break.

At Uno Park, Major Joe Fleming, a veteran of the South African War and the First World War, was found dead in a field of barley, clutching to his breast his Royal Canadian Regiment medals.

At Earlton Junction, however, Jim Elliott saved himself from the hot fog of carbon monoxide by slipping on the gas mask he'd used at Ypres.

When the fire's irreverent fingers reached into the synagogue at Englehart, the town's popular Jewish mayor, Dave Korman, risked his life in an attempt to save the holy scroll of the Torah. "Unfortunately, the synagogue was reduced to ashes," the nearly blind Korman recalls today. "In order to say our prayers for the Jewish high holy days, we had to use my Palace movie theatre as a substitute synagogue."

When the fire blow-torched into Haileybury, the citizens poured out into the streets, as Mayor Robert LeHeup phrased it, "like ants forced out of a blazing log." Seven hundred of its finest buildings were gutted into blackened and smoothly calcined shells. Left entirely untouched, curiously, was the "Millionaire Row" of wooden mansions proliferating along Lake Shore Road. The only thing left intact on Ferguson Avenue was a blistered red chewing-gum sign, displaying the ironic words, "Aids Digestion, Preserves the Teeth".

Some citizens stayed to battle the blaze on the streets (like fireman Gervaise Sutherland, who rescued two children, and then was found dead on the road beside one of the Fire Department's three abandoned pumpers). Some citizens stayed to fight for their homes (like George M. George, who successfully doused the flames around his frame house on Amwell Street with the pans of grape juice that his wife Alice was in the process of making into jelly).

Some citizens went hysterical in their greed (like the dozens who phoned the town's insurance agent, J. D. MacDonald, in a last-second effort to buy insurance even as the flames were devouring their offices and stores). And some citizens went calmly about their business (like William Edwards, printer for the *Haileyburian*, who coolly finished setting the type for the next day's lead story about the "mounting forest fire", before hot-footing it himself from the flames).

Thousands fled to New Liskeard or Cobalt, which were saved at the last minute by the suddenly veering wind (like Haileybury's undertaker, O. J. Thorpe, who piled his wife and seven children into the hearse and "drove away like mad"). Thousands more flocked to the lake (like the nuns of the Convent of the Sisters of the Assumption, who shepherded the 115 young girls under their charge into the cold water, while singing hymns).

The Catholic devout were the last to flee. At the Hospital of the Providence, seven Sisters of Mercy nurses were roasted to death while trying to save a little boy who was on the operating table under anaesthetic. Hundreds sought sanctuary in the Roman Catholic Cathedral, in the belief that its limestone walls were proof against fire; and they knelt before the high altar to pray for rain. They all scrambled out when the Gothic windows cracked — all except a sixty-two-year-old zealot, Mrs. Lucille St. George, stubborn in her faith. She was still praying at the altar rail when the great stone dome crumpled down on her.

208

Bishop Elie Latulippe, sixty-two and ill with a weak heart, insisted on burying the consecrated bread in the ground before fleeing in a Stutz car to North Cobalt. As he drove away into the smoke, the Bishop looked back and saw the ruins of his white palace shining in the afterglow of destruction. In North Cobalt, three hundred of his flock huddled together to sing vespers in the stone Roman Catholic College; and miraculously it was the only thing left untouched in devastated North Cobalt, except a white sign painted on a big rock by the roadway that read, "Christ Died for the Ungodly".

The people's awareness of impending peril was slow to come. At 3:15 P.M. Supreme Court Justice J. F. Orde was presiding at the non-jury assizes at the Haileybury court-house. He was hearing the leisurely legal arguments stated in a case concerning the custody of a child. The mother was seated in the witness-box, with her infant dozing on her lap. Then Sheriff George Caldbick begged leave to approach the bench. He whispered into Mr. Justice Orde's ear, "Fire has jumped over the railway tracks, and is attacking the T. & N.O. station. I urge you, sir, to take alarm."

"Court adjourned until nine-thirty tomorrow morning," said Mr. Justice Orde, giving the mother temporary custody of her baby. Then he strolled in stately fashion to the Vendome Hotel and packed his bags, refusing to hurry even when the hotel roof whirled away in flames.

One lawyer at the sittings who refused to stand on his dignity was R. S. Robertson, K.C., of the Toronto firm of Fasken, Robertson, Chadwick & Sedgewick. He ran for half a mile to a wallow of mud beside the lake. On the way he paused to help a boy who was tearfully tugging with a rope two Holstein cows that refused to budge, despite prodding in the rear from an umbrella wielded by the boy's mother. As a Good Samaritan, the lawyer gave his overcoat to a shoemaker, and protected himself from the shower of sparks by donning his black King's Counsel gown.

Seated in the Matabanic Hotel that afternoon was John R. Ross, a commercial traveller for R. M. Ballantyne, Limited, manufacturers of knitted garments in Stratford, Ontario. The short-sighted Ross peered through his pince-nez, and was worried when he saw pillars of black smoke twirling toward the hotel. So he packed his samples in his two large trunks, put them on the platform in front of the hotel's sample-room, and hurried back into the lobby.

He saw about twenty other travelling salesmen seated there unconcernedly, and exclaimed, "What are you fellows going to do? Sit here and get burned to a frazzle?"

They laughed heartily, and one taunted, "What kind of flowers would you like me to send to your funeral, buddy?"

Ross recalls, "Well, I thought there was no use of me getting all excited and kidded for being a worry-wart, so I sat down with them and relaxed."

Soon, however, Peter White, K.C., the Toronto lawyer, rushed in with news that the fire was raging not more than three hundred yards from the hotel. They all jumped to their feet. Indeed, the proprietor of the hotel, the beloved Arthur Ferland, became frantic because he had lost his family and could not find them; and White later said, "The poor fellow was running up and down like a madman."

Despite the hoots of the other commercial travellers, Ross announced he was determined to escape to Cobalt.

"You're crazy to try it," the others jeered. "They say the trolley car has stopped running, and the tracks are twisted into corkscrews."

"I'll walk it," said Ross.

Picking up his club bag, Ross started out. He struggled along the road for only three miles. He could not breathe, because the curtain of smoke seemed thick enough to cut. He could not see, because the wind was so furious, it kept whipping his pince-nez from his nose. He was just about to collapse into darting flames, when along came a seven-passenger Tin Lizzy, loaded with a dozen women and children. The driver said, "Stand on the running-board, and hang on for dear life, and we will try to make it to Cobalt."

Ross returned to the smoky ruins of Haileybury next morning, and found the Matabanic Hotel "as flat as a saucer. All that remained of my two trunks full of knitted garments was the hinges."

In Cobalt that afternoon, Harry Korson, the scrap dealer who owned the Northern Metal Company; his father-in-law, Aaron Cohen, owner of the Cobalt Rag & Metal Company; and a visiting French-Canadian junk dealer, were seated in Cohen's kitchen on Swamp Street in their shirt-sleeves. They were smoking cigars, and playing the card game known as 101.

Into the kitchen rushed Cohen's daughter Rebecca. She had staggered home through the smoke downtown, where she worked as stenographer for the Cobalt lawyers, Kelso Roberts and Col. Henry Edward McKee.

"All Haileybury is on fire!" she exclaimed.

The French Canadian put his cards down on the kitchen table. "Ah, well, *messieurs*," he sighed. "There'll be a lot of scrap for us to buy tomorrow in Haileybury."

When they heard that the fire had reached the Hudson Bay silver mine on the outskirts of Cobalt itself, however, the scrap merchants helped Cohen's six children put wet towels over their faces. Then they joined the throngs running through Cobalt's cliff-like streets, past window-panes smashing from the intense heat, down to the railway station. There they huddled and waited on benches for a rescue train.

As V. C. Hall, business manager of Frank Lendrum's Cobalt *Northern News*, later said of their panic, "We were all prepared to die. Personally, I went to get a gun, so I could shoot myself if I knew death was inevitable."

He was wrong; not all of them were prepared to die. Dick Fauteux, Cobalt's Lang Street butcher, looked up at the sky over Haileybury and saw that it was "red all over, just like a big red blanket". He turned to his wife, Leonie, a blue-eyed brunette of tweny-two, and said, "I'm going to hop into the flivver and go up to Haileybury. I smell trouble. Look after the two kids until I get back."

He was back twenty minutes later, his car loaded with refugees, and his eyes smarting from the smoke. He asked Leonie for a pair of goggles, and said, "I'm going to round up as many men with cars as I can, and ask them to follow me. There are only about fifty cars in all Cobalt, but I know they'll help when I tell them the people in Haileybury need help real bad."

Leonie remembers that her husband made about a dozen trips through the gauntlet of fire and smoke. Each time he returned, she was ready for him at the door with a bucket of cold water, into which he

211

would duck his head. Some of the refugees screamed angrily at him, as he would toss their bundles of clothing out the car window to make room for more people. Others insisted on salvaging such mementoes as a silver loving-cup or a portrait of Mother.

When Dick Fauteux's eyes couldn't take it any more, he drove his family to the Cobalt station. The women and children piled into a freight car, and waited for an engine that was supposed to arrive from North Bay.

Then Cobalt's Police Chief Sam Newton appeared at the station, and hollered, "The fire has reached the Cobalt bridge! If you men help put it out, there's a good chance that, with a shifting wind, we'll save the old town yet."

At midnight, the men returned, grimy and singed but grinning triumphantly, and Leonie Fauteux recalls, "My little family went back home, thanking God it was still standing there on Lang Street, humble though it was. After that, my husband was not a butcher in my eyes, but a hero."

The people of New Liskeard similarly conveyed refugees from Haileybury to their homes. C. W. Brown, then an accountant at the Royal Bank, recalls, "I made ten trips to Haileybury in my father's Model T Ford. Each time, I returned to New Liskeard with five passengers, mostly women and children. On one return trip, I overheard a lady passenger remark, 'I never dreamed I'd see the day when I'd be forced to accept New Liskeard hospitality!' I refrained from commenting."

In tormented Haileybury, the housewives themselves behaved heroically. Mrs. Florence Wesley, then a dark-haired, twenty-six-year-old mother, remembers putting wet cheesecloth over the faces of her children, Vincent, five, and Eileen, six, and marching them through the engulfing smoke to Haileybury High School on Latchford Street. She amused them there for hours by reciting funny fairy-tales, while her sister, Mrs. Anna Teresa Miller, the T. & N.O. telephone operator, stuck valiantly to her post at the switchboard. Florence's husband, Joseph Wesley, a tailor, meanwhile saved their two-storey wooden house on Rorke Street by sitting on the roof with a pailful of her cleaning water, and swatting the flames with a wet mop.

212

"I was panic-stricken," Mrs. Wesley recalls. "But I didn't dare show my terror, for fear of scaring the kiddies."

When fire headed toward her home on the outskirts of Haileybury, Mrs. Annie L. Craig, thirty-four year-old mother of four children, was baking bread, and had taken off her wedding ring and put it in a glass tumbler on the sideboard. Her husband Bill, a red-haired Scot, and her fire-ranger father, Samuel Stata, who lived nearby, were both away, and three of her children were at public school. Mrs. Craig's young sister rushed in to say the mayor had just ordered the town evacuated because of the fire.

"My heart almost jumped up into my throat," Annie Craig recalls. Ignoring her bread and her wedding ring, she snatched up her year-and-a-half-old son and his little yellow puppy from the floor. She got her mother and her sister's child, and collected her three children at school, and they ran a half mile to the lake shore. There a man in a lumberman's engine-driven boat agreed to take them to Farr's Island. They were three hundred yards from shore when the man dropped anchor, got into the canoe he had been trailing by a rope, and said, "I've got to go back for my sick wife. You stay here; I'll be back."

All night they stayed there, rocking wildly in the anchored boat, — three frightened women who couldn't operate the engine, and five wailing children.

"As great sparks and burning ash were flung into our faces by the howling wind," Mrs. Craig says, "I hastily threw overboard everything that might catch fire — two gallons of gasoline, two long straw seat cushions, and a big coil of rope. Even the fire-engine-red sun was blotted out in the smoke. We could hear the great bell towers of the Roman Catholic cathedral fall down with a jangling crash; barrels of gasoline on the dock burst into flames and went spinning high in the air, and we could hear dynamite exploding. A raft loaded with women and children passed by. A gaily trimmed lady's hat floated past. We were all chilled through with flying spray, and my young sister and I bailed water with old cans. My poor mother sat holding my baby in her arms, and kept him covered until morning with her heavy skirts."

At 9 A.M. their belated rescuer returned in his canoe in the falling snow. He got the engine going, and roared them to what was left of the town dock — a few charred timbers and cement pillars. A hungry-

213

looking man was seated on one desolate pillar, tearing a green cabbage apart and eating it.

"I knew how he felt, because we were ravenously hungry, too," says Mrs. Craig. "I looked around, and all I could see was a chill graveyard that had once been the prettiest town on the shores of Lake Temiskaming."

Perhaps the most vivid story is told by Rev. Robert Almon Spencer, the Haileybury Methodist minister, now eighty-seven, who has kept his diary all these years.

That morning the brown-moustached, brown-eyed minister had dug nine sacks of potatoes from his garden and put them on the verandah of his two-storey frame house on Main Street. That afternoon, he used some of the empty sacks in a vain effort to flog out the furious rain of sparks on the dry grass. His wife Elizabeth, the daughter of a Methodist minister herself, had fled to the lake with their four small children; but their fourteen-year-old daughter Eileen stayed behind to help her dad throw water on their flaming house with a hose.

When Rev. Spencer's neighbour, Gervaise Sutherland, warned him, "The town's doomed," the minister thrust a loaf of white bread into a prospector's packsack, grabbed a wool blanket striped red, white and blue, and raced to his smoke-wrapped red-brick church on the corner of Main Street. There he picked up the hymn-book and small Union Jack he'd carried all through the last war as a regimental captain; and he clutched Eileen by the hand, and they both ran to the lake shore, his moustache ablaze and his daughter's hair in flames.

The scene on the beach reminded him of some tale of the desert during a sand-storm, where men and beasts, caught in the grip of an elemental terror, had called an armistice, and crouched together in a blind instinct for protection. The grains of sand, lashed by the gale, were needles against the face, and the gusts of heat were a furnace; and big galvanized-iron shingles from a blazing pulp mill nearby whooshed through the air into the lake with an eerie *pu-u-ush-sh-sh-shhh!*

Rev. Spencer and his daughter waded into the icy water up to their necks. They stood there for more than two hours, the minister holding one side of the striped blanket and his daughter the other, and they would soak it, and hold it up over their heads as a shield against the

214

tempest of blazing brands and whirling shingles. "Don't be too scared, dear," he consoled his daughter. Inaudibly, he prayed, "Protect my family and myself, O Lord"; and he thought of the thirty-fourth Psalm, "The angel of the Lord encampeth around about them that fear him, and delivereth them."

At length the minister, utterly blinded by the smoke, was guided by his daughter's hand to the beach. They sat down on the sand to dry their clothes and tried to eat their loaf of bread, but they were too exhausted. Mr. Spencer overheard two bedraggled French Canadians talking; one said, "Well, Jean, how did you come out?" and the other answered, "We've lost all our possessions, but our lives are saved, so to hell with the rest." The minister later noted in his diary, "A rough speech, but we agreed."

Another refugee on the beach nearby was the carpenter's French-Canadian wife, Mrs. Lawrence ("Ed") Edwardson. She didn't know where her husband was, and her four small children were weeping; and, to add to her agony, she was nine months pregnant. Yet she had stood uncomplaining in the lake for hours, gripping a log, and gritting her teeth at the smoke and her mounting labour pains.

The expectant mother, the blinded minister and his trembling daughter, and the other refugees were taken on a wagon to the Lake Shore Road home of the public-school inspector, W. A. Wilson. Miraculously present there were Dr. Gordon Jackson, the Haileybury coroner, and Miss Kennedy, the nurse investigator for the Haileybury Mothers' Allowance Board. People in the crowded room discreetly held up a blanket to give the expectant mother privacy; and there, after fire and flood, Mrs. Edwardson gave birth to a nine-pound baby, later christened Wallace Kennedy Edwardson — the middle name in honour of the presiding nurse.

Mrs. Wilson made the minister lie down on the floor in the parlour, and bandaged his nearly blind eyes with damp cloths. But he couldn't lie still, for he kept brooding about the whereabouts of his wife Elizabeth and his four children. He got up and groped his way to the emergency registry office up the street, where he registered the fact that Eileen and himself were alive, and where his friend, the similarly burned-out Presbyterian minister, J. W. Watt, exclaimed, "I can't recognize you, Reverend! Why, you're charred black as an Ethiopian."

215

Then Mr. Spencer faltered his way back to the Wilson home. To his delight, he saw his wife Beth and their four children seated around the stove, drinking hot mugs of tea; and the rest was all kisses and embraces.

The minister and his family slept that night in the Methodist parsonage in New Liskeard. The next day, Mr. Spencer returned to Haileybury, to find his church a shambles of red brick; and all that remained of his home was nine sacks of roasted potatoes on the charred shell of the verandah.

He immediately had the Methodist Conference in Toronto send him, in sections, a portable church. Soon he was preaching "The Lord giveth and the Lord taketh away" to his congregation of three hundred souls, many of them living in the discarded street-cars that were shipped to Haileybury's refugees from Toronto's "boneyard of trolley chariots".

Mr. Spencer is now retired. His brown moustache is now silky white, and his brown eyes pouched behind his steel-rimmed spectacles. He stoops as he tends his garden of huge crimson peonies and yellow iris on the Lake Promenade in Long Branch, along the shore of Lake Ontario. Yet he is amazingly spry for a man of eighty-seven, and his hands do not tremble as he holds the diary recording the forest fire that happened so long ago.

"My experience taught me one thing," he reads aloud. "Ever since, I've had a better understanding of the three Hebrews, Shadrach, Meshach and Abed-nego, and their torment when they were thrown into the fiery furnace, because they refused to fall down and worship before King Nebuchadnezzar's golden idols and false gods."

_ 10 _

Vancouver's Bridge Collapse

O N THE DAY THE VANCOUVER BRIDGE TUMBLED down, a nineteen-year-old "high-steel punk" named Gary Poirier was the only one of the seventy-nine men working on that colossus of steel and concrete who had a premonition of impending death. The night before, in his small bedroom on East Pender Street, the apprentice had dreamed that the unfinished Second Narrows Bridge had collapsed into Burrard Inlet. In Poirier's dream, he was sliced clean in two by a snapping cable.

Now, in the butter-yellow sunshine next day, on the pleasantly warm Tuesday afternoon of June 17, 1958, the dream seemed preposterous, and Poirier tried to dismiss it from his mind. Yet it kept nagging him as he swayed catlike along the skeletal girder lacework high on the Second Narrows Bridge.

Poirier was teetering on the lip of a two-thousand-ton span. It was one of five such arms of steel clawing out from the North Shore, each supported on legs of concrete. His was the outermost anchor span thrust out over the water. Its red metal girders were being bolted together, while a gang of painters, lashed to the beams by safety belts, were flicking silver paint on the fourth span behind it. When these two spans, 375 feet long, were finished, work would start on the main cantilever arch of what was to be a $23 million web of steel spun out for two miles. Within six months, this most massive bridge in British Columbia would link North Vancouver to Vancouver proper in six-lane traffic.

One hundred and fifty feet below his roost, Poirier could see gulls wheeling over the angry grey waters of Burrard Inlet, which was now thirty feet deep and in perilous full rip tide. Poirier shuddered as he thought how those swirling waters had already swallowed two of the four high-steel men who had accidentally plunged to their death since work began on this bridge in February, 1956.

In the blue haze far off, Poirier could see the peaks of the twin coastal-range mountains, curved like couchant lions, arching their manes against the cloudless sky near Burrard Inlet's First Narrows. From them the Lion's Gate Bridge took its name. When that First Narrows Bridge was erected twenty years ago, its one mile of vaulting spans and soaring lines made it the longest suspension bridge in the British Empire. They hailed it as a symphony in steel and a poem in concrete marching across an ocean channel.

Now, Poirier could hear his own familiar symphony. Around him was the clang of steel pins being whacked, and the hammer of driving bolts. The high-steel workers, with their sunburned faces and their gnarled knuckles that looked beaten out on forges, seemed handcuffed to their daredevil toil.

At 3:35 P.M., the thirty-five-ton diesel engine — the "locie", the men called it — snorted up the tracks toward Poirier. It hauled two train cars, groaning with tons of steel beams, to the 155-ton crane already parked on Poirier's outjutting anchor span. The locie hooted its whistle, and the shriek grated on his jangly nerves. He mentioned his nervousness to another young worker on the bolting gang, George Schmidt.

Schmidt laughed. "If noise gets your goat, up here, then it's good-bye Charlie."

Poirier tightened his yellow safety jacket. He straightened his white "hard-boiled-egg" steel safety hat and settled his toes firmly inside his steel-capped black leather boots; and somehow the apprentice didn't feel quite so apprehensive. The dream, after all, must be just a dream.

At precisely 3:40 P.M., Poirier's dream turned into a living nightmare. With a cracking noise like two rifle shots, the anchor span twitched and quivered. It sagged down a few feet, hesitated, gave a convulsive shudder, and then plummeted down 150 feet to the rip-tide waters. It

218

carried the locie, the crane, tons of girders, and the astonished men with it.

The toppling anchor span violently whipped its supporting double pillar of concrete, tipping it fifteen degrees off vertical. This, in turn, tore free the fourth steel span, and it, too, crashed down into the water. It left silhouetted against the sunny blue sky an M-shaped ruin, with the two spans now macabre chutes dangling to the water from the cement pillars. The men were either clinging to the twisted girders like flies, or mangled as though by a giant egg-beater, or fighting for life in the rushing current.

After Poirier heard what he called the "double boom, boom", he felt himself hurtling down, down through the air, and he thought, "I've had it! I've had it! My dream was true." Then he felt himself sinking fifteen feet under icy water.

"When I came to the surface," he later said, "I found the impact had torn my yellow life-jacket almost off. But I managed to hang onto the jacket and a two-by-four, and I drifted in the swift current. And when I was fished out by a rescue boat ten minutes later, all I could think of was, 'I sure am lucky. All I've got is a possible fractured leg. I dreamed it all. Only in my dream I was killed. I'm mighty glad that part of my dream was wrong.'"

Nor was it "good-bye Charlie" for his fellow-worker, twenty-two-year-old George Schmidt. After his ride down with the span, Schmidt found himself among the tumbled grid of steel. He looked away from the dead and dying and down at himself. He saw that a flying girder had chopped off one of his legs, clean, just above the knee.

He unbucked his safety belt and made a tourniquet with it above the bloody stump. Then he lit a cigarette. He smoked it, and calmly waited. He was still puffing quietly when two men came along, and lifted him out of his steel bed of pain and into their row-boat.

"Thanks, fellas," was all George Schmidt said.

Garry Poirier and George Schmidt were two of the twenty tough-spirited bridge men hospitalized in Vancouver's worst single disaster. Eighteen others were killed almost instantly. A nineteenth man named Leonard K. Mott died later, while skin-diving for their bodies. Though he had been a professional stand-in for Peter Lorre in the movie

Twenty Thousand Leagues Under the Sea, the rip tide of Burrard Inlet was too powerful for Mott, and he was sucked to his death beneath the butchered bridge.

Newspapers called it Canada's most calamitous bridge collapse since August 28, 1907, when the cantilever Quebec City Bridge tumbled into the St. Lawrence River, killing seventy-five bridge-builders. Actually, its social repercussions were more akin to another Quebec bridge catastrophe — on January 31, 1951. Then four spans crumbled on the Duplessis Bridge, and plunged four men to their death in the St. Maurice River. The bridge was the pride of Premier Maurice Duplessis' home constituency of Three Rivers; it was named after his father, Superior Court Judge N. L. Duplessis. Because his pet bridge was supposedly as durable as his Union Nationale party, Premier Duplessis blamed its collapse on pernicious Communist workers. However, provincial opposition back-benchers charged that it was "built on the cheap" on a contract "padded with graft". Furthermore, they called the Premier's Highways Minister, Antonio Talbot, a "nitwit", "ruffian" and "rascal".

The Vancouver bridge collapse touched off similar blasts of purple political oratory. British Columbia's CCF Leader Robert Strachan demanded the immediate firing of Social Credit Highways Minister "Flying Phil" Gagliardi. He called for investigation of all major bridge and road projects built under Premier W. A. C. Bennett's régime. Bennett tried to dismiss his "smear" as "the usual wild statements from a wild man".

Even more significant, the Vancouver "bridge of sighs and tears" brought from British Columbia's militant trade-union movement a clarion call to protect labour's civil liberties. During a province-wide strike of the high-steel workers, Supreme Court Justice Alexander Malcolm Manson, the seventy-five-year-old former British Columbia Labour Minister, issued a controversial injunction. He enjoined the local union to direct its men back to work, because the unanchored bridge span was a "potential hazard" to citizens.

The union men said it was a free country and refused to be forced back on the job. They agreed that the bridge had, indeed, proved "hazardous" for their buddies who had died trying to build it.

Mr. Justice Manson promptly had seven union men arrested on contempt charges. During a stormy court session, punctuated by raucous outbursts from the gallery, Mr. Justice Manson exhibited a letter. It was signed "Steelworker", couched in "foul and obscene language", and threatened death for him and civil war by the union. Then Mr. Justice Manson imposed fines totalling nineteen thousand dollars on the union and its officials for defying his court order.

The British Columbia Federation of Labour retaliated by starting a defence fund to take the case to the Supreme Court of Canada. It also wired Prime Minister John Diefenbaker that this "involuntary servitude" was a breach of the civil liberties promised in Canada's constitution, the British North America Act. Two sympathetic Vancouver locals, the Painters Union and the Pulp and Sulphite Union, went further. They irately petitioned Canadian Justice Minister Davie Fulton to remove Mr. Justice Manson from the British Columbia Supreme Court bench.

Meanwhile, concurrent with a whole rash of crippling province-wide strikes, ranging from loggers to salmon fishers, the bridge-builders' strike raged unabated for more than fifty days. Management's spokesman, R. K. Gervin of the Structural Steel Association of British Columbia, likened labour's "hamstringing of British Columbia industry" to Communism. This just drew a laugh from the high-steel-union business manager, Tom McGrath, locked up in Oakalla Prison until he paid his three-thousand-dollar fine imposed by Mr. Justice Manson. "That," the labour leader scornfully told a Vancouver *Sun* reporter, "is the old Red scare."

The riotous results springing from the Vancouver bridge disaster were to be expected. British Columbia's leaders in politics and trade unionism have always been notable for their hot words and headstrong actions. In the phrase of the province's historian, Margaret A. Ormsby, "In no other part of Canada were working-men as radical as in British Columbia." They have consistently been the country's toughest labour-union bellwethers, battling for progressive working conditions and against what they call capitalist "boodlers".

The men chiefly responsible for the building of the bridge were Bennett and Gagliardi. What circuses were to the Roman emperors, bridges were to William Andrew Cecil Bennett, Social Credit Premier

221

of British Columbia. When the Roman populace cried for bread, they were given a circus; when the people of British Columbia complained about parliamentary improprieties or the unorthodox way of awarding contracts, they were given another bridge. Pointing to the roads and bridges spanning mountainous British Columbia, Bennett would solemnly declaim his slogan: "Social Credit gets things done!"

He was abetted by his Highways Minister, Flying Phil Gagliardi, no mean spellbinder himself. A former logging-camp bulldozer driver, who still serves as pastor of the Pentecostal evangelical church, the fiery Gagliardi says, "I talk fast. I act fast. I think fast." Arrested three times by traffic cops for speeding, Gagliardi talked about testing the curves of his dazzling new highways, and blithely raised the provincial limit from fifty to sixty miles an hour. The Highways Minister was wont to fly in his personal Government plane over a new bridge being erected, and exult about the Social Credit Party's "triumph of imagination over the hard, cold facts of engineering". The building of bridges and highways became such a provincial mania that CCF leader Robert Strachan was heard to mutter in disgust, "The people in British Columbia are getting so they prefer half a mile of black-top to democracy itself."

The erection of the new Second Narrows Bridge was to be the crowning toy for what their enemies called those "goldbrick twins", Bennett and Gagliardi. It would, after all, make a nice rhetorical flourish in speeches to stress that the Social Credit Party had spanned the very Burrard Inlet down which Captain George Vancouver had first sailed 160 years ago in his sloop of war, the *Discovery*. Besides, a new bridge was needed.

The old Second Narrows Bridge, already linking the North Shore to the South Shore, was a rickety wooden-and-iron thing. It trembled like a spavined old nag whenever a train rumbled along its spine. It was slung so low that every time a tug wanted to pass through the Narrows, all auto traffic on the bridge would grind to a halt to allow the wheezy bridge lift to be raised. Moreover, the toll charged by the old bridge was too cheap for what the traffic could bear: just twenty cents per auto.

Consequently, it was decided to build a $23 million humdinger of a new bridge a few dozen yards west of the old one. The decision was

222

made by the six-member British Columbia Toll Highways and Bridge Authority, a provincial Crown corporation, with Premier Bennett as chairman and Highways Minister Gagliardi's staff as technical guides.

Contracts were awarded to various bridge-erection companies, and the British Columbia Toll Authority retained as engineering consultants the top-calibre Vancouver firm of Swan, Wooster & Partners. Its senior partner, Colonel William George Swan, an expert with fifty years of experience in bridge designing, was described by Gagliardi as "the best consulting engineer in Canada". He had served as consultant for both the Pattullo Bridge and the Lions' Gate Bridge. For this new bridge, Colonel Swan recommended the cantilever design — a thing of grace and beauty, whose principle might be likened to a waiter holding a heavy tray of food aloft with a slender but powerful arm.

Unhappily, a mistake was made, and the temporary arms holding aloft the fifth anchor span were designed *too* slender. The mistake was later described by the Royal Commission inquiry, conducted by Chief Justice Sherwood Lett, as "a human mathematical error — a risk inherent in the engineering profession". The human error was made by two very human engineers. They made two slips in arithmetic while figuring out the design specifications for the "falsework grillage" — the platform and the temporary steel legs holding up the anchor span.

Over strenuous objections, the names of the two engineers were revealed to the Royal Commission. But by then it was too late to call them to account, for both men were working on the fifth anchor span on the day when the falsework buckled like a paper clip and tossed 330 tons of metal and men into the sea.

The disaster took all spectators by surprise, perhaps because death seemed so unexpected on a brilliant June afternoon, eighty-one degrees in the sunshine.

"That Tuesday was a sunny day, a warmish day, and the smoke haze drifted past on a gentle westerly," Jack Wasserman, columnist for the Vancouver *Sun*, recalls. "It was the kind of day that made you think of a cooling dip in a mountain lake. It was the kind of day for contemplating a holiday, or just getting home, taking off your shoes, and opening a cold bottle of beer."

Certainly, nobody in the news-room of the *Sun* expected this biggest scoop of the year to break. The deadline period was past then, and a

223

few reporters of the late-afternoon shift were standing around, waiting to go home.

The phone rang. Because the receptionists had all gone home, Jim Hazelwood, who covers the water-front, answered it. After agreeing, "Oh, yes," a couple of times, he put the receiver down.

"A woman says the Second Narrows Bridge fell down," Hazelwood said, with a laugh. Nobody got excited.

"We thought the woman was either joking or mistaken," recalls Audrey Down, a crack *Sun* reporter. "My first thought was that some joker was trying to play a trick on us. Like the joker a year before, who phoned up a local radio station to say the Second Narrows Bridge was on fire. After publishing an excited bulletin, the station had to correct it. Even after the calls started flooding in, and pandemonium began to mount around this red-hot story, we still thought it was the *old* Second Narrows Bridge that had done the splits."

Nor was the calamity expected by an amateur bridge-watcher named Jack Newman. He was peering at the high-steel workers through his binoculars from his nearby home on Edinburgh Avenue. He was admiring their goatlike agility, as they would scoot down diagonal girders by sliding on the balls of their feet. Then he sucked in his breath. It was an incredible sight — the new bridge was thundering down in a mushrooming cloud of dust, with a tumult that reverberated in downtown Vancouver.

"I couldn't believe it," said Newman, almost weeping as he told the story. "I felt as though I'd lost an old friend. I watched them build it through all these months. I even bought a new pair of glasses to become a better sidewalk superintendent. Just doesn't seem possible. My old friend, the bridge — gone . . ."

Nor was it expected by a professional bridge-watcher named Bill Lasko. His job, according to Workmen's Compensation Board regulations, was to circle underneath the bridge in a boat and keep an eye out for workers who might tumble accidentally into the water. Young Lasko was in his yellow twenty-two-foot-long barge, about 150 feet south-east of the end of the new bridge. Then he heard the loud crack, a momentary silence, an atomic roar — and then, as he later testified, "all of a sudden she just come right down." Lunch-baskets, hard hats, gloves, and oil drums showered down, and, like a flutter of dandelions, the yellow life-jackets.

A huge wash almost swamped his boat; and from that moment until 9 P.M., twenty-five-year-old Lasko moved like a man possessed. He raced his yellow barge among the jungle of twisted girders — first alone, and then with the aid of frogmen in an armada of sixty boats — desperately trying to rescue his fellow-bridgemen. He climbed up to the wharf for a while, where two Burnaby firemen gave him a cup of coffee and a cigarette; and they loosened his collar, and pleaded, "Please, Bill, knock off."

"No, I can't", he said; and at nine-thirty, he stood up on shaky legs and headed back for the yellow barge. "I saw a shirt with a life-belt on it, floating out there. It belongs to a guy I know. I'm going to find him." To himself, Lasko murmured, "I never dreamed the day would come that I would get more bodies than one."

To Jean Howarth, veteran star reporter of the Vancouver *Province*, who was on the spot screaming directions to the rescue boats from the edge of the fallen bridge, it all seemed utterly unbelievable — until she saw the boots of the dead men sticking out from blankets on the blood-stained boats

"The dead men did not look very real, or frightening, or sad," she later wrote in a memorable report. "But the big heavy boots were very real. They hurt."

She found some of the unreality of the dead men was in the living men, who had escaped and were still getting their hands back on life. "I was on that girder," said one of them, pointing. "I was on that girder, and I don't know how I got off it. I can't remember." He laughed a small silly laugh, and dug the heel of his hand into his face; and when the hand came away he was crying.

Another man, an elderly man, told her, "I was painting there. See where my bucket is? My God, it's still there! And when she started to go, I grabbed the girder I was on. A grabbed it so hard I think I broke two ribs." Yet he wouldn't go and have his ribs attended to. "I'm alive," he said. "When I climbed up from those pilings in the water, I got some slivers. My pants is pretty near dry already."

The caterpillar operator, G. W. Vanderbrink, who had watched the bridge "fall so slow, just like a falling tree", was still dazed. "It's funny," he said. "Around two-thirty in the afternoon, a man with a camera turned up at our work site. An amateur fan. Said he wanted to take some 'before' and 'after' shots of the bridge." Vanderbrink laughed hollowly. "Looks like the guy can take those 'after' shots now."

Hardened journalist that she is, Miss Howarth was most touched when a ten-year-old boy spoke to her. He had rushed down to see the sights when he heard the bridge go down like a cannon. He was beside her when the rip tide swept the first dead man into view, the man's hand caught in the webbing of his yellow life-jacket, his big steel-capped boots jutting out from the whirlpool.

Suddenly the boy was pressed very tight against Miss Howarth. "Would you put your arms around me?" he asked.

So she did, and the boy said, "The man's going to be all right, isn't he? Isn't he?"

And the reporter said, "Yes. They'll fix him up." Yet the boy continued to shiver in her arms, and he kept asking over and over, "Do you think he had any kids?"

The gang of twenty-four painters from the Boshard Company — most of them new Canadians, with their broods of children to worry about — were luckiest. They were spraying and touching up bright aluminum on girders of the fourth span, and they had a split-second warning when they heard the fifth anchor span crack ahead of them.

Their foreman, Juergen Wulf, was a hero with bleeding hands. He was standing on the bridge railway tracks, when he heard "a sort of rumbling noise", and saw the crane on the anchor span "slowly moving down and seeming to stop in midair"; and his own span shook, and he felt "like I was on top of a smokestack when an earthquake starts".

Death dogged his every footstep as Wulf raced 150 feet along the trembling steel. "Then I looked down," he recalled, "and I saw a guy struggling in the water and hollering for help."

Wulf grabbed a rope and slid one hundred feet down it; and when his hands were burned and torn raw, he let go. He dropped thirty feet into the rip tide, and rescued his struggling friend.

226

His friend, Anthony Romaniuk, a thirty-three-year-old painter, felt himself dragged ten feet below the surface, with his safety belt fastened to a beam. Romaniuk said: "I told myself, 'Don't panic, Tony. Keep cool, Tony.' And I unfastened my harness, and my life-jacket popped me up to the surface."

Another heroic painter, thirty-two-year-old Laci Szokol, had run out of paint, and was getting a refill when he felt a *snap, click, snap, click* under his feet. "I run thirty feet along the catwalk just like crazy," Szokol said. However, he stopped to throw down a rope and pull up his floundering pals, Michael Josefi and Tony Wohlfart.

"Afraid to go back to the job?" Szokol said. "No, not really. I like high places. The view is nice." And his rescued buddy, Tony Wohlfart, verified this: "Some people clean up streets. Some close up cans. We work in high places. Nobody forces us to do this. There will always be danger in high bridge work."

The forty-eight high-steel men working on the anchor span under the supervision of Big Jim English were aware of the danger. But they had no warning.

"I was sure I was finished," recalled twenty-four-year-old Don Gardiner. "As I whistled down through the air, I thought of my mother at home in Winnipeg. I had a big belt of tools, and it pinned me under water, and held me there for more than a minute. I didn't think I could make it up. I was *sure* I couldn't make it up. But then I fought, and I made it up."

As he catapulted through the air, trapped inside a criss-cross of steel beams, John Olynyk thought of his pretty brown-haired wife Edna, and of how he would see her no more. A husky two-hundred-pounder of six-foot-one, Olynyk had been working outside a diagonal beam. Then his partner, Al McPherson, with whom he'd once worked on the Rosedale Agassiz Bridge, inched outside the beam and said, "I'll spell you off, Johnny."

"I'd no sooner got inside the beam than I felt it plunging down," Olynyk recalled of his flight, during which he felt like a squirrel caught inside a whirling hollow log. "It's an awful feeling, when you're going down and you know you're trapped."

227

As it happened, the steel crushed his partner outside to death. Hardly more fortunate, Olynyk found himself eight feet under water, encased in a steel tomb. The burly fellow had barely enough room to turn himself around and start crawling up the incline. Panting for air, he squeezed himself up until he found an aperture. He poked his face through, and tried to heave himself out, but the opening was too small; his big shoulders would not go through.

"I shouted for help," he later said. "Someone on a passing boat heard me. 'Please,' I told them, 'get a cutting torch, or I'm done for.'"

Olynyk was sure he had no more than twenty minutes to live. "The water was already at my waist, and the tide was rising fast," he said. "I could do nothing to help myself. Just sit and wait."

He waited for fifteen minutes, until a gang of six welders, headed by Jim Fullager, arrived through the swirling waters in a work-boat. The water was up to his shoulders when they applied their torches to his steel cage, and tried to burn it away piece by piece. Olynyk said nothing, merely thinking to himself, "This is like living in hell."

When they finally pulled him free, just in the nick of time, Olynyk could hardly keep his face above water. He was treated for abrasions and then released to his wife Edna. She was calm in her joy that she was not the wife of one of the six other men cut out of the twisted beams by the the welders, who were released dead.

Margaret Chrusch was the wife of one of the men fatally trapped by the steel and the water. The Monday night before, just as they were preparing for bed, her Joe had taken her arm and said, "Listen, honey, if anything happens to me, you'll look after the kids?"

That Tuesday night, Margaret Chrusch sat numb at the kitchen table of their barren old house on Lakewood Drive, and for the sake of her four children tried not to cry.

Nine-year-old Diane, her arms withered by polio, stroked her mother's hair and comforted her. Five-year-old Linda, whom her husband used to call "my little pussy", was squabbling with six-year-old Gordon, who was exclaiming vigorously, "I'm the man in this house now." The oldest, ten-year-old Maureen, was wondering aloud how they'd pay the hundred-dollar-a-month rent, and the instalment payments of seventy-five dollars a month for their furniture, as well as the overdue hospital bills.

Mrs. Chrusch tried to explain that she could not yet think about the future. A neighbour told her that Workmen's Compensation would pay her seventy-five dollars a month for life, plus twenty-five dollars for each child. But Mrs. Chrusch, with one of Joe's handkerchiefs balled against her mouth, said, "Everything I do and every thought I think always comes back to the thought of Joe dead."

She recalled how they'd been getting back on their feet lately since Joe had brought the family west eight months ago from Lac du Bonnet in Manitoba, so he could work on the Kelowna and Creston and Second Narrows Bridges. True, he had been laid off for the two weeks just before last Christmas, and she'd had to work part time as a photo darkroom assistant. Still, things had been improving.

"I miss him so," Margaret said. "We always did things together. If it was the dishes to be done, I'd wash and he'd wipe. If it was the beds to be made, he'd take one side and I'd take the other. Joe was such a kind, easy-going man. We hardly ever argued. And when we did, it was me who started it."

"Honest, Marg, the police say Joe didn't drown," her neighbour tried to console her. "It was over for him very quickly."

Margaret Chrusch leaned her elbows on the unpaid-for table, and stared at the empty chair at the head of it, and finally broke into tears.

"It's looking at his chair," she said, "and not seeing him in it."

Violet Wright was the wife of one high-steel man who did not die; but the disaster crippled her Bill for eleven months. He endured a dislocated right hip, two broken ribs, a broken cheek-bone, and a dislocated left shoulder that continued to twinge with pain. Even today, he unconsciously rubs his shoulder as he talks.

Wright is a powerfully muscled six-footer from Red Deer, Alberta. Greying at fifty, he grins with a handsome, devil-may-care glint in his blue eyes. He has always been proud of being a high-steel man, ever since he got into the work in Trail, British Columbia, in 1934. He enjoys being one of the *élite* of construction workers, a bridge-building "cat" — a race reputedly so hardy that they "can chew nails and spit rust". He has helped erect such British Columbia bridges as Vancouver's Granville Street Traffic Bridge across False Creek, the Cottonwood Bridge near Quesnel, and the Pacific Great Eastern Railway Bridge at Abou.

"No two bridges are alike, and the work keeps you up in the fresh air," Bill used to say. "Risky? Why, a nice, wide six-inch girder is as easy to walk on as a city sidewalk."

However, his wife Violet, a slim, medium-sized woman, who wears glasses and whose greying hair is becomingly feather-cut, hates high places. Twice she tried watching her husband on the job as he was perched high on the girders. "I just can't stand watching him," Violet said, and she turned and ran.

But she has always been grateful that Bill, unlike other high-steel men who take their families gypsying from job to job with them, kept his home fixed in Vancouver, so his children would not always have to change schools. Violet keeps Dutch-clean their two-storey, rust-coloured stucco home. It is cream-trimmed, with a gabled roof and two chimneys that give it a character of its own, setting it apart from other houses on the street. Surrounded by a picket fence, it sits on a hill that commands a fine view of the new Second Narrows Bridge and the curving mountains, which Violet, a transplant from the Prairies, has grown to love.

When the bridge collapsed, Violet had cleaned the house and was ready to go out shopping. Her seventeen-year-old son Brian turned on his transistor radio and heard that there was a bad accident, but missed the details. Her twenty-one-year-old daughter Margaret rushed home after six ambulances passed by the Hastings Street bank where she worked. She feared that one of those ambulances was carrying her father.

Violet Wright was standing on the corner a few blocks away waiting for the red light to change, when Brian caught up to her on his bicycle. "The bridge has gone down," he told her, and they hurried home to wait.

"I tried to listen to the radio, but I couldn't," Violet recalls. "A reporter was interviewing a woman on the North Shore. She'd seen the bridge go down, and she was laughing, as though it were all a big joke. I couldn't *stand* it!"

230

She was lucky. Bill regained consciousness at the hospital long enough to mumble to a nurse to phone his wife. She knew by 5:30 P.M. where her Bill was, though he was on the lists as "missing" until eleven o'clock.

Bill was standing on a steel chord weighing more than fifty tons, atop the locie train, when the anchor span began to topple. The chord was attached to the crane boom, and the metal began to dance wildly under his feet.

"At first I thought the train had broken through," he told Violet. "It was a roar, just one big roar. I was swinging through the air on the chord. It went down, down, down, like a bat out of hell. I said to myself, 'This is it.'"

Bill was cursing to himself fiercely as he hit the water. He sank right to the bottom of Burrard Inlet, for he could feel the rocks scraping his feet; then his yellow life-jacket bobbed him to the surface. He snatched at two scaffold planks with his left hand — his right arm seemed frozen immobile — and groggily felt himself being washed several yards east. He was still swearing to himself when a pleasure boat veered into view; and then, needled with pain, he blacked out into unconsciousness.

"When I came to in the hospital," Bill says, "the first thing that swam into my vision was the frame over my bed, with poles across, and pulleys. I was thinking about this. Then my eye caught this man. He was standing at the foot of the bed with his hat in his hand. I thought I recognized him from somewhere. It was Highways Minister Phil Gagliardi, and he was saying, 'You will be well taken care of, sir.'"

It was indeed Highways Minister Flying Phil Gagliardi. When newspapermen had first broken the news to him in Victoria, he refused to believe it; he had laughed, "You're joking." When convinced it was true, he said he would visit the scene in Vancouver next morning. But Premier Bennett came out of a Cabinet meeting to order him to leave immediately.

Less than an hour later, Gagliardi landed in Burrard Inlet in his Government float-plane. After touring the wreckage, he said: "It's terrible. Steel and concrete don't matter. But men do. I estimate it'll cost $3.5 million and take six months to clean it up. But it won't cost British

231

Columbia one cent more. The bridge contractors are entirely responsible for everything that goes on here, until the bridge is completed and turned over to the British Columbia Toll Authority."

This didn't satisfy CCF leader Robert Strachan, who directed a blowtorch of withering scorn at Gagliardi. He accused him of interfering with the engineers, and demanded that Premier Bennett fire him.

"They can't blame me," Gagliardi protested. "All I am is a bystander. Was I holding it up and went for coffee or something?"

Nevertheless, he was much relieved when the Royal Commission inquiry, conducted by British Columbia's Chief Justice Sherwood Lett, submitted its report to the provincial Cabinet. It absolved the British Columbia Toll Authority from all blame.

Jubilantly, Premier Bennett announced that the probe "absolutely cleared" his dear friend, Highways Minister Gagliardi. He joined the latter in suggesting that CCF leader Strachan resign for trying to make "cheap political capital out of a tragedy".

Similarly, the consulting engineers said the striking high-steel workers were trying to make capital out of emotionalism when they refused, a year later, to bolt the unanchored bridge span. "Only three days' work will safely bolt it up," they pleaded, as members of Local 97 of the Ironworkers Union took up picketing placards instead of their tools, and demanded higher wages.

If a high-steel worker went back on the job without being assured the bridge was safe, Local Business Agent Norm Eddison declared, "he would tempt fate. I would rot in jail rather than withhold this information from our membership."

When officials scoffed that it was certainly safe to work on, the workmen raised the cry: "You said it was safe before."

That cry echoed when Supreme Court Justice Alexander Malcolm Manson had seven union men arrested on contempt charges for defying his second court order. "Can you always believe the engineers?" a high-steel man named Isaac Hall asked the court. "The engineers said the same thing last June, but my pal got killed on the bridge."

The fifty-day strike ended after the union won a 57c-an-hour increase to add to their current basic rate of $2.62 an hour. While they

232

appealed Mr. Justice Manson's contempt conviction of nineteen thousand dollars in fines, the union men went back to building their unfinished bridge.

"Naturally, the crew talks about the accident," said Big Jim English, the job superintendent, who had tumbled unconscious into the rip tide himself. "But they don't talk about it morbidly. Sometimes a man will pat a section and say, 'This is where I was working,' or 'This is what I was hanging onto.'"

Nor was there anything morbid about the July memorial service held for the doomed men in Vancouver's Empire Stadium. The widows and children, who had been helped by the fifty-thousand-dollar "Families Fund" donated by warm-hearted Vancouver citizens, gathered in the oval stadium to mourn for the dead. As the band played "O God, Our Help in Ages Past", "The Lord's My Shepherd", and "Abide with Me", they could see the tip of the wrecked bridge jutting out below the jagged peaks of the North Shore Mountains.

Afterwards, from a barge in the Burrard Inlet, Rev. George Turpin, the chaplain of Shaughnessy Hospital, scattered nineteen scarlet roses one by one on the dark waters around the "bridge of sorrow". The roses were tied with a golden ribbon, which the Reverend Mr. Turpin called a spanning symbol of unbroken friendship with their fellow workers: "We remember single acts of bravery, when someone will respond to a sudden emergency. But today we are remembering the daily courage of men whose tasks take them into dangerous places. They all shared a common danger, and now they will live on in our hearts and minds."

To Bill Wright, the high-steel union man, who was off work crippled for eleven months, the broken bridge will always be symbolized by his broken arm. While he was off the job, he got Workmen's Compensation of $250 a month — about half his salary. But that doesn't bother him. He is now back at construction work, but no longer at the bridge-building he loves so much, because his sore arm won't allow him to climb high steel as he used to. He is today ridden by a passion "to get back into the shape I was before" — although, he concedes wryly as he rubs his shoulder, "none of us bridge men will ever be what we were before."

This fearless man's concern about high places has become an obsession. In the spring of 1960, still crippled, he was lying on the lawn and

233

watching his wife Violet climb a ladder to clean the outside windows of their home.

The ladder began to shake, and his wife began to shake, and Bill Wright began to shake.

"Get down!" he cried. "Get down! It's dangerous up there."

ACKNOWLEDGEMENT

In addition to sources mentioned in the body of the book, information was received from the people listed below, and is hereby gratefully acknowledged.

Mrs. J. F. Adamson, Stratford, Ont.
G. S. Alcock, Valois, Que.
Meta Cheves Allen, Quebec City
Joseph Anthony, Kingston, Ont.
Mrs. M. Avison, Macdonald College, Que.
A. T. Baker, Calgary
Dan J. Barrett, London, Ont.
Alison Bartle, Grand Falls, Nfld.
Clara Beam, Pasadena, California
Eddie Bell, Regina
Patricia V. Berger, Montreal
H. F. Bezanson, Halifax
J. A. Bibeau, St. Boniface, Man.
Mrs. J. R. Bird, Broadview, Sask.
Paul Bjarnason, Vancouver
E. Jervis Bloomfield, Vancouver
Auguste A. Bolte, Toronto
Joseph Bradley, Toronto
J. D. Brady, Timmins, Ont.
Jessie Bryan, West Vancouver
Ona Burgess, Norland, Ont.
George Cadogan, Durham, Ont.
Lorne Gordon Campbell, Oakville, Ont.
Mrs. Eileen Campinvro, Greenfield Park, Que.
Mrs. Noel Caron, St. Noel, Que.
George A. Chapman, Richmond, Que.
Marielle Chauvin, Montreal
Hubert R. A. Clark, Calgary
Joan Cohen, Winnipeg
Mrs. A. Connally, Montreal
Mrs. John A. Connors, Halifax
E. Q. Constain, Vancouver
Mrs. George Cook, Vancouver
W. H. Cook, Orillia, Ont.
Doris Cooper, Hamilton
Arthur C. Coote, Halifax
William A. Corbett, St. John's, Nfld.
Victor Corby, Toronto
M. L. Costigan, Stettler, Alta.
T. F. Cote, St. John's, Nfld.
Dean W. J. Cousins, Lethbridge, Alta.
Sam Cowan, Port Arthur, Ont.
Cecil Cox, Toronto
Mrs. B. L. Craig, Delta, Ont.
Mrs. R. K. Cruickshank, St. Mary's, Ont.
Arthur Curotte, Verdun, Que.
Ada Currie, Guelph, Ont.
Thomas A. Dealy, Brantford, Ont.
John Decker, Fort Erie, Ont.
Mildred Denby, Toronto

Stella Desrochers, Montreal
B. Doerksen, Regina
Hope Donaldson, Toronto
J. Alex Edmison, Ottawa
Agnes Elliott, Montreal
S. L. Elliott, Lachute, Que.
V. Elsden, Three Rivers, Que.
L. E. F. English, Museum Curator, St. John's, Nfld.
Alec C. Ferguson, Guernsey, Channel Islands
Jean Fern, St. John's, Nfld.
Byron Fisher, Montreal
Ron Fleischman, Montreal
Joseph T. Foreman, Verdun, Que.
John Fowler, Vancouver
Ray Gardner, Vancouver
Mrs. George M. George, Sault Ste. Marie, Ont.
Richard H. Gluns, Toronto
Florrie Green, Islington, Ont.
Mrs. R. Gregoire, Capreol, Ont.
C. D. Grover, Winnipeg
Harry E. Grundy, Sherbrook, Que.
Mrs. Murray Hahn, Toronto
Norman A. Hall, Regina
F. P. Hanrahan, Port Arthur, Ont.
Mrs. George H. Harper, Waterloo, Ont.
Stella Harvey, Regina
Mrs. W. K. Hennig, Vancouver
Senator John G. Higgins, Ottawa
Mrs. C. Jacobson, Kenora, Ont.
Marjorie Jenkins, Toronto
Clyde C. Jessup, Nanton, Alta.
James Johnson, Norfolk, Nebraska
Beatrice L. Johnston, Montreal
Beatrice Wyatt Johnston, Montreal
Mrs. W. R. Jones, London, Ont.
Hazel Kaiser, Calgary
Charlotte Keens, Toronto
Lieut.-Col. Alfred Keith, London, Ont.
Lillian Kidd, Halifax
Dorothy H. Kingston, Bourlamaque, Que.
Ovila Kirouac, Ste. Anne de la Pocatière, Que.
Lulu M. Kneeland, Montreal
Fran Korson, Toronto
O. A. Kummer, Preston, Ont.
Mrs. R. Glenna Larimer, Beaconsfield, Que.
Mrs. James Lawrence, Kitchener, Ont.
Andrew P. Leslie, Toronto

Rev. J. Lofthouse, Hamilton
W. Longworth, Port Arthur, Ont.
Mrs. M. McAuley, Regina
Norah McCullough, Regina
Mrs. A McCully, Lachine, Que.
G. A. Macdonald, Timmins, Ont.
Hugh MacDonald, Montreal
T. E. Mackey, Toronto
L. C. McLean, Montreal
Viola MacMillan, Toronto
Leonard MacNeil, Toronto
Herbert Manning, Toronto
William Marlow, Montreal
A. J. Marshall, Montreal
R. W. Marshall, Westville, N.S.
E. Grace Martyn, London, Ont.
E. S. Merrett, Montreal
John Miller, Toronto
Don Mole, Winnipeg
Eric Moon, St. John's, Nfld.
Don Morris, St. John's, Nfld.
D. Murray Murphy, Montreal
May Neal, Regina
Mabel E. Neale, Beaconsfield, Que.
Mrs. J. Nickiford, Calgary
George D. Noonan, Regina
Norberta O'Rourke, Woodbridge, Ont.
Nelle Overgarde, Moose Jaw, Sask.
H. A. Pagnuelo, St. Hyacinthe, Que.
Clifford W. Parkin, North Hatley, Que.
Andrew Paterson, Montreal
S. L. Pearson, Hollywood, Florida
Mary Pedersen, Bedford, N.S.
Fred Perks, Montreal
E. P. A. Phillips, Port Arthur, Ont.
Grace M. Pugmire, Atlanta, Georgia
Mrs. R. Ralton, Winnipeg
R. G. Ray, Ottawa
Jean McCrimmon Reeves, Burlington, Ont.
William Godfrey Reise, Hamilton
J. E. Religa, Bell Island, Nfld.
Kathleen A. Rex, Toronto
Mrs. E. Rowe, Orillia, Ont.
Emily M. Rowe, Orillia, Ont.
Marjorie M. St. George, Woodill, Halifax
Johnny Sandison, CKCK, Regina
Mrs. Emily Scarr, Winnipeg

Mrs. Rita Seligman, Montreal
Eric Seymour, St. John's, Nfld.
T. Sheehan, Montreal
Trevor Slapak, Blairmore, Alta.
Mrs. D. M. Smith, Hamilton
Mrs. Rose Smith, Winnipeg
G. F. Stevenson, Ottawa
Lindsay Barclay McGall Stewart, Regina
Frank Storrs Stocking, Montreal
A. M. Sturton, Quebec City
Anne Swann, Toronto
A. R. Sykes, Ottawa
Mrs. G. Tenbrummeler, Toronto
J. D. Theriault, Rivière du Loup, Que.
A. I. Tolhurst, Montreal
E. Y. Tomkins, Montreal
Thomas W. Topping, Deseronto, Ont.
Frank Tumpane, Toronto
B. Turner, Regina
Mrs. H. R. M. Turner, Welland, Ont.
Mabel L. Tylasky, Bawlf, Alta.
Mrs. H. Tyler, Toronto
C. G. Urquhart, Winnipeg
Raymond Varela, Brockville, Ont.
Robert H. Vaughan, Perth, Ont.
Henri Vincent, Daveluyville, Que.
Margaret Vincent, Dundas, Ont.
Harold C. Walby, Montreal
Ellen Walker, Victoria
S. A. Wallace, Q.C., Windsor, Ont.
John S. Walsh, Montreal
John A. Warr, Ste. Thérèse de Blainville, Que.
Robert Watt, Montreal
Earl Weinert, Toronto
Mrs. Ralph Weinrauch, Montreal
Ruth M. Welch, Leonardville, N.B.
Gerald C. J. Whitten, Gander, Nfld.
Ethel Williamson, St. Catharines, Ont.
Clifford Wilson, Montreal
Mrs. Mildred Wilson, Toronto
James B. Winder, Montreal
Anne Woods, Vancouver
James A. Wright, Granby, Que.
Mrs. Margaret Wylie, Lachine, Que.
H. A. Yeo, Rivière du Loup, Que.
Bessie Young, Toronto
Brigadier Wilfred Yurgensen, Montreal

BIBLIOGRAPHY

Bell, Lieut.-Col. F. McKelvey, *A Romance of the Halifax Disaster;* Halifax, privately published, 1918.

Billings, Henry, *Bridges;* New York, Viking Press, 1956.

Black, Archibald, *The Story of Bridges;* New York, Whittlesey House, 1936.

Borrett, William C., *Historic Halifax;* Toronto, Ryerson Press, 1948.

Bothwell, Jessie Robson, *Pioneers! O Pioneers!;* Regina, Service Printing Co., 1958.

Cahill, Brian, and Smallwood, Joseph R., *This Is Newfoundland;* Toronto, Ryerson Press, 1949.

Canadian Red Cross pamphlet, *Call 320;* Winnipeg, 1950.

Drake, Earl, *Regina the Queen City;* Toronto, McClelland & Stewart, 1955.

Dunfield, Sir Brian, *Special Commissioner Report on Destruction by Fire of Knights of Columbus Hostel;* St. John's, Nfld., Robinson & Co., Ltd., 1943.

Fay, Dr. C.R., *Life and Labour in Newfoundland;* Toronto, University of Toronto Press, 1956.

Gard, Robert E., *Johnny Chinook;* Toronto, Longmans, Green & Co., 1945.

Giddings, Prof. F.H., *A Civic Community Study of the Disaster City;* New York, Columbia University Press, 1920.

Hamilton, Robert M., *Canadian Quotations and Phrases;* Toronto, McClelland & Stewart, 1952.

Hardy, W.G., editor, *Alberta Golden Jubilee Anthology;* Toronto, McClelland & Stewart, 1955.

Hoffman, Arnold, *Free Gold;* New York, Rinehart & Co., 1947.

Holbrook, Stewart H., *Burning an Empire;* New York, Macmillan, 1943.

Howay, F.W., *British Columbia, the Making of a Province;* Toronto, Ryerson Press, 1928.

Hutchison, Bruce, *The Unknown Country;* Toronto, Longmans, Green & Co., 1948.

Kelsy, Vera, *British Columbia Rides a Star;* Toronto, J.M. Dent & Sons, 1955.

Kerr, Kay and Jack, *The Story of the Great Landslide at Frank, 1903;* Frank, Alta., pamphlet of New Turtle Mountain Hotel, 1958.

LeBourdais, D.M., *Metals and Men;* Toronto, McClelland & Stewart, 1957.

Lett, Chief Justice Sherwood, *Royal Commission Report on the Second Narrows Bridge Collapse;* Vancouver, 1958.

Liddell, Ken E., *This is Alberta;* Toronto, Ryerson Press, 1952.

Liddell, Ken, *This Is British Columbia;* Toronto, R y e r s o n Press, 1958.

MacDougall, J.B., *Two Thousand Miles of Gold;* Toronto, McClelland & Stewart, 1946.

MacLennan, Hugh, *Barometer Rising;* New York, Duell, Sloan & Pearce, 1941.

McKelvie, B.A., *Pageant of B.C.;* Toronto, Thomas Nelson & Sons, 1955.

Marshall, Logan, *Tragic Story of the Empress of Ireland;* Montreal, privately published, 1914.

Mitchell, W.O., *Who Has Seen the Wind?;* Toronto, Macmillan Co. of Canada, 1947.

Moon, Robert, *This Is Saskatchewan;* Toronto, Ryerson Press, 1953.

Morrow, R.A., *Story of the Great Disaster at Springhill Mines, Feb. 21, 1891;* privately published, 1891; property of Jane Field, Stellarton, N.S.

Ontario Department of Lands and Forests, *A Statistical Reference of Lands and Forests Administration;* T o r o n t o, 1959.

Ormsby, Margaret A., *British Columbia: A History;* Toronto, Macmillan Co. of Canada, 1958.

Pollard, William Correll, *Life on the Frontier;* London, England, Stockwell Publishers, 1905.

Prince, Samuel Henry, *Catastrophe of Halifax;* Columbia University Press, 1920.

Raddall, Thomas Head, *Halifax, Warden of the North;* Toronto, McClelland & Stewart, 1948.

The Red River Flood of 1950 (photo booklet); Steinbach, Man., Derksen Printers Ltd., 1950.

Roberts, Leslie, *Noranda;* Toronto, Clarke Irwin, 1956.

Sloane, Eric, *The Book of Storms;* New York, Duell, Sloan & Pearce, 1956.

Smallwood, Joseph R., *The New Newfoundland;* New York, Macmillan, 1931.

Smith, Stanley, K., *The Story of Stricken Halifax;* New York, Gerald E. Weir Ltd., 1918.

Steinman, David B., and Watson, Sara Ruth, *Bridges;* New York, Dover Publications, 1941.

Wechsberg, Joseph, *Avalanche!;* New York, Alfred A. Knopf, 1958.

Wright, Jim F. C., *Prairie Progress;* Saskatoon, Modern Press, 1956.

Young, Scott, *The Flood;* Toronto, McClelland & Stewart, 1956.

Zucker, Paul, *American Bridges and Dams;* New York, Greystone Press, 1941.

INDEX